Against the Consensus

In June 2008 Justin Yifu Lin was appointed chief economist of the World Bank, right before the eruption of the worst global financial and economic crisis since the Great Depression. Drawing on experience from his privileged position, Lin offers unique reflections on the cause of the crisis, why it was so serious and widespread, and its likely evolution. Arguing that conventional theories provide inadequate solutions, he proposes new initiatives for achieving global stability and avoiding the recurrence of similar crises in the future. He suggests that the crisis and the global imbalances both originated with the excess liquidity created by US financial deregulation and loose monetary policy, and recommends the creation of a global Marshall Plan and a new supranational global reserve currency. This thought-provoking book will appeal to academics, graduate students, policymakers, and anyone interested in the global economy.

JUSTIN YIFU LIN is Professor and Honorary Dean of the National School of Development at Peking University. He was Chief Economist and Senior Vice President of the World Bank between 2008 and 2012, and was the first economist from the developing world to hold this position. Prior to joining the World Bank, Professor Lin served for fifteen years as Founding Director and Professor of the China Centre for Economic Research at Peking University. He is a corresponding fellow of the British Academy, a fellow of the World Academy of Sciences for the Developing World, and the author of twenty-three books, including *The Quest for Prosperity: How Developing Countries Can Take Off* (2012), *New Structural Economics: A Framework for Rethinking Development and Policy* (2012), *Benti and Changwu: Dialogues on Methodology in Economics* (2011), *Economic Development and Transition: Thought, Strategy, and Viability* (2009), and *Demystifying the Chinese Economy* (2011).

Against the Consensus

Reflections on the Great Recession

JUSTIN YIFU LIN

CAMBRIDGE UNIVERSITY PRESS
Cambridge, New York, Melbourne, Madrid, Cape Town,
Singapore, São Paulo, Delhi, Mexico City

Cambridge University Press
The Edinburgh Building, Cambridge CB2 8RU, UK

Published in the United States of America by Cambridge University Press, New York

www.cambridge.org
Information on this title: www.cambridge.org/9781107038875

First published 2013

Printed and bound in the United Kingdom by Bell and Bain Ltd

A catalogue record for this publication is available from the British Library

Library of Congress Cataloging in Publication data
Lin, Justin Yifu, 1952–
Against the consensus: reflections on the great recession / Justin Yifu Lin.
    pages   cm
Includes bibliographical references and index.
ISBN 978-1-107-03887-5
1. Global Financial Crisis, 2008–2009.   2. Recessions – History – 21st
century.   3. China – Economic policy.   I. Title.
HB37172008.L57   2013
330.9′0511–dc23

                                                              2012050469

ISBN 978-1-107-03887-5 Hardback

Contents

Figures

Tables

Boxes

Preface

I was the first person from the developing world to be appointed chief economist of the World Bank, a position traditionally held by renowned economists from the West. My tenure started in June 2008, right before the eruption of the worst global financial and economic crisis since the Great Depression. The position at the World Bank required me to explore the causes and a way out of the crisis. In this book I present a perspective that may be new to people accustomed mainly to Western points of view.

Let me explain why I wrote this book.

As an intellectual from the developing world, I used to believe, like the monk in the classic Chinese epic novel *Journey to the West*, that the West had a holy sutra, which I needed only learn and apply to help my native country modernize and prosper. I felt fortunate to have the opportunity, just as China was beginning to transition from a centralized economy to a market economy, to study modern economics with the masters – including several Nobel laureates – at the University of Chicago, a global center of modern economic research.

Soon thereafter, PhD in hand, I was ready to apply my knowledge to real-world problems at home. Instead, I was confronted by events that contested the very applicability of modern economics in my country. In 1988, after a decade of reforms, China experienced its first episode of double-digit inflation. The orthodox inflation-fighting response would be to raise interest rates to cool down overheating investment and discourage consumption. Instead, the government adopted a retrenchment program and administratively cut back many investment projects, leaving them wastefully uncompleted. Evaluated against macroeconomic theory, the government's behavior was irrational.

Modern economics is premised on rationality – the belief that all economic agents act rationally. If the Chinese government had acted irrationally, the modern economics would be inapplicable in China. But, if the Chinese government did act irrationally, how did its policies lead to a decade of 10 percent average annual growth following the reforms begun in 1979? The answer, clearly, is that it acted rationally in response to constraints that differed from those assumed in the existing theoretical models taught in school.

Theodore W. Schultz, my mentor at the University of Chicago, had a similar experience. Before his seminal work, peasants in agrarian economies were considered irrational because they would not save and invest like "rational" famers in modern society. His research found that in fact it was rational for peasants in a traditional agrarian economy not to save, because without technological advances the marginal return to saving was close to zero. His insight revolutionized agricultural economics and policy.[1]

So, assuming that the Chinese government acted rationally, why was it reluctant to raise interest rates and why did it create other market distortions? Because the survival of many large state-owned enterprises depended on the implicit subsidies supplied through low-interest-rate loans and other intentional distortions. These large state enterprises, capital-intensive in defiance of China's comparative advantage in labor-intensive activities, were not viable in an open, competitive market. They were a product of China's strategy during the 1950s, when it was still a poor agrarian economy, to overtake the United Kingdom in ten years and catch up with the United States in fifteen years.

Following modern macroeconomic theory to raise interest rates or implementing shock therapy to remove other distortions based on the Washington consensus would have bankrupted most state enterprises, resulting in widespread unemployment and social and political unrest. Although academia dismissed China's dual-track approach to transition (protecting nonviable firms in the old priority sectors while liberalizing entry into sectors consistent with China's comparative advantages), the Chinese government saw it as the only approach that could achieve both stability and dynamic growth. I wrote about this insight in *The China Miracle: Development Strategy and Economic Reform*, published in 1996, and later in *Demystifying the Chinese Economy*, published in 2011.

---

[1] The previous policy recommendation was to change farmers' irrational behavior in order to modernize agriculture in traditional economies. Schultz's finding suggested that the right policy should be providing farmers with modern technology (Schultz 1964).

The enlightenment from China's response to the inflation of 1988 inspired me to adopt a *changwu* attitude, observing the world as though seeing it for the first time through a newly born baby's eyes, without preconceived notions. When considering a policy issue, instead of applying current theories or conventional interpretations of experience, I tried to construct a causality model anew by myself each time by identifying the agents behind the phenomenon, the goals they wanted to achieve, the constraints they faced, and the options they had, as I describe in my recent book *Benti and Changwu: Dialogues on Research Methodologies in Economics.*

China's miraculous growth and increasing global influence in the world helped propel me to the position of chief economist of the World Bank. My mandates were to be the World Bank president's chief economic advisor, to lead the World Bank's intellectual work on development economics, and, by helping developing countries achieve sustainable, dynamic, and inclusive growth, to rid the world of poverty. Despite the rise of multiple growth poles in the first decade of the new century that include some emerging market economies, most countries in Africa and other parts of the world remain trapped at low income levels, unable to narrow the income gap with advanced economies. Before the crisis erupted, I thought my main challenge was to find ways to help these poor countries improve their development performance.

I started my job by visiting South Africa, Rwanda, and Ethiopia in the first week of my tenure. But my plans for devoting myself to promote economic development in poor countries were soon interrupted by the collapse of Lehman Brothers and the ensuing global financial and economic crisis. Its depth and length were not foretold by conventional economic theories. *Changwu* helped me understand the crisis and propose a way out.

When I arrived in Washington in June 2008, the surge in food and fuel prices was grabbing all the headlines. I asked my colleagues whether deflation was likely to follow once inflation had been arrested. Most economists found the question bewildering, because of their confidence in the Great Moderation – a phenomenon believed to reflect the high-income country governments' mastery of macroeconomic policies to smooth the business cycle in the last two decades before the crisis. As conditions worsened after the collapse of Lehman Brothers in September 2008, I suspected that the world might suffer from a protracted recession due to the large excess capacity built up during the extraordinary boom before the crisis. I proposed a global initiative to invest in bottleneck-releasing, productivity-enhancing infrastructure projects – what I called "beyond Keynesianism" – as a countercyclical measure to restore growth. Believing that the crisis would last three to seven quarters at most, like other crises in the past half-century, most economists advised governments to follow conventional measures, relying on automatic stabilizers while strengthening social safety nets to protect the poor and vulnerable. Through the coordinated efforts of the G20 (Group of Twenty leading economies) governments, there was a green sprout of recovery in the first half of 2010. When the International Monetary Fund recommended in fall 2010 that crisis-afflicted countries retrench fiscally, I argued that the focus should be on improving the quality of fiscal stimulus instead, otherwise slowing growth and mounting fiscal deficits would likely follow. Today the world's attention is fixed on the Eurozone debt crisis, but I worry that, if we don't take the beyond Keynesianism measure that I advocated at the onset of the crisis now, the entire world may be on the road to a protracted "new normal" or even "lost decades."

This book presents my analysis of the roots of the economic crisis and stalled growth and proposes win-win solutions that will lead to global stability and sustainable development.

I conducted most research in the book during my tenure as chief economist of the World Bank. I would like to thank my World Bank colleagues, Vandana Chandra, Jean-Jacques Dethier, Doerte Doemeland, Shahrokh Fardoust, Vivian Hon, Celestin Monga, Zia Qureshi, David Rosenblatt, Volker Treichel, James Trevino, and Yan Wang, for their invaluable contributions to my research and preparation of the book. I am also grateful to Meta de Coquereaumont and Bruce Ross-Larson for an excellent editorial review.

Overview

Monolithic explanations of international development increasingly fall short in describing today's diverse, multipolar world. This book reflects an attempt to "emancipate our minds, seek truth from facts, proceed from reality in everything," as Deng Xiaoping famously said, by presenting a view that may be new to people accustomed mainly to Western perspectives. The book analyzes the roots of the current global crisis and proposes win-win solutions that will lead to development and global stability.

In fall 2008 the world was rocked by the eruption of the worst global financial and economic crisis since the Great Depression. Unless we can understand the roots of this Great Recession and its likely evolution, the correct policy responses to prevent a recurrence will elude us. The commonly accepted explanations for the crisis are inconsistent with the empirical facts. Had the academic and policy community understood or been willing to face the true causes and taken prompt and effective action, the crisis could have been prevented or moderated.

What caused the 2008–9 global crisis?

The recent crisis began in the United States with a financial system meltdown following the bursting of the housing bubble. The crisis was preceded by a dramatic rise in current account imbalances, which was commonly accepted as the cause of the crisis. These global imbalances were believed to originate in East Asian economies' export-oriented strategies and accumulation of foreign reserves as self-insurance after the 1998 crisis and especially in China's undervalued exchange rate. These global imbalances and the purchase of Treasury bills with excess reserve accumulations, so the thinking went, led to cheap credit and a housing bubble in the United States.

Global imbalances did not arise in East Asia...

Though plausible at first glance, there were good reasons to doubt these explanations. East Asian economies had been pursuing similar development strategies for more than half a century, but trade surpluses ballooned only in the decade before the crisis. If East Asian self-insurance and China's undervalued currency were the causes of the global imbalances, countries competing with the East Asian economies should have reduced their trade surpluses and reserves. Yet, in the decade before the crisis, other economies' trade surpluses rose as well, shrinking East Asia's contribution to the US trade deficit from 51 percent in the 1990s to 38 percent in the 2000s. Almost all countries except the United States increased their trade surpluses or reserves. Globally, reserves rose from $1 trillion in 2001 to $7 trillion in 2007. The only way for all countries to increase their reserves simultaneously was for the reserve currency countries (mainly the United States) to increase the supply of reserve currencies.

I have a different view. The combination in the United States of financial deregulation (starting in the 1980s), which allowed high leverage, and low interest rates (following the bursting of the dot-com bubble in 2001) led to a large increase in liquidity and fed the housing bubble of the 2000s. The wealth effect from the housing bubble and from financial innovations that sprung up under lax supervision supported excessive household consumption. This new consumption surge, along with deficit financing of the wars in Iraq and Afghanistan, generated large US trade deficits and global imbalances. The United States was able to finance the large-scale imbalances for so long only because the dollar was the main reserve currency.

The excess liquidity sloshing around the United States also contributed to large gross capital outflows to other countries, supporting growth and booms in their investments and equity markets. The dollars obtained through trade surpluses and capital inflows in nonreserve currency countries could not circulate directly in their domestic markets but had to be converted to the local currency and held as central bank reserves. Those reserves then flowed back to the United States to buy US Treasury bills or to invest in US financial markets. These return flows fed the impression that low US interest rates were caused by the excess accumulation of reserves in nonreserve currency countries. When the housing bubble burst in the United States and the financial system collapsed, a global crisis erupted.

Financial deregulation and liberalization also swept over Europe. Major European banks established branches in eastern and southern Europe, using high leverage to support housing bubbles and consumption booms. The booms also benefited from the adoption of the euro. When the banks started to deleverage after the crisis, eastern and southern Europe suffered severely, and several countries remain mired in a sovereign debt crisis.

...or in China

As early as 2003 academics and policymakers in high-income countries began pointing at China as the culprit behind the mounting global imbalances, even though China did not begin to amass a large trade surplus until 2005.

China's large current account surplus reflects mainly its high domestic savings. The hypotheses about China's high saving rate – such as its aging population and the lack of a well-developed social safety net – focus on incentives for household saving. But these cannot be the main explanations, because, at an amount equivalent to 20 percent of gross domestic product (GDP), household savings are no higher in China than they are in India and many other countries. What makes China's saving pattern unique is the large share of corporate savings, a result of surplus labor in the traditional sector, and continuing distortions that favor large state corporations, a legacy of China's dual-track reform. Surplus labor kept corporate profits and savings high by preventing wages from rising as the production of tradables expanded rapidly. Corporate savings also benefited from implicit subsidies to large corporations (a result of the financial system serving big firms), low taxation of natural resources, and unregulated monopolies in some sectors.

A win-win path to recovery

The world's attention is concentrated on whether countries in the Eurozone can produce stabilization packages large enough to rescue the southern European countries in debt crisis and whether those countries will roll out structural reforms to boost their competitiveness.

Without structural reforms, stabilization measures just buy time; problems will inevitably recur, and with ever greater ferocity.

The challenge of structural reforms

But here is the challenge: structural reforms are contractionary and may cut more deeply into jobs, economic growth, and government revenues already hurt by the recession, at least in the near term, with dire social and political consequences. This means that structural reforms are not politically feasible in many countries. And, even if implemented, reforms may not shrink the fiscal deficit. Social spending generally increases in response to rising unemployment and the drop in fiscal revenue that occurs when growth slows. The market will respond negatively to the rising public debt, especially if the reforming country's currency is not a reserve currency or if the country has no independent monetary policy, as in the Eurozone, and is unable to monetize its debt.

The standard recommendation by the International Monetary Fund (IMF) has long been to offset the contractionary effects of structural reforms by devaluing the currency to increase export demand. And, for a small economy, that policy prescription can work if the global economy is sound. But devaluation is not an option for individual countries in southern Europe, despite being theoretically feasible for the Eurozone as a whole. And any attempt at currency devaluation in the Eurozone to create space for structural reform could trigger competitive devaluations, as Japan, the United States, and many other countries are also beset with high unemployment and structural problems.

Without structural reform, the debt-ridden countries in southern Europe are likely to require repeated and increasingly large rescue packages, which will unavoidably be monetized by the European Central Bank. And, unless Japan and the United States undergo their own structural reforms, they will continue their loose monetary policies to keep interest rates low so as to support the financial system, help indebted households, and reduce the cost of raising and serving public debt. The likely outcome is that the Eurozone, Japan, and the United States will all be trapped in a protracted new normal of slow growth, high risk, and low returns to financial investment. Low interest rates will also encourage short-term speculative capital flows to international commodity markets (resulting in volatile prices) and to emerging economies (causing asset bubbles, currency appreciation, and difficulties in macroeconomic management).

Beyond Keynes: global investment in infrastructure

To avoid these dismal consequences, high-income countries must stimulate demand to create the space for structural reforms. With a glut in housing stock and excess capacity in construction and manufacturing in almost every high-income country, public or private debt restructuring and fiscal consolidation should not be the priority. Countries should instead promote sustainable job creation and growth through investment to create demand for construction and capital goods and restore consumer confidence.

To avoid the rapid accumulation of public debt, as in Japan during its "lost decades" after 1991, countercyclical fiscal stimuli should be applied in a way that goes beyond Keynes, as I advocated at the beginning of the global crisis. Fiscal policies should be proactive and countercyclical, focusing on projects that create jobs today and enhance productivity tomorrow, especially in infrastructure, green sectors, and education. Monetary policy should accommodate fiscal needs. Because the resultant faster growth and higher government revenue in the future can be used to pay back the costs incurred today, paying for these policies will not become a tax burden on future generations.

Domestic productivity-enhancing investment opportunities are limited in high-income countries and may not be large enough to pull them out of the crisis. In developing countries, however, opportunities for productivity-enhancing infrastructure investments abound. In today's closely connected world, investments in developing countries will generate demand for the exports of high-income countries, with an effect similar to that of currency devaluation. Except for a few emerging market economies, however, most developing countries are constrained by a weak fiscal position or low foreign reserves and require outside investment funds. Thus the second implication of the beyond Keynes approach is for the advanced economies to create facilities for supporting investments in developing economies in order to reap gains for both sets of countries.

The world needs a Marshall Plan to stimulate global investment in infrastructure to release bottlenecks to growth in developing countries and to create space for structural reforms in high-income countries. Instead of simply putting out one fiscal fire after another in sovereign debt crisis countries through emergency IMF financing and other rescue packages, the G20 should provide parallel funds to multilateral development banks, including the World Bank and regional development banks, with the capacity to design and implement infrastructure investment projects. The investment funds should come from reserve-issuing and reserve-rich countries. In today's global economy, infrastructure projects are good investments for private sector funds, including pension funds and sovereign wealth funds. In addition to an active role in selecting and designing projects and making them attractive to private investors, the multilateral development banks and governments could create innovative arrangements to leverage private funds. Such infrastructure investments on a global scale are a win-win strategy for developed and developing countries alike – for today and tomorrow.

How poor countries can catch up: flying geese and leading dragons

A global push for infrastructure investments in developing countries will work only if developing countries can grow dynamically in the coming decades. But do they have the space to do so in today's uncertain, stressful global economy? And, if so, how do they seize the opportunity and then sustain their growth?

The low- and middle-income traps

Before the Industrial Revolution, per capita income was fairly evenly distributed; it was only a few times higher in the richest countries than in the poorest. Then incomes began their great divergence. A few Western industrialized countries took off and came to dominate the world economic and political order. Until 2000 the G7 contributed about two-thirds of global GDP measured in market exchange rates and about one-half measured in purchasing power parity (PPP).

Since 2000 we have seen the rise of a multipolar world, with China and a few other large developing countries driving global growth and recovery in the current global crisis. But only a handful of East Asian economies have advanced from low-income agrarian economies to middle-income newly industrialized economies and toward high-income advanced industrialized economies. Between 1950 and 2008 only twenty-eight economies reduced their per capita income gap with the United States by at least ten percentage points – and only twelve of these were neither western European countries nor oil- or diamond-producing small countries. The other 150 plus countries have been trapped at the middle- or low-income level.

The rise of a multipolar growth world is thus the result of dynamic growth in just a few middle-income countries with large populations. Whether the new growth pole countries can avoid the middle-income trap and whether other developing countries can maintain dynamic growth are crucial questions for global recovery and for the viability of a global infrastructure initiative. The main global development challenges remain reducing poverty, achieving the Millennium Development Goals, and narrowing income and other human development gaps between low- and middle-income countries and high-income countries.

Flawed development theories

Developing countries have for decades been trying to catch up with the industrialized high-income countries – to achieve sustained dynamic growth. Under the prevailing development thinking, governments have been advised to adopt import substitution policies, intervening to overcome market failures, and to accelerate industrialization since World War II. This early development thinking can be labeled "development economics 1.0." Countries following this approach had some initial successes, but these were quickly followed by repeated crises and stagnation. The dominant development thinking then shifted to neoliberalism, as summed up in the Washington consensus in the 1980s. Reforms in governance and the business environment were intended to transfer to developing countries the idealized market institutions of industrialized high-income countries. These policy prescriptions can be labeled "development economics 2.0." The result was lost decades of growth in developing countries.

Responding to the persistence of poverty in developing countries, the global development community focused its aid increasingly on education and health programs, seen as important humanitarian concerns. As these human development programs failed to achieve their intended project results, development research began to emphasize randomized controlled experiments to improve service delivery. This trend can be labeled "development economics 2.5." North Africa's experience with strong education advances but lagging growth and job opportunities calls into question the validity of this approach.

The few developing economies that industrialized and grew dynamically after World War II – most of them in East Asia – followed an export-oriented development strategy rather than the prevailing import substitution strategy. Cambodia, China, Mauritius, and Vietnam, which achieved stability and dynamic growth in their transition from a planned to a market economy, followed a gradual, dual-track approach rather than the shock therapy advocated by the Washington consensus. They continued to protect firms in priority sectors while liberalizing entry in other sectors, but they often perform poorly on governance and business environment indicators. The successful developing countries made enormous advances in education, health, poverty reduction, and other human development indicators, and none used randomized controlled experiments to design their social and economic programs.

A better way: comparative advantage – following industrialization

The lesson? We need to rethink our economic development theories and policies. The rapidly widening income gap between Western countries and the rest of the world is a result of their rapid increase in per capita income, reflecting the accelerated structural changes in industry and technology made possible by the Industrial Revolution. The few countries that were not oil- or diamond-producing economies that greatly narrowed the income gap with the United States also achieved similar structural changes. Modern economic development is a process of continuous change in structure, including technologies, industries, and institutions.

Development thinking has focused on what developing countries do not have and developed countries do (capital-intensive industries), on what developing countries cannot do well and developed countries can (Washington consensus policies and governance), and on areas that do not contribute directly to structural change in developing countries but are viewed as humanitarianly important by high-income countries (health and education). The shift in development thinking and projects away from trying to understand the determinants of structural change and to facilitate these changes is a shift too far. Development economics should build on Adam Smith's insights (remember that he called his book *An Inquiry into the Nature and Causes of the Wealth of Nations*), looking closely at the causes of structural change and the process of economic development, which reflect the nature of modern economic growth. I propose a move to "development economics 3.0," which focuses on what developing countries have (their endowments) and areas in which they can do well based on their (latent) comparative advantage (as determined by their endowments), to allow them to initiate a process of dynamic structural change.

In a globalized world, a country's optimal industrial structure – one in which all industries are consistent with the country's comparative advantages and are competitive in domestic and international markets – is endogenous to its endowment structure at a specific time. Achieving that optimal structure requires a well-functioning market so that firms can follow the country's comparative advantages in their choices of activities and technologies. If firms can do that, the economy will be competitive, capital will accumulate as rapidly as possible, the economy's endowment structure and comparative advantages will change, and the economy's industrial structure will need to become more capital-intensive. Changing the industrial structure requires upgrading hard and soft infrastructure to reduce transaction costs. Upgrading entails externalities and coordination issues that firms cannot internalize in their individual decisionmaking, so governments will need to be actively involved.

Successful economies in East Asia and western Europe followed the flying geese pattern in dynamically industrializing their economies and narrowing the gap with developed countries. In US and western European industrialization, the United Kingdom was the lead goose and Germany, France, and the United States were the followers. By following carefully selected lead countries, latecomers can emulate the flying geese pattern that has enabled trailing economies to catch up since the eighteenth century, by building up industries that are growing dynamically in more advanced countries with endowment structures similar to theirs. The economic failures of many developing countries after World War II stemmed from their misguided attempts to adopt comparative-advantage-defying import substitution strategies instead. This strategy not only prevented them from benefiting from the latecomer advantage in upgrading to their areas of comparative advantage but also generated distortions and induced rent-seeking practices to protect nonviable firms in priority sectors. Washington consensus reforms such as privatization and financial sector liberalization failed because they overlooked the endogeneity of the distortions and the need for the government to facilitate industrial upgrading.

China had adopted a comparative-advantage-defying strategy before the 1979 reforms, and performed poorly. Its performance turned around after 1979, however, when it adopted a dual-track approach to transition, giving transitory protections to nonviable firms in old priority sectors and facilitating private firms' entry to new latent comparative advantage sectors. Other countries that followed a similar transition strategy also performed well. Now, as China absorbs its surplus labor and wages rise accordingly, it will need to transition from labor-intensive industries to increasingly more capital- and technology-intensive sectors. Due to China's huge size, this will open a large space for low-income developing countries still in their labor-intensive industrialization development phase. This new phenomenon has been called the "leading dragon" pattern. If Brazil, India, Indonesia, and other large middle-income countries maintain their current pace of growth, the same opportunities for low-income countries can emerge in other regions.

If governments set up a policy framework for private sector activities that is attuned to a country's comparative advantage, poorer countries in sub-Saharan Africa and southeast Asia could also start a process of labor-intensive industrialization, growing at 8 percent or more for several decades. The "Growth Identification and Facilitation Framework," which I developed at the World Bank, advises governments on how to facilitate this development.

Toward a brave new international monetary system

The 2008–9 global economic and financial crisis highlighted major deficiencies in the international monetary system. And, although the system appears to have weathered the initial shock, it remains fragile. The global imbalances arising from the excess liquidity created by financial deregulation and monetary policy in the United Sates were so large and lasted so long because of the reserve currency status of the

US dollar (US current account deficits and capital outflows create the global supply of US dollar reserves).

The US dollar became the primary reserve currency mainly through a process of "benign neglect."[1] After World War II industrial economies focused on reconstruction. The memory of the Great Depression weighed heavily on policymakers, who established new institutions to oversee international transactions and promote the growth and stability of international trade and finance – the Bretton Woods system. For nearly two decades the Bretton Woods system maintained fixed exchange rates tied to gold. Then, in the mid-1970s, the international economy entered a period of drifting global economic governance. Countries followed their own monetary and exchange rate regimes, and the US dollar established itself as the predominant international reserve currency.

The emerging multireserve currency system is inherently unstable

The world is now moving toward a more diversified set of reserve currencies. Either gradually (as the US economy's share in the world economy shrinks) or through a sudden debilitating shock, the US dollar's central role is expected to diminish. Two key questions arise. First, how will this evolution toward a multireserve currency system affect global monetary and economic stability? Will it be more or less stable than the current system? Second, is there an alternative system, such as the creation of a new international reserve currency, that might be more favorable to the global economy? A new international reserve currency will be acceptable only if it is a win-win for both developed and developing countries.

Driving the need for reform of the international monetary system is the fact that it is out of sync with the evolution of the real economy globally and appears to be a major source of financial instability. Some economists think that a multireserve currency system would be more stable because competition among major reserve currencies could become a discipline mechanism for resolving the incentive incompatibility between national and global interests under the current system. If a reserve currency country conducts its monetary policy in support of

[1] Rogoff (1983).

domestic interests at the expense of global interests, reserve holders can switch out of that reserve currency and into others.

This argument has merit if all the major reserve currency countries have strong and healthy economies. It is more likely, however, that they will all have severe structural weaknesses. When these weaknesses become apparent in a reserve currency country, they can trigger the flight of short-term funds to other reserve currencies, causing them to appreciate sharply, as recently happened to the Swiss franc and the Japanese yen. The currency appreciation then weakens the real economy and worsens its structural weaknesses, inducing short-term funds to move yet again to another reserve currency. As a result, such a multireserve currency system is likely to be highly unstable as multiple currencies compete for reserve status and use in international transactions. It is a lose-lose situation, for reserve currency countries and other countries alike.

A bold proposal to restore stability to the international monetary system

Stability can be restored – and the conflict of national and global interests inherent in using national currencies as reserve currencies resolved – if all countries adopt a single supranational reserve currency. I propose replacing the system of national reserve currencies with a global reserve currency called "paper gold" ("p-gold"). P-gold would be issued by an international monetary authority following Milton Friedman's k percent rule.[2] Each country's central bank would use p-gold as its reserve currency and issue its domestic currency with a fixed exchange rate against p-gold. P-gold would be used in international trade and capital flows (as the US dollar is now). The increase in p-gold each year – global seigniorage – could be used to pay for the operating costs of the international monetary authority and for global public goods agreed on by all countries. The system would avoid the fatal limitation of a gold standard (the supply of gold cannot expand to meet the needs of a growing global economy) and national reserve

---

[2] The supply of p-gold would follow Friedman's k percent rule (or a modified Taylor rule) based on a projected measure of global economic and asset transaction growth. The value of k could be tied to growth in world GDP and world trade and could be reviewed periodically by an expert panel for any needed adjustments.

currencies (the inherent conflict between national and global interests). The p-gold system would have a disciplining effect on national monetary authorities while avoiding the dilemma that Greece faces now: an inability to devalue its currency.

P-gold is an improved version of Keynes's proposal for a new international currency called the bancor. That proposal never took off because countries had confidence in the US dollar; the US economy was strong and dominated the global economy (at more than 50 percent of global GDP), so other countries had no compelling reason to push for change. Today the US economy's share of global GDP is around 20 percent, and the international monetary system is wobbly. A global currency such as p-gold could become a win-win for all countries by eliminating instability, which is bad for reserve currency countries and nonreserve currency countries alike.

PART I

What Caused the 2008–9 Global Crisis?

The global financial crisis of 2008–9 caused the greatest contraction in the global economy since the Great Depression. The crisis began in the United States with a meltdown in the financial system following the bursting of the housing bubble and the collapse of Lehman Brothers. Government actions helped avoid the worst possible scenario, but the world economy remains fragile, with high unemployment and large excess capacity in the advanced economies and high levels of sovereign debt in Eurozone countries.

The economic crisis took almost everyone by surprise. As late as April 2007 the International Monetary Fund (IMF) was affirming that risks to the global economy were extremely low and that there were no issues of great concern.[1] Despite large and widening global imbalances in current accounts, confidence prevailed – confidence in the US financial and political system and its financial regulations, in a capital market that was the largest in the world,[2] and in monetary policy institutions that had always engendered trust.[3] The world economy was seen as robust, and global imbalances were considered sustainable. Few economists expressed serious concerns about the US housing bubble and a disorderly unwinding of rising global imbalances.

But there were a few doomsayers, and their concerns were dramatically validated when the financial crisis erupted in September 2008.[4] The coordinated policy response by the G20 countries – cash infusions, debt guarantees, and other forms of assistance on the order of $10

---

[1] IMF (2007).   [2] Reinhart and Rogoff (2009: 214).   [3] Bernanke (2005b).
[4] The most vocal criticism came from Raghuram Rajan (2005), chief economist of the IMF, who warned of a collapse of the financial system in his Jackson Hole speech in August 2005, and Nouriel Roubini, who, in 2005, clearly forecast that housing prices were riding a speculative wave that would soon sink the economy. See, for example, Roubini (2008).

1

trillion[5] – helped avoid a global depression. But the causes of the crisis remain the subject of fierce debate.

A dramatic rise in global imbalances had preceded the crisis. They were widely viewed as its cause, but economists disagree about how important the imbalances were. Some economists consider them to be the primary cause of the crisis, while others view them as only facilitating its development.[6]

Many observers believed that the imbalances arose from East Asian countries' export-oriented strategies and accumulation of foreign reserves as self-insurance following the 1997–8 regional financial crisis, and especially from China's undervalued exchange rate. The global imbalances and reserve accumulations, so the thinking went, led to cheap credit and a housing bubble in the United States. But there is another explanation. The combination in the United States of financial deregulation (starting in the 1980s), which allowed higher leverage, and low interest rates (following the bursting of the dot-com bubble in 2001) led to a large increase in liquidity, which fed the housing bubble. The wealth effect from the housing bubble and innovative financial instruments supported excessive household consumption. This consumption surge and the fiscal deficits needed to finance the wars in Iraq and Afghanistan generated large US trade deficits and global imbalances. The United States was able to maintain these severe imbalances for as long as it did because of the dollar's reserve currency status.

The excess liquidity in the United States also contributed to large gross capital outflows to other countries, supporting booms in their investments and equity markets and growth. The dollars obtained through trade surpluses and capital inflows were converted into local currencies and were held as reserves by the central banks. Those reserves then flowed back to the United States, to buy Treasury bills or to invest in US financial markets, giving the impression that low US interest rates were caused by the excessive accumulation of reserves in those nonreserve currency countries. When the housing bubble burst in the United States and the financial system collapsed, a global crisis resulted.

---

[5] IMF (2009: tables 3 & 4).

[6] See Portes (2009) and Krugman (2009a) for arguments that global imbalances were the primary cause of the crisis; see Rajan (2010), Lin, Dinh, and Im (2010), Roubini and Mihm (2010), Laibson and Mollerstrom (2010), and Obstfeld and Rogoff (2010) for arguments that the imbalances only facilitated its development.

Meanwhile, financial deregulation and liberalization also swept over Europe. Major European banks established branches in eastern and southern Europe, using high leverage to support housing bubbles and consumption booms. The adoption of the euro exacerbated intra-European imbalances, whose unsustainability became evident only in the aftermath of the global financial crisis, triggering the sovereign debt crisis. Fiscal positions that had been manageable before the crisis, when government revenues were rising, became unsustainable in the recession following the global financial crisis. The recession and the fiscal stimulus packages adopted to counteract it resulted in a ballooning of fiscal deficits and a massive deterioration in debt indicators, setting the stage for the sovereign debt crisis in the Eurozone that began with Greece in early 2010.

As early as 2003 many academics and policymakers in high-income countries were pointing at China as the culprit behind the mounting global imbalances, even though China did not begin to amass a large trade surplus until 2005. In fact, China's large current account surplus reflects mainly its high domestic saving rate. Had the academic and policy communities understood the real causes of the crisis and dealt with them earlier, the crisis could have been averted or at least mitigated. Only if we understand the roots of the crisis and its likely evolution can we design an appropriate policy response to prevent a recurrence.

1 | The world economy and the 2008–9 crisis

The world economy grew rapidly between 2000 and 2008. Unemployment and poverty declined as advanced, emerging, and developing economies alike recorded high growth rates. Strong demand for raw materials from fast-growing developing and emerging market economies pushed up commodity prices, to the benefit of resource-rich countries. The world was experiencing a period of widespread euphoria.

The dampening in recent years of the volatility of business cycles in advanced industrial economies also bred optimism about economic prospects and the sustainability of economic growth (Figure 1.1). Recessions were shorter and their impacts milder. For example, the 1987 US stock market crash did not lead to a recession, and the 1990–91 recession was fairly short and shallow. Similarly, the bursting of the dot-com bubble in 2001 resulted in only a mild recession and a sluggish recovery. At the same time, expansions were lasting longer. Some refer to this success in stabilizing the business cycles and ushering in an era of low inflation, high growth, and modest recessions as the "Great Moderation."[1]

Business and financial deregulation and innovative financial instruments were credited with creating a more flexible and adaptable economic system, enabling the Great Moderation. Financial assets were considered less risky than beforehand, prompting more financial intermediation, which fueled economic growth and spurred financial innovation, especially through hedge funds. Business cycles were less volatile because of abundant global liquidity – partly reflecting surplus savings in some emerging market economies – giving the false sense that

---

[1] The term "Great Moderation" was coined by James Stock and Mark Watson (2002).

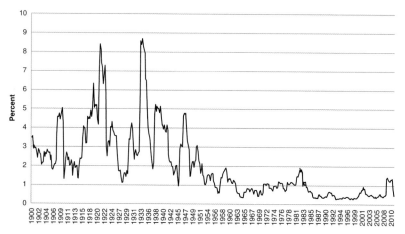

Figure 1.1 Standard deviation of growth in US gross national product
Source: Gordon (1990); the time series was extended to 2010 by the author.

stability was attributable to structural improvements in the financial system. In addition, expanding globalization and free trade – boosted in part by China's entry into the World Trade Organization in 2001 – and the buoyant growth of China and newly emerging market economies were expected to keep inflation at bay even as global growth accelerated.[2]

As the subprime crisis spread in the United States, economists expected that the rest of the world would "decouple" – a concept propounded by Jim O'Neil of Goldman Sachs and rapidly taken up by others. Decoupling contended that Brazil, China, India, and the Russian Federation, shielded by their own strong domestic demand, would not be affected by the meltdown in the US subprime market. For example, in September 2008 the German minister of finance, Peer Steinbrueck, declared: "The crisis is above all an American problem. The other G7 ministers share this opinion."[3] Clearly, many policy-makers were unaware how closely linked US and European financial industries had become.

As the global economy was expanding rapidly, so were global imbalances, with large current account surpluses in East Asia (and, to a lesser extent, in Europe) and a widening current account deficit in the United States. Views on the importance of these global imbalances differed

---

[2] Roubini and Mihm (2010: 26–31).   [3] Roubini and Mihm (2010: 115).

sharply. Economists such as Fred Bergsten and Miranda Xafa viewed the imbalances as a threat to world economic stability.[4] In testimony before the US Congress, Bergsten asserted that "the global imbalances probably represent the single largest current threat to the continued growth and stability of the US and world economies."[5] Others, such as Ben Bernanke, considered imbalances to be the natural outcome of underdeveloped financial systems in developing countries, which prompted growing demand for US dollar–denominated financial assets, but he did not think that they presented a major risk to the global economy.[6]

But it was US domestic policy that was largely responsible for the global imbalances and the country's real estate bubble. The loose monetary policy introduced in 2001 in response to the bursting of the dot-com bubble, magnified by financial deregulation and innovations in financial instruments, resulted in a boom in the US housing market. The wealth effect from the housing boom coupled with the financial innovations that allowed households to capitalize the gains in housing prices led to household overconsumption and overindebtedness. Rapidly rising household debt and public indebtedness to finance the Iraq and Afghanistan wars resulted in a large US current account deficit, made possible by the dollar's reserve currency status.

In hindsight, the loose monetary policy response to the recession brought on by the bursting of the dot-com bubble in 2001 went too far and lasted too long. Moreover, when the US trade deficit became a growing concern to policymakers in 2003, the policy response could have been better tailored to the causes of the global imbalances had policymakers acknowledged the role of excess US demand instead of pointing to other countries to explain rising US imports. The US housing boom could have been restrained and financial regulation

---

[4] Miranda Xafa, a member of the IMF's executive board, argued before the crisis: "The rising US current account deficit has increased concerns among policymakers about a possible abrupt disruption and disorderly unwinding, involving a major sell-off of dollar assets, a sharp increase in US interest rates, and an associated sharp reduction in US absorption. Such an abrupt unwinding of imbalances, triggered by a sudden loss of market confidence in the dollar, would obviously have negative spillover market effects on financial markets and the global economy" (Xafa 2007).
[5] Bergsten (2007).   [6] Bernanke (2005a).

tightened much earlier, thereby avoiding the global crisis, or at least moderating its more harmful impacts.

Eruption, evolution, and consequences of the crisis

The global financial crisis erupted on September 15, 2008, with the collapse of Lehman Brothers, largely as a result of accumulating defaults on mortgages and derivative products. The ensuing financial crisis led to a sharp decline in credit to the private sector and a steep rise in interest rates. As more US financial institutions collapsed, so did equity markets and international trade and industrial production, with the effects now spreading to other advanced economies and to emerging market and developing economies as well (Figure 1.2). With real growth around the world well below projected rates, the advanced economies entered a recession. Only China and developing Asia maintained strong growth.

By most measures, the crisis reached proportions not seen in modern economic history. Barry Eichengreen and Kevin O'Rourke, two respected economic historians who documented the global financial

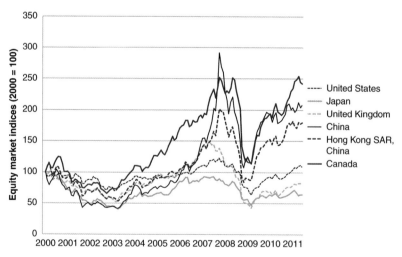

Figure 1.2 Collapse of equity markets
Source: World Bank's "Global economic monitor" database: http://data. worldbank.org/data-catalog/global-economic-monitor.

crisis, have compared it with the Great Depression of the 1930s.[7] World output and world trade collapsed, unemployment soared, credit dried up, and stock markets nosedived.

The bursting of the US real estate bubble triggered the crisis. Housing prices fell precipitously in the second quarter of 2007, but growth in housing prices had been slowing since 2005. Housing prices had begun to rise sharply in the late 1990s, increasingly deviating from market fundamentals as underwriting standards weakened.[8] Prices peaked in April 2006. When the US Federal Reserve Board tightened monetary policy, banks stopped offering teaser rates on subprime mortgages (so-called "NINJA"[9] loans, made without documentation of borrowers' income) and started insisting that borrowers pay off debt. As housing prices continued to plunge, mortgage delinquencies, charge-offs, and defaults accelerated. The liquidation of foreclosed housing accelerated the already rapid decline in the real estate market. Alarmed by the expanding housing glut, banks that were overextended in the housing market cut back sharply on new mortgages. As housing prices continued to fall, increasing numbers of borrowers with adjustable-rate mortgages defaulted, further endangering the position of financial institutions that held subprime loans securitized through new instruments such as collateralized debt obligations (CDOs, discussed below).

As the bottom fell out of the CDO market, large-scale sell-offs of these instruments and of assets connected to the defaults followed.[10] Hedge funds that dealt in these instruments had become highly leveraged, with the riskiest having debt to equity ratios as high as 20 to 1. By summer 2007, for example, two hedge funds run by Bear Stearns, which had invested several billion dollars of short-term loans in highly illiquid

---

[7] Eichengreen and O'Rourke (2010).

[8] According to Paul Krugman and Robin Wells (2010), it was synthetic mortgage securities and the degradation of underwriting standards that contributed most to the housing market crisis. Mortgage originators – which in many cases had no traditional banking business – made housing loans and then immediately sold the loans to other firms, which pooled and repackaged the loans and then sold shares in these security pools. Rating agencies gave AAA ratings to the most senior of these securities – those that had first claim on interest and principal repayment. As the housing bubble continued to inflate, making enormous profits for those involved, no one wanted to think about the risks inherent in a future housing bust. When the bust came, much of that AAA paper was worth just pennies on the dollar.

[9] "NINJA" stands for "no income, no job, or assets."   [10] Lewis (2010).

subprime CDO tranches, were rapidly losing most of their value. Banks responded by withdrawing the short-term loans that the hedge funds had used to finance the CDOs. The collapse of those two funds presaged the fate of hundreds of other hedge funds and of other institutions in the shadow banking system that perform banking functions but are not regulated as banks, such as mutual funds and money market mutual funds.[11]

The first signs of a serious crisis emerged in late 2007, when rising mortgage defaults led to the collapse of two international banks, the German IKB Deutsche Industriebank and the UK Northern Rock. In response, the central banks of Canada, the European Union, Switzerland, and the United States announced a plan in December 2007 to provide at least $90 billion in short-term financing to banks. Shortly thereafter the European Central Bank injected $500 billion into the financial system.

In March 2008 Bear Stearns filed for bankruptcy and was bought by J. P. Morgan for less than a tenth of its precrisis value. The crisis erupted in full force in September 2008, when Merrill Lynch, Lehman Brothers, and the insurance companies AIG and HBOS filed for bankruptcy, largely as a result of their exposure in the real estate market.[12] The banks were so highly leveraged that they were vulnerable to even a small decline in housing-related markets. Lehman Brothers' collapse was the largest bankruptcy in US history. With Lehman's fall, all credit between financial institutions ended abruptly, as the uncertainty of balance sheet positions made intrabank lending too risky. This sudden halt in credit, which triggered a liquidity crisis and bank runs, can be seen by the dramatic jump in 2008 in the spread between the London Interbank Offered Rate (LIBOR) and the overnight indexed swap rate (Figure 1.3).

With leading US banks, insurance companies, and pension funds facing bankruptcy, the US government responded swiftly with a $700 billion bank bailout to forestall complete financial system collapse. To encourage banks to resume lending among themselves and to businesses and consumers, Congress authorized the Treasury to insure or purchase up to $700 billion in commercial or residential mortgage securities or related financial instruments under the Troubled Assets Relief Program. To save AIG, the largest insurance company in the world,

---

[11] Roubini and Mihm (2010).   [12] Roubini and Mihm (2010).

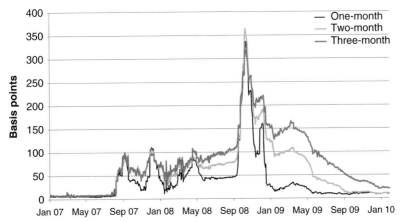

Figure 1.3 Spread between LIBOR and the overnight indexed swap rate
Note: The LIBOR–overnight indexed swap rate spread measures the risk of default associated with lending to other banks.
Source: Bullard (2010), based on daily data from the *Financial Times* and Reuters for 2007 to 2010.

from a liquidity crisis and help financial institutions restore credit, the Federal Reserve Board lowered effective interest rates to a nominal rate close to 0 percent. Shortly before the collapse of Lehman Brothers, the government had taken over Fannie Mae and Freddie Mac, whose sales of mortgage securities in the secondary mortgage market had gotten them into financial trouble.[13]

The financial crisis severely damaged the real economy. Consumer credit, which had been growing steadily during the boom years, dried up. Companies with expansion plans could not raise the capital to finance them. Worldwide, the number of start-ups tumbled, as lending for new projects became too risky.

The US recession started in December 2007 and lasted eighteen months, when growth finally began to pick up, though still sluggishly. US gross debt climbed from 62 percent of GDP before the crisis to almost 94 percent in 2010, largely reflecting a sharp downturn in tax revenue because of the recession. Demand fell in all sectors after September 2008,

---

[13] Fannie Mae and Freddie Mac are US government-sponsored enterprises created to expand the secondary mortgage market by securitizing mortgages (mortgage-backed securities), thus allowing lenders to reinvest their assets in more lending and increase the number of lenders in the mortgage market.

but the decline was larger for goods than for services. Retail sales collapsed as consumers, uneasy about the future, postponed durable goods purchases and vacations. The automobile sector was hit particularly hard, with capacity utilization rates at historic lows of less than 40 percent. Restructuring became inevitable for most automobile companies, and many filed for bankruptcy. When Chrysler and General Motors did so in the middle of 2009 they were rescued by the US Treasury, which became an equity shareholder as part of the American Recovery and Reinvestment Act of 2009, a $787 billion fiscal stimulus package.

Employment also declined precipitously in the United States, but the distribution of job losses was uneven across sectors, skills, and states. More than 8.1 million jobs were lost, almost 7 percent of total employment. Construction and durable goods were the most severely affected; at the trough of the cycle, the construction industry employed almost 30 percent fewer people than it had at the beginning of the recession. The downturn was harsher in states that had experienced a large housing boom and in the already depressed "Rust Belt," where manufacturing has been a major employer. Unemployment rose more for workers without qualifications, who tended to work in sectors hit hardest by the crisis (construction, leisure, and transport). Long-term unemployment as a share of total unemployment reached unprecedented levels.

The recession in the United States quickly spread to other advanced economies and then to developing countries, triggering fears of a depression. A few statistics demonstrate the depth of the crisis. In 2009 output fell 1.9 percent globally and 3.4 percent in high-income countries (5.2 percent in Japan, 4.9 percent in the United Kingdom, 4.3 percent in the European Union, and 2.6 percent in the United States). GDP growth fell to about 0.5 percent in emerging market economies, while staying above a reasonably strong 4 percent in developing countries. World trade was 50 percent lower in 2009 than in 2008. Equity markets collapsed. Unemployment rose sharply around the world, surpassing 15 percent in Greece and Spain, where unemployment was already high before the crisis.

The global slowdown exposed vulnerabilities. Countries that had experienced housing booms, such as Ireland and Spain, or had high fiscal deficits before the crisis, such as Greece and Portugal, now teetered on the brink of a sovereign debt crisis and required support from the European Central Bank (ECB) and IMF. The sovereign debt crisis in the Eurozone had potentially calamitous consequences for the world economy.

How the crisis spread around the world

The crisis spread globally through several channels. One was money markets. The collapse of Lehman Brothers in September 2008 rendered its short-term debt effectively worthless, triggering panic among investors and a run on the money market funds that financed the commercial paper market. This intensified perceptions of default risk and sowed panic throughout the global financial system. Following strenuous efforts by central banks to inject liquidity into the system, commercial banks lowered their lending rates.

Trade was another channel. Letters of credit and commercial paper guaranteeing that goods in transit between trading partners would be paid for when they reached their destination were no longer available after the Lehman collapse.[14] As a result, global trade came to a standstill. At the peak of the crisis, in early 2009, exports were down 30 percent year on year in China and Germany, 37 percent in Singapore, and 45 percent in Japan.

Remittances were yet another channel. Total remittances dropped only marginally, but remittances from some groups of workers shrank substantially, particularly remittances from Central American migrants working in the US construction industry. Many, laid off because of the crisis, stopped sending money home altogether, causing aggregate demand and GDP growth to contract in their home countries.

The crisis also spread as a result of the collapse in international commodity prices, especially oil, as demand in advanced economies shrank, throwing oil-exporting countries into fiscal crisis. Oil prices collapsed to $40 a barrel in 2009, down precipitously from a real price of $110 a barrel (in 2005 dollars) a year earlier. In the run-up to the crisis, commodity price hikes added to the effects of the collapse in the financial sector and pushed the advanced economies deeper into recession. Loose monetary policy also contributed to the precrisis hikes by diverting demand from US Treasury bills.[15] Tight commodity markets and declining interest rates engendered a perverse incentive to convert commodities into assets.

---

[14] Roubini and Mihm (2010).   [15] Caballero, Farhi, and Gourinchas (2008).

2 | The real causes of the crisis

Several years after the crisis there is still no consensus on its root cause. Debate focuses on global imbalances and the relative importance of domestic and international factors in the emergence of the US housing bubble. Two main hypotheses have been proposed.

One hypothesis is that East Asian and Chinese economic policies led to a global savings glut that lowered interest rates, stimulating unbridled financial sector growth and inflating the US housing bubble. The export-led growth strategies, efforts to self-insure against a future balance of payments crisis, and the undervaluation of the Chinese currency resulted in large and unmanageable current account surpluses and international reserves. Systematic export promotion by China and East Asian economies through a variety of macroeconomic and microeconomic policies, including dumping, was viewed as the main cause of the global imbalances. Contributing factors were the desire to self-insure by accumulating international reserves as a buffer against a repeat of the 1998 balance of payments crises, when many of these countries had to request financial assistance from the International Monetary Fund. The claim that the Chinese authorities were keeping the value of the yuan artificially low to boost export competitiveness has been repeatedly mentioned as a key factor behind China's rising trade surplus and global imbalances.

An alternative hypothesis is that the US housing bubble was primarily homemade, reflecting the expansion of the mortgage market to low-income segments of the population, the loose monetary policy following the bursting of the dot-com bubble of the 1990s, and failures in the regulation, incentives, design, and structure of the mortgage and financial markets, including the rise of a shadow banking system largely outside the purview of bank regulators.[1] Household overconsumption, made

---

[1] Laibson and Mollerstrom (2010), Lin, Dinh, and Im (2010), and Obstfeld and Rogoff (2010) find that global imbalances and the financial crisis originated primarily in the economic policies of a few countries (including the United States)

possible by the wealth effect of the housing bubble, and rising public debt, brought about by US fiscal policy tied to the Iraq and Afghanistan wars and the tax cuts of the administration of George W. Bush, led to large current account deficits. The United States could finance these large deficits because the dollar was a reserve currency. This hypothesis attributes the crisis to US policies that encouraged unsustainable overconsumption and triggered global imbalances.

Hypothesis 1: global imbalances led to the housing bubble and the global financial crisis

Three policies pursued by China and East Asian economies have been proposed as causes of a global savings glut that put extreme downward pressure on interest rates, stimulating the real estate booms and risky innovations in the financial sector that transmitted the financial crisis worldwide. All three policies – export-led growth strategies,[2] foreign currency reserve accumulation for self-insurance,[3] and China's exchange rate policy[4] – could theoretically create artificially high trade and current account surpluses. If the export-led growth strategy hypothesis were true, trade surpluses should have emerged almost immediately and been reduced by exports from countries competing with East Asian exports, possibly even leading to trade deficits. If the self-insurance argument really explained global imbalances, the imbalances should have come from a rise in trade surpluses primarily in countries that have accumulated reserves for self-insurance and not in

during the 2000s and in distortions that influenced the transmission of these policies through US financial markets and, ultimately, through global financial markets. Specifically, they argue that it was the toxic interaction of the Federal Reserve Board's monetary stance, global real interest rates, credit market distortions, and financial innovation that made the United States the epicenter of the global financial crisis.

[2] Klein and Cukier (2009) exemplify this argument.

[3] Aizenman (2008) and Aizenman and Lee (2008) provide evidence of self-insurance motives in East Asia. Ben-Bassat and Gottlieb (1992) also support this viewpoint, with a general model tested using data on Israel.

[4] Goldstein and Lardy (2009) review this position and argue that a 40 percent appreciation could eliminate China's global current account surplus. Jeanne (2011) presents a model in which savings and capital controls are used to undervalue the real exchange rate.

countries whose currencies are a reserve currency and so do not have to be concerned about a balance of payments crisis. And, if China's exchange rate policy is to blame for global imbalances, its external surplus should be correlated with its exchange rate. Moreover, trade surpluses should have declined or become deficits in developing countries that compete with China's exports.

Export-led growth strategy

Although China and East Asian economies have dramatically increased their trade surpluses in recent years, they have followed export-led growth strategies since the 1960s. Sustainable export-led growth strategies have not been based on targeting an ever-expanding trade surplus but on increasing integration with international markets, leading to more imports as well as exports and generating higher quality jobs in the tradables sector. Therefore, these strategies could not have been the root cause of the large global imbalances since 2000 (Figure 2.1).

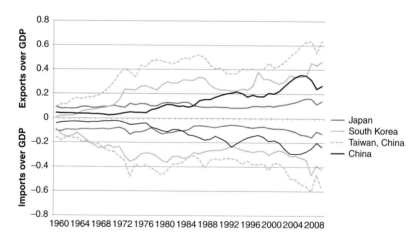

Figure 2.1 Decomposition of the trade balance (exports and imports as a percentage of GDP)

Sources: IMF's "World economic outlook" database, OECD's "National accounts" data, Council for Economic Planning and Development (2011), and World Bank's "National accounts" data.

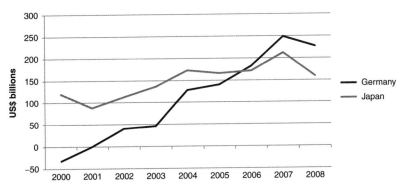

Figure 2.2 Current account surplus
Source: World Bank's "World development indicators" database: http://data.worldbank.org/data-catalog/world-development-indicators.

The self-insurance motive

After the financial crisis of the late 1990s, current account surpluses and foreign reserves mounted in the East Asian emerging market economies. The self-insurance hypothesis views this rise as deliberate, motivated primarily by a desire to accumulate foreign reserves to avoid recourse to international lenders. But this argument is not credible. Other countries, such as Germany and Japan, that do not need to self-insure, because their currencies are fully convertible, also substantially increased their trade surpluses and thus also contributed to rising global imbalances (Figure 2.2).

Self-insurance thus does not explain the widening trade surpluses of economies without a self-insurance motive. Moreover, at more than $3 trillion, China's reserves are now well beyond any need for self-insurance. Some economists attribute the rise in reserves to hot money inflows as well as foreign direct investment (FDI), which augmented the impact of growing current account surpluses.[5]

China's exchange rate policy

China's exchange rate began to be considered a main cause for the global imbalances in 2003, but China did not have a large trade surplus

---

[5] Obstfeld and Rogoff (2010).

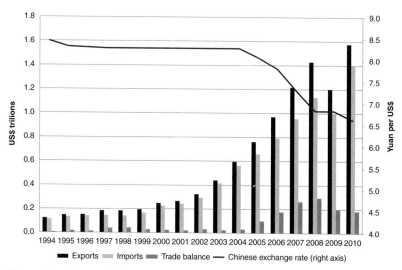

Figure 2.3 China's global trade and exchange rate
Source: IMF's "International financial statistics" database: http://elibrary-data.
imf.org/FindDataReports.aspx?d=330610e=169393.

until 2005, and its trade surplus in 2003 was smaller than in 1997 and 1998 (Figure 2.3). Indeed, in 1998, when the yuan was still pegged to the US dollar, China's currency was viewed as substantially *over*valued.[6]

The argument that China's exchange rate policy was the root cause of the global imbalances rests on the belief that the Chinese authorities kept the value of the yuan artificially low in order to boost exports and reduce imports.[7] A bill co-sponsored by US senators Charles Schumer and Lindsey Graham in 2005 (later withdrawn) calling for a 27.5 percent tariff on Chinese imports reflected this belief.

The over- or undervaluation of the yuan is a subject of intense debate. Estimates of undervaluation range from 3 percent[8] to 50 percent,[9]

---

[6] Lardy (2005).

[7] Krugman (2010a, 2010b) argues that the undervaluation of the yuan caused the large US trade deficit and that the subsequent Chinese purchase of US Treasury bonds lowered interest rates in the United States and caused the real estate and equity bubbles that led to the financial crisis. Low real interest rates also provided investment banks with a strong incentive to structure new and complex financial instruments that helped multiply the effect of failing mortgages throughout the entire financial system during the crisis. See also Lardy (2005).

[8] Funke and Rahn (2005).   [9] Ferguson and Schularick (2009).

depending on the model. Most empirical calculations of undervaluation rely on the theory of purchasing power parity (the same good should have the same price in different countries). Although intuitively appealing, this notion has proved to be unreliable. Labor-intensive goods are consistently less expensive to produce in developing countries than in developed countries, and capital-intensive goods are more costly to produce in developing countries than in developed countries. Some analyses aim at estimating the yuan's value by controlling for *predictable* divergences from purchasing power parity, but even these divergences are subject to considerable uncertainty.

Another approach is based on the fundamental equilibrium exchange rate method. It estimates the exchange rate adjustment that would be needed to attain a current account value in line with its fundamental value.[10] Obviously, such estimates depend on judgments of the fundamental value of the current account as well as of the relationship between a change in the value of the exchange rate and the current account balance. Overall, there seems to be little consensus on how much the yuan deviates from its equilibrium value.

Moreover, the theoretical underpinnings of an expected exchange rate appreciation are unclear. The Balassa–Samuelson theorem, which postulates that an economy's exchange rate appreciates in real terms over the long term when the tradables sector expands rapidly, is one of the major theoretical foundations for the claim that the yuan is undervalued. In a paper co-authored with two colleagues, I show that the real exchange rate in an economy with a rapidly growing tradables sector and large surplus labor in the traditional sector may not appreciate until the surplus labor is depleted.[11] China had abundant labor in its rural areas, so the fact that the exchange rate had not appreciated substantially was not a sign that China was manipulating its exchange rate.

More fundamentally, several economists argue that the effect of an exchange rate appreciation on the current account may be ambiguous. Ronald McKinnon contends that the exchange rate plays little role in adjusting the current account but simply reflects savings–investment balances, which are determined by structural factors that may not be

---

[10] John Williamson (1983) introduced the fundamental equilibrium exchange rate (FEER). For an application of the FEER model to China, see Wang (2004).

[11] Lin, Ju, and Liu (2011).

systematically related to the exchange rate.[12] He argues that, under financial globalization, forcing a creditor country such as China to appreciate its currency is neither necessary nor helpful for reducing its trade surplus. The trade balance is by necessity equal to the difference between savings and investments, but savings and investments are related to macroeconomic balances. Therefore, focusing on the exchange rate as determining savings and investments is misguided. For example, US net saving will not necessarily rise when the US dollar loses value.

Finally, if undervaluation of the yuan caused the global imbalances, the following three empirical phenomena should have occurred.

- When the yuan appreciated by 20 percent between 2005 and 2008 the US trade deficit with China should have declined. It did not happen.
- The US trade deficit with other countries competing with China should have declined, causing other countries to reduce their trade surpluses. This did not happen.
- China's trade surplus with other countries should have increased. Again, this did not happen.

First, the US current account deficit with China rose until 2007, despite the 20 percent appreciation of the yuan after 2005 (see Figure 2.3). In part, this reflected the fact that US import prices remained unchanged or increased after the yuan's appreciation. The large and growing export share of Chinese producers gave them rising market power and allowed them to pass on the higher cost in dollars to wholesalers.[13] And it would have been even more expensive for the United States to import from countries other than China.

Second, if undervaluation of the yuan was the main reason for the rising US trade deficit and China's trade surplus, the US trade deficit with countries that compete with China should have declined. But most other developing countries substantially increased their current account surpluses and reserves over the same period (Figure 2.4).

Third, if undervaluation of the yuan was the main reason for the US trade deficit and for China's trade surplus, China's trade surplus with other advanced economies – such as Germany, Japan, South Korea, and

---

[12] McKinnon (2010).   [13] Goldstein and Lardy (2008: 24).

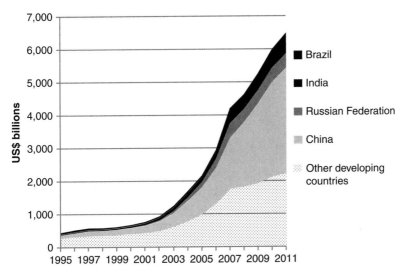

Figure 2.4 Foreign exchange reserves of developing countries
Source: World Bank's "World development indicators" database: http://data.
worldbank.org/data-catalog/world-development-indicators.

Taiwan, China – should also have grown. To the contrary, China's trade with other advanced economies turned into a deficit.

This evidence shows that the exchange rate does not seem to be a significant determining factor in the evolution of the US current account deficit with China. Over the last decade US imports from China rose continually. This trend was not affected by the depreciation of the US dollar–yuan real effective exchange rate from 2001 to 2004 or by its appreciation from 2005 to 2008. Key reasons were structural changes in China's economy and related structural changes in other Asian economies, as well as US monetary and fiscal policies.

The three hypotheses all imply that China and the East Asian economies are driving the global imbalances. If any one of the three (or a combination of the three) is the cause of the global imbalances, US trade deficits with the East Asian economies as a share of total deficits should have increased. While the US trade deficits with China rose substantially, however, US trade deficits with East Asia declined significantly (Figure 2.5). Therefore, although the three commonly accepted causes may have contributed to the global imbalances, they cannot be the fundamental cause.

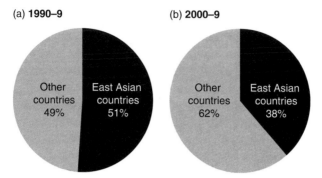

Figure 2.5 Average share of East Asian economies in the US trade deficit
Source: United Nations' "Commodity trade statistics" database: http://comtrade.un.org/db.

The global savings glut and interest rates

Interest rates have been considered one of the most important channels through which global imbalances led to the global economic crisis.[14] The hypothesis is that the global savings glut put extreme downward pressure on interest rates, catalyzing the real estate boom in many countries and the risky financial innovations that were crucial to the crisis's global contagion. But recent research shows that the global savings glut might not have been related to the downward pressure on interest rates and the financing of housing booms.[15]

Financial flows can affect world interest rates, but current accounts and net capital flows shed no light on financing because they have little to say about the underlying changes in gross flows and their contributions to existing stocks, including trade in financial assets.[16] As a result, current account imbalances provide little information about a country's role in international borrowing, lending, and financial intermediation; about how its real investments are financed from abroad; or about the impact of cross-border capital flows on domestic conditions.

The link between current account balances and long-term interest rates also appears tenuous. For example, US dollar long-term interest rates increased between 2005 and 2007 with no apparent

---

[14] Krugman (2009a), Summers (2008).
[15] Borio and Disyatat (2011), Laibson and Mollerstrom (2010).
[16] Borio and Disyatat (2011).

reduction in either the US current account deficit or net capital outflows from surplus countries, such as China. Moreover, the sharp fall in US long-term interest rates after 2007 occurred against a backdrop of improvements in the US current account deficit, and thus smaller net capital flows.[17]

The link between the US current account deficit and global savings appears weak (Figure 2.6). Although that deficit began to deteriorate in the early 1990s, the world saving rate did not begin to trend downward until the end of 2003. And the stabilization and reduction in the US current account deficit since 2006 occurred against a backdrop of a continuing upward drift in savings in emerging market economies.[18] Furthermore, there does not seem to be a clear link between the global saving rate and real interest rates or term premia. Real world long-term interest rates and term premia have both trended downward no matter what was happening with the global saving rate.

The impact of the global savings glut on the housing bubble in the United States has also been questioned.[19] Global saving rates did not trend strongly upward during the inflation phase of the housing bubble. Moreover, a large investment boom should have accompanied a global savings glut – to the tune of at least 4 percent of GDP – because US households would have chosen to invest a large share of those funds. But the US investment rate did not rise from 1995 to 2005 and ended only 1.6 percentage points higher in 2005 than in 1995. Moreover, when Federal Reserve Board chairman Ben Bernanke formulated his global savings glut hypothesis,[20] the investment rate was lower than in 1996. In fact, the boom was in consumption, not investment.

Hypothesis 2: US policies led to the global financial crisis

The other key hypothesis is that global imbalances reflected policies and structural factors affecting savings in the United States rather than

---

[17] Obstfeld and Rogoff (2010) also note that data do not support a claim that the proximate cause of the fall in global real interest rates starting in 2000 was a contemporaneous increase in desired global saving, given that global saving fell by 1.8 percent of world GDP from 2000 to 2002 and aggregate global saving did not rise until later in the decade.

[18] Laibson and Mollerstrom (2010) also make the point about falling interest rates coinciding with a falling global savings rate.

[19] Laibson and Mollerstrom (2010).   [20] Bernanke (2005b).

policies in China and the East Asian economies. To be correct, this hypothesis requires a causal link between US monetary, fiscal, and housing policies and the large and growing US current account imbalances. In several papers, I have argued that the housing bubbles were triggered by the Fed's low interest rate policy following the bursting of the dot-com bubble in 2001, magnified by financial deregulation in the 1980s.[21] These policies, in combination with policies aimed at expanding the availability of mortgages to low-income borrowers in the subprime market, led to excessive risk-taking and leverage, resulting in excess liquidity and bubbles in the housing and equity markets alike. The wealth effect of these bubbles enabled US households

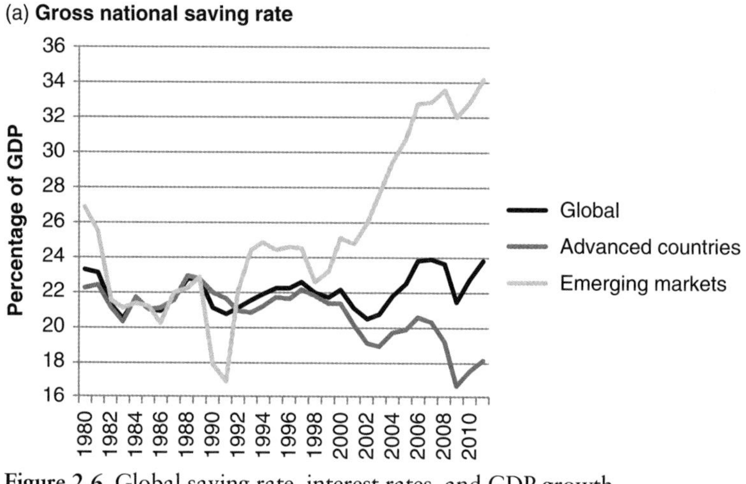

(a) **Gross national saving rate**

Figure 2.6 Global saving rate, interest rates, and GDP growth
Notes: The US term premium and the Eurozone term premium are nominal ten-year term premia based on zero-coupon real and nominal yields calculated on the basis of estimates from a modified version of the term structure model of Hördahl and Tristani (2007). The OECD interest rate is a 2005 GDP PPP-weighted average of real long-term (mainly ten-year) interest rates for Australia, Canada, Denmark, the Eurozone, Japan, New Zealand, Norway, Switzerland, the United Kingdom, and the United States.
Sources: Borio and Disyatat (2011); IMF's "International financial statistics" database: http://elibrary-data.imf.org/FindDataReports.aspx?d=330610e=169393; and OECD's "International development statistics" database.

[21] Lin, Dinh, and Im (2010).

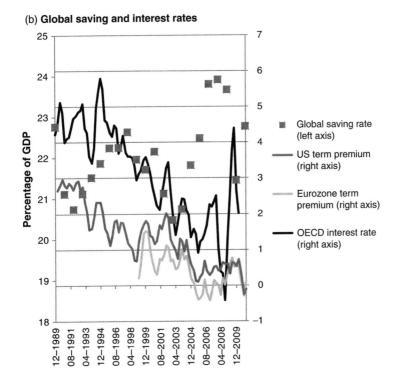

(b) **Global saving and interest rates**

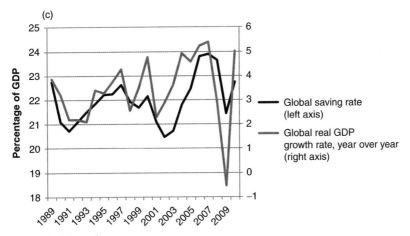

Figure 2.6 (cont.)

to overconsume and, together with the public debt arising from spending on the Afghanistan and Iraq wars and a range of tax cuts, caused US current account deficits to rise.

Aggregate demand pressures emanating from the accommodative monetary policy were initially reflected in oil and other commodity prices and finally led to an increase in headline inflation. The consequent tightening of monetary policy resulted in a correction in housing prices, triggering defaults on subprime loans, large losses for banks and financial institutions, sharp increases in risk aversion, a loss of confidence and trust among market participants, and substantial deleveraging and capital outflows from emerging market economies. The earlier financial excesses were thus reversed in a disruptive manner.

Loose monetary policies and low interest rates

The Fed's monetary policy, already fairly loose since the 1980s, became even more expansionary when the technology bubble burst in early 2000 and caused a recession. In the run-up to the bursting of the bubble, stock prices continued to climb, but the Fed did not intervene. When the bubble burst, consumers experienced a large loss of wealth. With consumption and economic activity plummeting and the economy heading toward recession, the Fed adopted an aggressive monetary policy to mitigate these effects, reducing the federal funds rate twenty-seven times, from 6.5 percent in March 2001 to 1 percent in June 2003 (Figure 2.7).[22] Testifying before Congress on July 15, 2003, Federal Reserve Board chairman Alan Greenspan stated that the economy was not "showing convincing signs of a sustained pickup of growth," so a further easing of interest rates could encourage growth without "ultimately stoking inflationary pressures." Other events reinforced the decision to keep interest rates low, including the terrorist attacks on the United States in 2001. The US stock market fell sharply after the attacks, raising concerns about the health of the US economy. Thanks to the active monetary policy, the US economy recovered quickly, and the dot-com recession was short-lived.[23]

---

[22] Rajan (2010).

[23] According to the National Bureau of Economic Research (2010), the 2001 recession lasted eight months (from March to November), shorter than the average duration of US recessions in the postwar era.

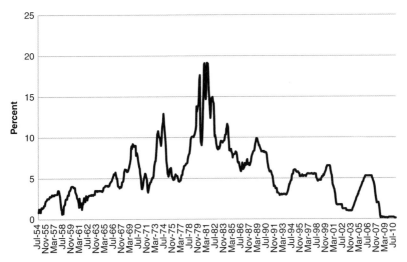

Figure 2.7 Long-term effective federal funds rate
Source: US Federal Reserve Board (2009).

The Fed's monetary policy and low interest rates had a strong impact on the US housing market. A 2008 paper from the Federal Reserve Bank of St Louis observed that "monetary policy has significant effects on housing investment and house prices and that easy monetary policy designed to stave off the perceived risks of deflation from 2002 to 2004 contributed to a boom in the housing market in 2004 and 2005."[24] Specifically, the Federal Reserve assured markets of its willingness to maintain easy monetary conditions and to step in to provide liquidity should financial markets run into trouble – the so-called "Greenspan put."[25] These assurances, along with a range of housing policies, helped boost lending considerably, including to borrowers who were barely (or even not at all) creditworthy.[26] Rajan notes that "sustained easy monetary policy that is maintained while jobs are still scarce has the effect of

---

[24] Jarocinski and Smets (2008: 362).
[25] This is a term coined by the *Financial Times* in a January 4, 2001, article that referred to Greenspan's statement that the Fed would intervene ex post to smooth the effects of the burst bubble but could not know about it ex ante (*Financial Times* 2001).
[26] Jeffrey Sachs (2009) and Maurice Obstfeld and Kenneth Rogoff (2010) also note that the overly accommodative Fed policy starting in 2001 played a key role in the expansion of the housing market and global imbalances.

increasing risk taking and inflating asset-price bubbles, which again weaken the fabric of the economy over the longer term."[27] Household borrowing shot up from 66 percent of GDP in 1997 to 100 percent a decade later. The protracted period of low short-term interest rates in combination with financial innovation also lowered long-term interest rates by dampening inflationary expectations and making financial assets appear less risky. That led to excess liquidity and to a housing price boom beginning in 2002.

As a result, the US economy surged, but domestic production could not keep up with rising domestic consumption. Imports bridged the supply gap in consumer goods, including imports from oil-exporting countries, leading to current account deficits with these countries. As China had become the main producer of labor-intensive processed consumer goods by 2000, the United States ran an increasingly large deficit with China, which in turn ran trade deficits with many East Asian economies that provided it with intermediate products.

The loose monetary policy and low interest rates not only fed the housing bubble in the United States but also encouraged an aggressive search for higher yields on a global scale, reflected in a record $1.2 trillion in capital flows to developing countries in 2007 (up from $200 billion in 2000). Financial liberalization in many developing countries contributed to these large capital flows and to record-high investment-led growth in these countries.[28] This accelerated growth jacked up demand for (and the prices of) natural resources and increased trade surpluses in natural-resource-exporting countries, stimulating a boom in commodity prices that further accelerated growth in natural-resource-exporting developing countries. As a result, many advanced capital-goods-exporting countries, such as Germany and Japan, amassed large trade surpluses. The foreign reserves accumulated through trade and capital account surpluses flowed back to the United States, a reserve currency country, as countries purchased Treasury bills

---

[27] Rajan (2010).

[28] The World Bank (2010) notes that the fall in borrowing costs from 2003 to 2007 was associated with almost 70 percent of the increase in capital flows into developing countries and 80 percent of the increase in domestic consumption. In addition, on average, investment to GDP ratios in developing countries increased 5.2 percentage points from 2000 to 2007. More than half the 1.4 percentage point increase in potential output growth rates in developing countries from 2003 to 2007 was directly attributable to the capital deepening during this period.

or other financial investments. This led in turn to a capital account surplus in the United States.[29]

Wealth effects of the real estate boom and rising stock market

Real estate and equity investments increased rapidly, and, as mortgages became more readily available, housing prices rose far higher than economic fundamentals warranted; the housing boom had become a bubble.[30] The price of a median house rose 124 percent between 1997 and 2006. The national median home price rose from 2.9 times to 3.1 times median household income in the two decades ending in 2001 and then to 4.0 times in 2004 and 4.6 times in 2006.[31] In a book entitled *Irrational Exuberance*, Robert Shiller points out how far housing prices had deviated from what economic fundamentals would suggest (Figure 2.8).[32]

---

[29] Most scholars emphasize that the high demand for US Treasuries from trade surplus countries allowed the US government to borrow more cheaply than otherwise – a phenomenon often referred to as the "exorbitant privilege" (Eichengreen 2011a). More important than this privilege, however, is the fact that, as long as the US dollar is an accepted reserve currency, the funds to support the trade deficits will recycle back to the United States as Treasury bill purchases or other forms of financial investments. The resulting US capital account surpluses offset the current account deficits. This may give the appearance that investors prefer the US dollar (Bernanke 2005a; Bernanke *et al.* 2011), but it is actually because the US dollar is a reserve currency that outflows (through the US current account deficit and gross capital exports and held as reserves by other central banks and as private sector savings in nonreserve currency countries) must recycle back to the United States as investments in Treasury bills or other financial instruments; otherwise, the central banks and private sector would earn nothing on their holdings of reserve currency, because it cannot circulate directly within the receiving countries.

[30] IMF (2008: 17): "The countries that have experienced the largest unexplained increases in house prices over the past decade are Australia, Ireland, and the United Kingdom; house prices in these countries were 20 to 30 percent higher in 2007 than can be attributed to fundamentals. A group of other countries – including France, Italy, the Netherlands, and Spain – have house price gaps of 10–20 percent. The estimated gap for the United States – about 7 percent – is smaller than for most other countries and has been narrowing compared with earlier estimates, partly reflecting the decline in US house prices over the past 18 months."

[31] Steverman and Bogoslaw (2008).   [32] Shiller (2005).

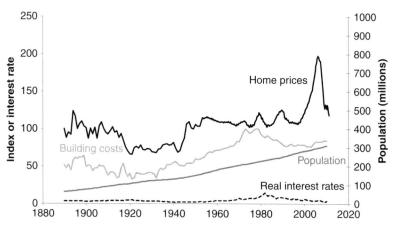

Figure 2.8 US home prices and economic fundamentals
Source: Shiller (2005).

Because housing and real estate constitute an important share of household wealth,[33] the wealth effects from the booming real estate market and the recovery of the equity market made households feel richer and consume more. While disposable personal income rose between 1986 and 2009, net worth fell from 1999 to 2002 before rising from 2002 to 2006. The US stock market rose more than 50 percent from June 2003 to October 2007.[34] Financial innovations allowed households to refinance their mortgages and capitalize their wealth gains in the housing markets. Household debt rose rapidly with consumption, from 100 percent of household disposable income in 2001 to 132 percent in 2007. Household consumption accounted for most of this 32 percentage point increase.

The increase in housing prices contributed to the consumption boom primarily through home equity loans and mortgage refinancing cash-outs.[35] A study using micro-data to estimate the elasticity of consumption to housing and financial wealth from 1989 to 2001 found empirical evidence of a link between housing wealth and consumption, with a

---

[33] Data from the US Federal Reserve Board (2009) on US flow of funds accounts indicate that the share of real estate in the total net worth of households and nonprofit organizations was less than 30 percent in 2000, peaked at 40 percent in 2005, then dropped to 37 percent in 2008 and 34 percent in 2009 (Q3).
[34] World Bank (2010).   [35] Greenspan and Kennedy (2008).

substantially larger marginal propensity to consume from housing wealth than from financial wealth.[36] Another study, using panel data for fourteen countries, found that "changes in housing prices should be considered to have a larger and more important impact than changes in stock market prices in influencing household consumption in the US and in other developed countries."[37]

Housing equity can be extracted through three channels: cash available to home sellers, which is equal to the difference between the sale price of a home and any mortgage debt paid off at the time of sale and closing costs; home equity loans,[38] which are equal to originations minus repayments resulting from other forms of equity extraction; and cash-out refinancing, which is refinance originations minus repayments of first liens resulting from refinancing. During the period from 1991 to 2006 cash from these liquidity channels alone averaged an estimated $590 billion annually,[39] about 67 percent of it from equity extracted through sales of existing homes, 20 percent from home equity loans, and 13 percent from cash-out refinancing.

A study using an empirical model to examine the nexus of the asset price boom, consumption, and the current account balance found that asset price movements explained a substantial share of the cross-sectional variation in international financial flows.[40] In regressions with real housing price appreciation as the independent variable and the accumulated balance of trade as the dependent variable, the study found that movements in residential home prices explained about half the variation in accumulated current account deficits in a sample of eighteen Organisation for Economic Co-operation and Development (OECD) countries plus China. While acknowledging that the regressions cannot identify causality, the authors point to preliminary evidence that causality runs from asset bubbles to current account deficits, based on the finding that the consumption boom was financed largely by real estate loans.

---

[36] Bostic, Gabriel, and Painter (2006).
[37] Case, Quigley, and Shiller (2005: 26).
[38] Home equity loans enable borrowers to use the equity amassed in their home as collateral. A home equity loan creates a lien against the borrower's house and reduces actual home equity.
[39] Greenspan and Kennedy (2008).   [40] Laibson and Mollerstrom (2010).

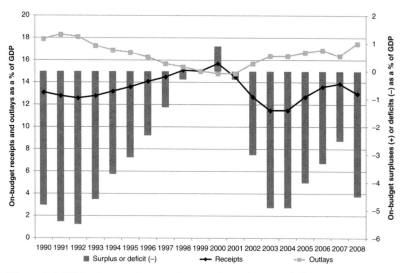

Figure 2.9 US budget receipts, outlays, and surpluses or deficits
Source: US Office of Management and Budget (2010).

One more factor contributed to the large US current account deficits: public sector dis-saving. The wars in Afghanistan starting in 2001 and Iraq starting in 2003 and the tax cuts enacted by the George W. Bush administration in 2001 and 2003, compounded by the reduction in tax revenues because of the recession, moved the US budget from a surplus of almost 1 percent of GDP in 2000 to a deficit of 4.5 percent in 2008 (Figure 2.9).[41] All else equal, this increase in the budget deficit implies a fall in public sector savings and national savings and a corresponding swing of 5.5 percentage points of US GDP in the current account.

---

[41] US Office of Management and Budget (2010). The deficit defined here excludes Social Security funds.

3 | Financial deregulation and the housing bubble

Behind the low US saving rates and the asset bubble in the real estate market were the expansionary monetary and fiscal policies of the United States, the key factor in the emergence of the global imbalances. This asset bubble fueled an extended consumption spree and rising current account deficits, which the United States was able to finance because of the dollar's international reserve currency status. But the housing and financial sector policies for opening the mortgage market to borrowers not previously considered creditworthy – the subprime mortgage market – and the financial innovations created to support the subprime mortgages were the primary causes of the rising and bursting of the housing bubble. The financial deregulation and low interest rates brought about by the Federal Reserve's monetary policy fostered expansion and innovation in the financial sector, and increasingly complex financial derivatives allowed the risks associated with the new instruments to be underestimated and fueled the housing bubble.[1] When the housing bubble burst, these new financial instruments led to financial crises in the United States and the world. How did this happen?

New financial instruments and the housing bubble

Starting in the 1970s, US policy emphasized deregulation in order to encourage business activity. It also reduced oversight and the disclosure of new activities undertaken by banks and other evolving financial institutions. Savings and loan (S&L) associations specialized in taking deposits with short-term maturities and making mortgage loans with long-term maturities. This asset–liability mismatch made them especially vulnerable to the costs of high interest rates. When the Fed

[1] Sachs (2009).

increased interest rates to combat inflation in the late 1970s, most thrift institutions reported large losses. By 1982 many institutions had failed, but no systemic reforms were taken.[2] Despite the signs of increasing financial distress, the S&L industry continued to expand rapidly. As investors, seeing substantial potential for profits, invested in real estate, S&L institutions shifted from home mortgage loans to higher-risk loans funded by deposits attracted by above-market interest rates. When the Tax Reform Act of 1986 eliminated most of the tax shelters that had made real estate an attractive investment, many deposits were withdrawn, and hundreds of institutions failed. The subsequent bailout of the S&L industry cost some $210 billion.

The rise in increasingly risky financial transactions went hand in hand with growing consolidation in the financial industry. Banks realized that the larger they became, the better their prospects of being bailed out by the government if their increasingly risky businesses failed (they had become "too big to fail"). Between 1990 and 1998 the number of banking institutions shrank 27 percent as banks merged to reduce their risk.[3] In 1994 the Riegle–Neal Interstate Banking and Branching Efficiency Act eliminated restrictions on interstate banking and branching, thus supporting even greater banking consolidation.[4] Then, in 1999, the Glass–Steagall Act regulating banks was replaced by the Gramm–Bliley–Leach Act, essentially eliminating the separation between traditionally conservative commercial banks and the more risk-tolerant investment banks.[5] Banks could now simultaneously offer the services of a commercial bank, an insurance company, an asset manager, a hedge fund, and a private equity fund. With access to deposit insurance and Federal Reserve support, banks pursued high-risk activities that endangered the entire financial system.

In 2004 the US Securities and Exchange Commission relaxed the net capital rule, enabling investment banks to increase the debt they could

---

[2] Sherman (2009).   [3] Mallaby (2010: 11).

[4] One example of such consolidations occurred in April 1998, when Travelers Insurance Group and Citicorp, the parent body of Citibank, announced plans to merge and form Citigroup, Inc., taking in the combination of banking and securities dealing. Although the merger was not entirely compliant with the spirit of the Glass–Steagall Act, bank executives structured it in a way that conformed to the Federal Reserve's increasingly liberal interpretation of the act.

[5] Roubini and Mihm (2010: 74).

assume vastly and fueling growth in the mortgage-backed securities that supported subprime mortgages. These mortgage-backed securities – collateralized mortgage obligations, collateralized debt obligations (CDOs), collateralized loan obligations, and CDOs of CDOs of CDOs (CDO3s), which assembled multiple credit default swaps to mimic an underlying CDO – were divided into tranches of various levels of risk. These securities and the risk they implied became difficult to value, ratcheting up the risk level in the financial system. This lack of transparency enabled even quasi-public institutions such as Fannie Mae and Freddie Mac, and prospective borrowers, to avoid scrutiny. In this opaque environment, it became increasingly common for borrowers to misrepresent their income and to fail to provide documentation.

There was no clearinghouse for trades in most of the new derivative instruments, as there was for stocks, bonds, and options, and the Commodity Futures Modernization Act of 2000 ensured that derivatives remained unregulated. Derivatives trading expanded swiftly, rising from an outstanding nominal value of $106 trillion in 2001 (1,039 percent of US GDP and 331 percent of world GDP) to $531 trillion in 2008 (3,688 percent of US GDP and 868 percent of world GDP).[6] The legal and technological infrastructure of the industry was unable to handle this enormous expansion in derivatives volume, especially in the absence of regulation.[7]

Mortgage-backed securities thrived in this shadow banking system, which grew dramatically in the run-up to the crisis (Figure 3.1). This growth was partly the result of a perceived decline in the profit-making opportunities of traditional commercial banks. Facing competition from nonbanks and their products, such as junk bonds and commercial paper, the traditional commercial banks had begun transforming themselves in ways that reduced regulatory scrutiny.[8] A new shadow banking system emerged that included nonbank mortgage lenders, structured investment vehicles and conduits, investment banks and broker-dealers, money market funds, hedge funds and private equity funds, and state- and local-government-sponsored pools of auction rate securities and tender option bonds. The common denominator of

---

[6] Semiannual over-the-counter derivatives statistics at end-June 2011 (Bank for International Settlements [BIS] 2012).
[7] Goodman (2008).   [8] Gorton and Metrick (2010).

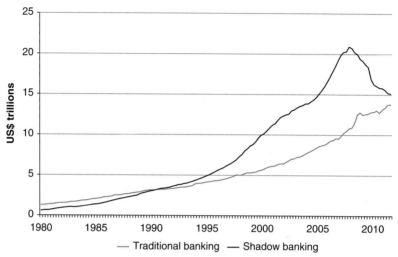

Figure 3.1 Traditional and shadow banking systems
Note: Shadow banking funding includes commercial paper and other short-term borrowing (banker acceptances), repo liabilities, net securities loaned, liabilities and pool securities of government-sponsored enterprises, liabilities of asset-backed securities issuers, and money market mutual fund assets.
Sources: Financial Crisis Inquiry Commission (2011); US Federal Reserve Board (2009).

these new institutions was that they acted as banks but were not regulated as banks, encouraging further opacity in the financial system.[9]

This lack of transparency was a danger, because institutions in the shadow banking system borrowed in short-term liquid markets but invested in long-term illiquid assets. The vulnerabilities emanating from this severe maturity mismatch between assets and liabilities were compounded by the fact that none of the institutions in the shadow banking system had access to a lender of last resort or to deposit insurance. This lack of backstopping vastly increased the threat of bank runs, and explains the collapse of the shadow banking system as the crisis unfolded.

Rating agencies overlooked these vulnerabilities, effectively encouraging even riskier behavior, for three main reasons. A large part of the transactions had been moved off the balance sheet and therefore eluded

---

[9] Roubini and Mihm (2010).

attention. Rating agencies found it increasingly difficult to assess the risk involved with new instruments and valued them using mathematical models that relied on optimistic assumptions that minimized measured risk.[10] And ratings were skewed upward because the rating agencies depended on the financial institution for employment and contracts.

Multiple moral hazard problems further encouraged excessive risk-taking. Traders were rewarded for betting on a CDO but were not punished if the bet failed. Traders and bankers at investment banks, hedge funds, and other financial services firms were rewarded for their performance by a system of constantly rising annual bonuses that depended on whether investment returns exceeded those of a risk-appropriate benchmark (the "alpha"). Investment banks found that such returns were more likely if the investment was associated with tail risk – an event that was very unlikely to occur. It is in the nature of a tail risk event, however, that its likelihood of occurring increases exponentially with the number of people acting on the assumption that it will not occur.[11]

The Federal Reserve Board's approach to bubbles: the "Greenspan put"

The Federal Reserve's reluctance to regulate markets was yet another part of the flawed governance framework in the financial sector. In a 2004 speech on risk and uncertainty in monetary policy, Federal Reserve Board chairman Alan Greenspan said in reference to the technology bubble: "Instead of trying to contain a putative bubble by drastic actions with largely unpredictable consequences, we chose, as we noted in our mid-1999 congressional testimony, to focus on policies 'to mitigate the fallout when it occurs and hopefully ease the transition to the next expansion.'"[12] Greenspan advocated an approach to monetary policy that viewed the risks of intervening in potential bubbles at a time of exuberant expectations as greatly outweighing the benefits. Because it was not possible to know a priori whether a bubble existed, it was only possible to intervene ex post. This view was based on the belief that structural economic changes, in particular rising

---

[10] Roubini and Mihm (2010).   [11] Rajan (2010).   [12] Greenspan (2004: 4).

productivity, had contributed to uncertainty about the economic environment in which monetary policy was operating.

This policy, which came to be known as the "Greenspan put," led to a
belief among traders that the government would always bail them out
after a bubble had burst but would not intervene to keep the bubble from
building.[13] Effectively, the Federal Reserve was providing insurance
against the possibility of a market crash – a situation one analysis of
the Greenspan put referred to as a "meta moral hazard," citing evidence
from two investor surveys.[14] One was a national opinion survey in 2001
of more than 2,000 investors for the Securities Investor Protection
Corporation.[15] The other was a small survey in 2000 of fund managers
and chief economists in London and New York, which asked about
whether "confidence in an ever-increasing stock market is due to the
belief that monetary policy will be used to support the market and that
corrections will elicit reductions in interest rates until the market turns
around."[16] Respondents believed that the Fed reacted more to a stock
market fall than to a rise. Nearly all respondents believed that this type of
reaction was partly responsible for the high valuations on the US stock
market. This asymmetric conduct by the monetary authorities reduced
the risk premium and helped propel the market ever higher. Investors
behaved as though diversified equity instruments were insured subject to
a deductible – a market floor slightly below current prices but with no
ceiling.[17] The Federal Reserve, viewing the subprime market as a benefit
of letting markets go free, refused to intervene even after warnings of
impending danger surfaced.[18]

These financial innovations resulted in a market that lacked transparency, underestimated risk, and had little idea how the new financial
products might behave under conditions of severe stress – a perfect

---

[13] *Financial Times* (2001).   [14] Miller, Weller, and Zhang (2002).
[15] ORC (Opinion Research Corporation) International (2001).
[16] Cecchetti *et al.* (2000: 75).
[17] Miller, Weller, and Zhang (2002) provide empirical evidence for a decline in the
risk premium. The survey was conducted by the company Securities Investor
Protection Corporation.
[18] Inner City Press reported on September 28, 2008: "For example, Bronx-based
Fair Finance Watch commented to the Federal Reserve about the practices of
now-defunct nonbank subprime lender New Century, when US Bancorp bought
warrants for 24 percent of New Century's stock. The Fed, rather than take any
action on New Century, merely waited until US Bancorp sold off some of the
warrants, and then said the issue was moot" (Lee 2008).

environment for the housing and mortgage bubbles to build. Essentially, by injecting vast amounts of money into the economy and letting it stay there too long, the Federal Reserve muted the effect of the bursting of the technology bubble by inflating an entirely new one. The critical condition for the emergence of the global economic crisis, however, was the expansion of the subprime mortgage market.

Expansion of the subprime mortgage market

Long-standing policies making housing mortgages more available to low-income households received new prominence in 1992 with the passage of the Federal Housing Safety and Soundness Act, which aimed at reforming housing agencies and promoting home ownership among low-income and minority groups. The Department of Housing and Urban Development (HUD) was asked to develop affordable housing goals for the agencies and to monitor progress.

Two key tools of the government's policy to promote lending to subprime borrowers were government-sponsored Freddie Mac and Fannie Mae. Freddie and Fannie guaranteed an increasingly large share of mortgage-backed securities and enjoyed an implicit guarantee by the US Treasury. Foreign investors treated these securities as nearly equivalent to US Treasury bills. The supervision of Freddie and Fannie was loose. Since the regulator was funded through congressional appropriations, any effort to enforce quality standards exposed the regulator to the risk of budget cuts. The unwholesome combination of an activist Congress, government-supported private firms, and a weak regulator allowed the subprime market to overheat.

As housing boomed, Freddie Mac and Fannie Mae found the high rates available on subprime lending particularly attractive, while their lack of experience with low-income lending allowed them to ignore the additional risk. Under the administration of Bill Clinton, HUD steadily increased the share of funding that agencies were required to allocate to low-income housing.[19] Stronger enforcement of the Community

---

[19] HUD had begun loosening mortgage restrictions in the mid-1990s, enabling first-time buyers to qualify for loans that they had been unable to get before. In 1995 Freddie Mac and Fannie Mae began receiving affordable housing credit for purchasing mortgage-backed securities, which included loans to low-income borrowers, and they soon began purchasing subprime securities. In 1996 HUD

Reinvestment Act of 1977 under the Clinton administration[20] encouraged further increases in mortgages to low-income borrowers,
especially in highly visible and politically sensitive metropolitan areas.

Subprime lending received another big boost under the George W.
Bush administration, which raised the low-income lending mandate for
Freddie Mac and Fannie Mae to 56 percent of their assets in 2004, even as
the Federal Reserve started to increase interest rates and express concerns
about the housing boom.[21] The accounting scandals at Freddie Mac and
Fannie Mae that were exposed in 2004 made them even more compliant
with Congress's demands for more low-income lending.[22]

But increased lending from government-sponsored agencies alone does
not explain the boom in the subprime mortgage market. Lobbying by the
financial sector seems to have had a major role in legislative changes
supporting subprime lending. One study exploring the effects of financial
industry lobbying on financial regulation in the run-up to the global
economic crisis found strong evidence of positive connections between
both financial sector spending on lobbying and network connections
between lobbyists and legislators and the probability of a legislator
deciding to support deregulation.[23] This lobbying led to a host of new
government policies favoring lending to subprime borrowers.

Special interests, as measured by campaign contributions from the
mortgage industry and constituent interests and by the share of subprime
borrowers in a congressional district, influenced US housing policy during the subprime mortgage credit expansion of 2002 to 2007.[24] From
2002 mortgage industry campaign contributions increasingly targeted

directed Freddie and Fannie to provide at least 42 percent of their mortgage
financing to borrowers whose incomes were below the median in their area. The
target was raised to 50 percent in 2000 and 56 percent in 2004. In addition, HUD
required Freddie and Fannie to provide 12 percent of their portfolio to "special
affordable" loans (loans to borrowers with less than 60 percent of their area's
median income). This target was raised to 28 percent in 2008.

[20] Bhutta (2008).
[21] US National Archives and Records Administration (2004); see also US
Department of Housing and Urban Development (2004).
[22] Financial Crisis Inquiry Commission (2011).   [23] Igan and Mishra (2011).
[24] Mian, Sufi, and Trebbi (2010). Key legislation adopted by Congress includes the
American Dream Downpayment Act of 2003 (US Congress 2003), which aimed
to increase homeownership among low-income communities by providing
assistance with down payments and closing costs. In addition, a number of laws
that would have prevented predatory lending and weakened protection by the
government in the case of default were discussed but were never put to the vote,
including the Responsible Lending Act of 2005 (US Congress 2005c), the Prohibit

US representatives from districts with a large fraction of subprime borrowers. Both subprime mortgage lenders and subprime mortgage borrowers influenced government policy. Since the composition of the districts did not change, while financial sector lobbying for key legislative changes peaked around 2003 to 2006, it seems likely that lobbyists were the most important factor explaining the expansion in government support for the subprime market in the run-up to the crisis.[25]

As more money from Fannie Mae and Freddie Mac flooded into financing low-income housing, real estate prices generated ever higher returns. The new financial derivatives developed in the shadow banking system gave the false impression that risks associated with mortgage lending had fallen. These conditions attracted more private sector lending to low-income borrowers. The share of subprime loans insured by Fannie Mae and Freddie Mac fell as the bubble grew, from 44 percent in 2003 to 22 percent in 2005, while private sector loans came to account for 84 percent of subprime mortgages by 2006.[26] In that year 25 million mortgage loans out of a total of 55 million were subprime.[27] One study found that the number of mortgages obtained in a particular zip code was *negatively* correlated with household income growth.[28]

The subprime mortgage market was also fueled by public and private sector investments from Germany, Japan, and China and a range of other emerging market economies that had large surplus savings as a result of US current account deficits. With government debt yielding very low returns, most investments were directed to the subprime market. Foreigners bought 40 to 50 percent of the securities generated by US financial institutions.[29] Investor confidence was boosted by the high ratings that rating agencies gave to the mortgage-backed securities and collateralized debt obligations that securitized subprime mortgages and derived their value from mortgage payments and housing prices.

The US financial system, in particular the shadow banking system, was also a key element in transmitting the crisis abroad, especially to Iceland and Ireland. Both countries relied on the US financial system for

Predatory Lending Act of 2005 (US Congress 2005b), and the Federal Housing Finance Reform Act of 2005 (US Congress 2005a).

[25] Rajan (2010) argues that it was the increase in income disparity since the 1990s that led politicians to expand the mortgage market to low-income households, so that they could win the support of their low-income constituents. The empirical evidence here does not support his argument.

[26] Duhigg (2008).   [27] Mian and Sufi (2009).

[28] Mian, Sufi, and Trebbi (2010).   [29] Reinhart and Rogoff (2009).

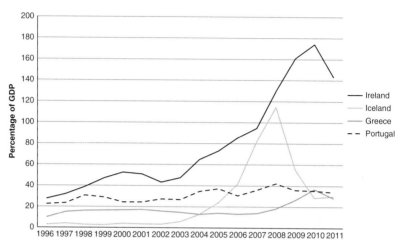

Figure 3.2 Foreign-owned bank sector liabilities
Sources: BIS (2011b); IMF (2010a).

funds, usually as short-term debt, foreign-owned bank deposits, or foreign-owned portfolio equity. Fueled by a rapid expansion of credit, the housing market in both countries began heating up in 2000, resulting in a boom in property investment and construction. The wealth effect from the boom spurred consumption and helped sustain high growth rates. Buoyed by the real estate boom, Ireland's banking system ballooned to five times the size of the economy, and by the end of 2010 its external debt had soared past the 1,000 percent of GDP level.[30]

When the crisis hit, US funds dried up, throwing the banking system in the United States, the Eurozone, and many other countries into a liquidity crunch and slowing credit to the real estate market. As the cost of borrowing rose, demand for housing fell, prices dropped, and the supply of housing mounted. This put pressure on the balance sheets of banks, many of which had relied extensively on profitable mortgage loans to boost earnings. The bailout or purchase of failing banks led to a crisis of confidence and an outflow of foreign assets from some countries (Figure 3.2). The crisis exposed Ireland's vulnerabilities to financial contagion. Iceland collapsed a few months before Ireland, mostly because Ireland refinanced through the European Central Bank (see Chapter 4).[31]

---

[30] IMF (2010a).   [31] Lane (2011).

4 | *What's wrong with the Eurozone*

Although 2010 and 2011 saw the beginnings of a recovery from the global economic crisis, driven primarily by growth in emerging markets, the simmering sovereign debt crisis in the Eurozone still looms large – and could even spark a renewed global financial crisis. What were the roots of Europe's sovereign debt crisis? How important was the global financial crisis to the evolution of that crisis, and how important were factors internal to the Eurozone, especially the adoption of the euro?

The European crisis reflects primarily the reaction of financial markets to overborrowing by private households, the financial sector, and governments in noncore Eurozone countries.[1] The crisis led to economic adjustment programs, sponsored by the European Union and the IMF, in Greece, Ireland, and Portugal. Many analysts – along with the public in some core countries – blame the European debt crisis on fiscal profligacy in noncore Eurozone countries, driven primarily by the expansion of a welfare state model and rising public sector wages.[2] If countries had balanced their budgets and avoided the temptations of a welfare state, this view claims, there would have been no excessive private spending, and investors and banks would have been more aware of the risks. That being the case, noncore countries should renounce their welfare objectives and adopt a more realistic fiscal policy. In this view, such fiscal discipline would strengthen the euro without the need for more fiscal stimulus. Germany strongly endorses fiscal austerity for ending the crisis. Under Germany's leadership, the G20 summit in Toronto in June 2010 established fiscal consolidation as the new policy priority.[3]

---

[1] The noncore Eurozone countries are Greece, Ireland, Italy, Portugal, and Spain. The core countries are Austria, Belgium, France, Germany, and the Netherlands. Other euro countries are Cyprus, Estonia, Finland, Luxembourg, Malta, the Slovak Republic, and Slovenia.

[2] For an example, see Weidmann (2012).

[3] Parkin and Czuczka (2010); Wolf (2012).

Deregulation and financial integration in the Eurozone

But a deeper analysis of the dynamics underlying the euro crisis shows that the deregulation that allowed the banks in core Eurozone countries to increase their leverage and the availability of their funds for lending to support housing bubble and excess consumption in noncore countries was a major cause of the crisis in the noncore countries. Much as in the United States, financial deregulation prompted the development of new financial instruments and derivatives and spurred the real estate and consumption boom.[4] The adoption of the euro, which facilitated financial integration and lowered currency risk in periphery countries, also contributed to the large inflows of capital from core countries into noncore countries. Similar issues of housing bubble and excess consumption made possible by increasing bank lending from core Eurozone countries also occurred in countries beyond the Eurozone, such as Iceland and Hungary and other countries in eastern Europe. The increases in housing investment and consumption led to an economic boom and rising wages in private and public sectors before the crisis in the noncore countries. Initially, fiscal revenue increased along with wages and real estate prices, keeping deficits in line with the Maastricht criteria (except in Greece) despite governments' rapidly escalating spending to cover their rising wage bills and social transfers. With growth driven more and more by unsustainably high domestic consumption, noncore countries lost export competitiveness and manufacturing sectors shrank. At the same time, in the core countries wage restraint and undervaluation of the euro (compared with their former national currencies) boosted competitiveness and external surpluses.

The global financial crisis of 2008–9 led to a recession in Europe (Figure 4.1) and the bursting of the real estate bubble. The recession and the fiscal stimulus packages adopted to counter it resulted in ballooning fiscal deficits and a massive deterioration in debt indicators, setting the stage for the sovereign debt crisis in the Eurozone that began with Greece in early 2010.

A deeper look at the dynamics between the core Eurozone countries (especially Germany) and the noncore countries reveals some similarity to the dynamics between East Asian surplus economies and the United States during the run-up to the global financial crisis.[5] Excess

---

[4] See Chapter 3.   [5] Lin and Treichel (2012).

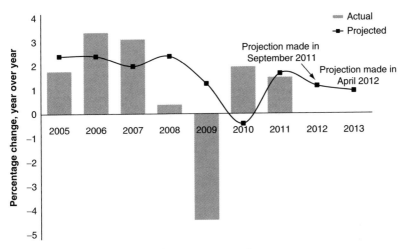

Figure 4.1 Projected and actual Eurozone growth
Note: Projection data from previous year of actual GDP growth.
Source: IMF, World Economic Outlook, various years.

consumption in the United States brought about by a real estate boom and low interest rates allowed East Asian economies to expand their exports until the real estate bubble burst – and the ensuing financial crisis triggered a global recession. The US consumption boom went hand in hand with a decline in economic competitiveness, especially in manufacturing.

The euro and financial deregulation

Since 1957 Europe has been moving toward greater financial integration. In the 1970s and early 1980s most countries began to lift capital controls and deregulate interest rates under various EU directives, with a view to creating a single market in banking and financial services. Not until the late 1980s and early 1990s, however, did most countries embark definitively on financial liberalization, spurred by the Single European Act of 1987 (Table 4.1).

The Financial Services Action Plan of 1999, a five-year financial harmonization program, was a major step toward European financial integration. The plan aimed to develop a single market for wholesale financial services, create open and secure retail markets, establish clear

Table 4.1 *Financial liberalization and integration in Europe*

Country	Lifting of capital controls	Interest rate deregulation	First Banking Directive	Second Banking Directive
Belgium	1991	1990	1993	1994
Denmark	1982	1988	1980	1991
France	1990	1990	1980	1992
Germany	1967	1981	1978	1992
Greece	1994	1993	1981	1992
Ireland	1985	1993	1989	1992
Italy	1983	1990	1985	1992
Luxembourg	1990	1990	1981	1993
Netherlands	1980	1981	1978	1992
Portugal	1992	1992	1992	1992
Spain	1992	1992	1987	1994
United Kingdom	1979	1979	1979	1993

Source: Buch and Heinrich (2002).

and efficient prudential rules and supervision of financial services, and establish the conditions for an optimal single financial market. The Lisbon Agenda of 2000 and the Lisbon Strategy's 2005 relaunch reinforced the goal of creating a single financial market. A measure of capital account openness (the Chinn–Ito index) indicates that the Eurozone countries achieved a fully integrated financial market after the euro was adopted in 2002 (Table 4.2).

Following the adoption of the euro and the marked increase in financial integration, bilateral bank holdings and transactions increased some 40 percent among Eurozone countries.[6] In contrast, bank holdings and transactions increased only 25 to 30 percent, if the group of countries is expanded by the three EU countries that did not adopt the euro (the United Kingdom, Denmark, and Sweden).

This elimination of currency risk, together with the easier access to international capital markets that came with the currency union, led to a drop in interest rates in noncore Eurozone countries and a convergence with rates in core countries (Figure 4.2).

[6] Kalemli-Ozcan, Papaioannou, and Peydro (2010).

Table 4.2 *Chinn–Ito index of capital account liberalization for selected EU country groups*

EU country group	1990–4	1995–9	2000–4	2005–9
Core euro countries	83.2	96.1	97.4	100.0
Noncore euro countries	19.5	80.5	96.6	100.0
Other euro countries	−37.9	−9.5	24.7	81.3
Noneuro countries	8.8	39.0	66.9	87.9

Notes: The Chinn–Ito index is expressed in terms of its highest value for all countries considered in their sample. A value of 100 thus means complete liberalization. Core countries are Austria, Belgium, France, Germany, and the Netherlands. Noncore countries are Greece, Ireland, Italy, Portugal, and Spain. Other euro countries are Estonia, Malta, the Slovak Republic, and Slovenia. Noneuro countries are Sweden and the United Kingdom.
Source: Chinn and Ito (2008).

Financial integration also facilitated cross-border capital flows in the Eurozone. These cross-border flows were largely dominated by claims from core country banks on the banks of noncore countries, however. Lending by German and French banks to noncore countries' banks was by far the most important factor in this increase, as indicated in Figure 4.3, and benefited from financial deregulation and liberalization akin to that having taken place in the United States. Total claims by core countries on noncore countries increased by 433 percent from 1999 to the peak in 2008. Countries outside the Eurozone were also significant recipients of lending from core countries. In two striking cases, core bank claims on Iceland increased by 1,113 percent over the same period, while core bank claims on Hungary increased by 603 percent.[7]

Increased lending by core country banks without a consequent rise in interest rates was made possible by dramatic increases in leverage ratios (measured as total assets over total equity) for these lending institutions, which peaked in 2007 at 33 to 1.[8] Other measures for leverage, such as value of return to equity ratios and tier 1 capital leverage ratios, showed stable or declining levels during the period before the crisis, which, in hindsight, suggested that "risk weights were perhaps too low, especially for positions in the trading book."[9]

---

[7] BIS (2012).   [8] BIS (2009).   [9] BIS (2009: 5).

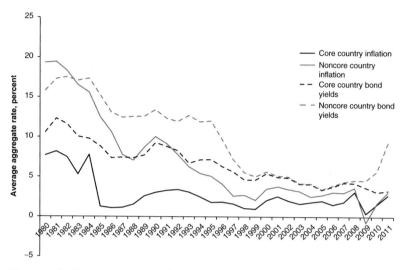

Figure 4.2 Convergence in inflation rates and long-term bond yields in Eurozone countries

Note: Core countries are Austria, Belgium, France, Germany, and the Netherlands. Noncore countries are Greece, Ireland, Italy, Portugal, and Spain.

Source: IMF's "International financial statistics" database: http://elibrary-data. imf.org/FindDataReports.aspx?d=330610e=169393.

As with the United States, this increase in leverage was encouraged by the creation of derivatives whose risk profile could not be properly assessed. At the same time, risk management was weakened through the shadow banking system, which was only marginally under the supervision of bank regulatory authorities.[10]

Notable in this regard is that, while these balance sheet ratio levels were not greater than those seen in past business cycles, *off-balance sheet bank leverage* increased rapidly and significantly contributed to the build-up of financial leverage prior to the crisis of 2007. Many segments of the asset-backed commercial paper (ABCP) markets, such as structured investment vehicles, collateralized debt obligations, single-sell ABCP conduits, and securities arbitrage programs, grew exponentially during this timeframe in both the United States and Europe. Covered bonds played an important role in increasing leverage,

---

[10] Carbó-Valverde, Marques-Ibanez, and Rodríguez Fernández (2011).

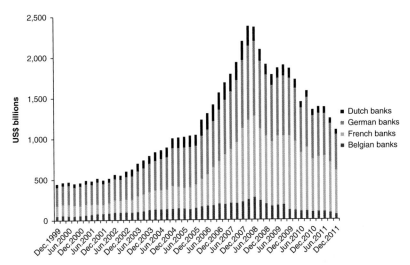

Figure 4.3 Claims by core Eurozone countries on noncore countries' banking systems
Note: Noncore countries are Greece, Ireland, Italy, Portugal, and Spain.
Source: BIS's "Locational banking statistics" data: www.bis.org/statistics/bankstats.htm.

especially in Spain, where the amount outstanding increased from fewer than 10 billion in 2000 to more than 125 billion in 2005. Crucial to this increase in volume was legislation allowing for low risk-weighting for this class of assets, allowing banks to take on greater exposure to liquidity risk.[11] These higher leverage ratios amplified the rate of return on assets for core countries during the run-up to the crisis.[12]

In addition, the sharp increase of bank funds and fall in interest rates led to a huge increase in consumer lending, much of it funneled into real estate in Ireland, Spain, and Greece, inflating the housing bubbles whose later bursting led to the economic crisis (Figure 4.4). Housing prices rose an average of 12.5 percent a year in Ireland, 9 percent a year in Greece, and 8 percent a year in Spain between 1997 and 2007, well

---

[11] Avesani, Pascual, and Ribakova (2007).
[12] Beck and Demirgüç-Kunt (2009) show that the rate of return on assets in core countries increased from 0.3 percent between 1990 and 1995 to 1.0 percent between 2002 and 2007.

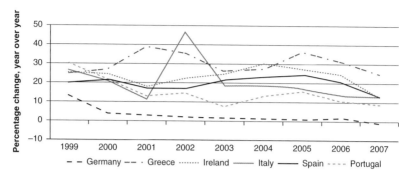

Figure 4.4 Growth rate of mortgage loans for selected Eurozone countries
Source: ECB (2009).

higher than the 4.6 percent annual increase in the United States during its housing bubble. Over the same period, construction as a share of gross output rose from 9.8 percent to 13.8 percent in Spain, from 7.9 percent to 10.4 percent in Ireland, and from 6.0 percent to 7.1 percent in Greece,[13] again well higher than in the United States, where it rose from 4.6 percent to 4.9 percent.[14] The channeling of funds into real estate allowed bubbles to emerge whose bursting was at the core of the economic crisis.

As in the United States, financial deregulation in Europe encouraged the creation of derivatives whose risk profile could not be properly assessed. At the same time, the large shadow banking system, only marginally supervised by bank regulatory authorities, weakened risk management. In Spain, in particular, securitization (mortgage- and asset-backed) may have had a large and lasting effect on housing prices.[15]

The housing investment and consumption booms were not without (temporary) benefits. For example, Greece's economy, after averaging 1.1 percent annual GDP growth from 1980 to 1997 – the slowest in eventual Eurozone countries – averaged 4.0 percent annually over the next ten years, the third fastest rate in the Eurozone. Spain averaged 3.8 percent growth from 1997 to 2007, 1.3 percentage points higher than in the 1980–97 period. Ireland, at an average annual rate of 6.8 percent

[13] The first year with data available for Greece was 2000.   [14] Dadush (2010).
[15] Carbó-Valverde, Marques-Ibanez, and Rodríguez Fernández (2011).

from 1997 to 2007, had the fastest growth in the Eurozone, an improvement over its already impressive 4.6 percent from 1980 to 1997. Only Portugal grew more slowly in the later period than in the earlier one, with an average rate of 2.3 percent between 1997 and 2007 compared with 3 percent between 1980 and 1997, on account of its poor competitiveness.

After the euro had been adopted, a false sense of prosperity soon took over in the low-risk environment created by the free flow of capital throughout Europe and elsewhere, low borrowing costs, easy access to liquidity through leveraging and an increase in lending from core banks to noncore banks, and the absence of exchange rate risk. The prosperity was artificial, because there were no matching improvements in productivity or the business environment – the foundations of sustained long-term growth. To the contrary, the suddenly abundant financial flows in noncore Eurozone countries worsened the already weak competitiveness in these countries.[16]

Rising wages and government spending in noncore Eurozone countries

A key factor contributing to the loss of competitiveness was the sharp rise in wages in noncore Eurozone countries. Between 2001 and 2011 per unit labor costs rose 33 percent in Greece, 31 percent in Italy, 27 percent in Spain, and 20 percent in Ireland; they grew 11 percent in the United States and just 0.9 percent in Germany.[17] This increase was driven primarily by rising wages in private and public sectors as a result of the false prosperity. Government spending increases were considered manageable because of the substantial drop in sovereign borrowing costs after the adoption of the euro and the rapid rise in revenue resulting from the increase in economic activity and the real estate boom (Table 4.3 and Figures 4.2, 4.5, and 4.6).

Rising wages and government spending in noncore Eurozone countries increased aggregate demand. In Greece, for example, aggregate demand grew 4.2 percent a year between 2002 and 2007, well above the 1.8 percent Eurozone average.[18] The increase was financed by foreign borrowing, which stoked inflation. Consumer prices in Greece rose

---

[16] Gwartney, Hall, and Lawson (2010).   [17] Dadush (2010).
[18] Dadush (2010).

Table 4.3 *General government deficit, selected Eurozone countries (percentage of GDP)*

Country	2000	2001	2002	2003	2004	2005	2006	2007	2008	2009	2010	2011
Greece	-3.7	-4.5	-4.8	-5.6	-7.5	-5.2	-5.7	-6.5	-9.8	-15.6	-10.3	-9.1
Ireland	4.7	0.9	-0.4	0.4	1.4	1.7	2.9	0.1	-7.3	-14	-31.2	-13.1
Italy	-0.8	-3.1	-3.1	-3.6	-3.5	-4.4	-3.4	-1.6	-2.7	-5.4	-4.6	-3.9
Portugal	-3.3	-4.8	-3.4	-3.7	-4.0	-6.5	-4.6	-3.1	-3.6	-10.2	-9.8	-4.2
Spain	-0.9	-0.5	-0.2	-0.3	-0.1	1.3	2.4	1.9	-4.5	-11.2	-9.3	-8.5
France	-1.5	-1.5	-3.1	-4.1	-3.6	-2.9	-2.3	-2.7	-3.3	-7.5	-7.1	-5.2
Germany	1.1	-3.1	-3.8	-4.2	-3.8	-3.3	-1.6	0.2	-0.1	-3.2	-4.3	-1.0

Source: Eurostat: epp://eurostat.ec.europa.eu.

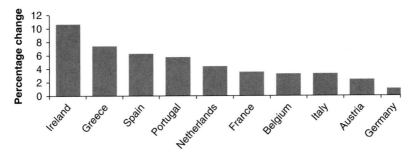

Figure 4.5 Annual growth of government expenditure, selected Eurozone countries, 1997–2007 average
Source: Eurostat: epp://eurostat.ec.europa.eu.

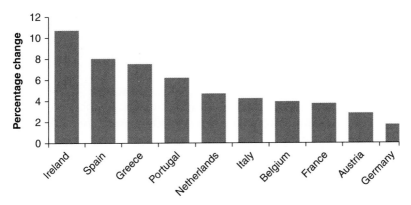

Figure 4.6 Annual growth of government revenue, selected Eurozone countries, 1997–2007 average
Source: Eurostat: epp://eurostat.ec.europa.eu.

47 percent from 1997 to 2009, nearly double the Eurozone average of 27 percent. From 2003 to 2011 Greece's real effective exchange rate appreciated 17 percent, eroding competitiveness and increasing the current account deficit.

This loss of external competitiveness led to a shift from manufacturing toward services and nontradables. From 2000 to 2007 the share of manufacturing in GDP fell 10 percentage points in Ireland, 4 percentage points in Spain, 3 percentage points in Portugal and Italy, and 1 percentage point in Greece (from its already low 10 percent; Table 4.4).

Table 4.4 *Manufacturing value added, selected Eurozone countries (percentage of GDP)*

Country	2007	Change since 2000
Germany	24	1
Ireland	22	−10
Italy	18	−3
Spain	15	−4
Portugal	14	−3
Greece	10	−1

Source: World Bank (2009a).

In Germany, meanwhile, the share of manufacturing in GDP rose 1 percentage point (from an already very high level), reflecting the country's rise in overall surplus position with other Eurozone countries.

At the heart of the euro debt crisis is an intra-area balance of payments crisis caused by a severe imbalance in competitiveness and the associated, largely private, cross-border debt flows. The large increase in lending to noncore countries made possible by rising bank leverage in core countries and the common currency were central to the balance of payments crisis, through its impact on interest rates (for both public and private debt), financial integration, and the encouragement of export-led growth in core countries and consumption-led growth in noncore countries.

In the aftermath of the global financial crisis, most European countries fell into recession. As the real estate bubble burst, nonperforming loans rose sharply, and public debt ballooned as governments bailed out the financial sector and then rolled out stimulus packages to counteract the recessionary impacts of the crisis. As output contracted, government revenues dropped sharply, adding another layer of debt to finance the widening deficits (Figures 4.7 and 4.8).

As in the United States, the financial deregulation increased the bank leverage and availability of funds in the core Eurozone countries. The adoption of the euro facilitated the large financial flows from core countries to noncore countries, and interest rates in noncore countries converged to those in core countries. The sharp increase in the low-interest funds set off consumption and real estate booms in noncore countries, boosting growth and swelling government spending and

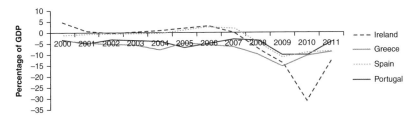

Figure 4.7 Evolution of general government deficits, selected Eurozone countries
Source: Eurostat: epp://eurostat.ec.europa.eu.

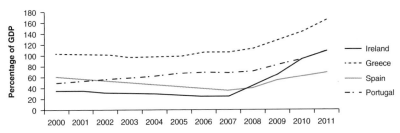

Figure 4.8 Evolution of general government gross debt, selected Eurozone countries
Source: Eurostat: epp://eurostat.ec.europa.eu.

revenue. The resulting real appreciation reduced the competitiveness of noncore countries, shrinking exports and resulting in current account imbalances. Fiscal positions had remained manageable before the global financial crisis because government revenues were rising, but the recession following the crisis caused budget deficits to mount rapidly and debt indicators to worsen. Meanwhile, core countries, particularly Germany, maintained a competitive edge through wage restraint, allowing them to increase exports to noncore countries and their banks to profit from increased lending to noncore countries.

5 | Why China's reserves have risen so much

If the global imbalances resulted from the excess liquidity created by reserve currency countries – particularly the United States, through its expansionary monetary and fiscal policies and its housing finance policies – rather than a global savings glut brought about by the economic policies of China and East Asian economies, why did China's current account surplus rise so much and attract so much attention? What was the role of China's policies and saving rate in the evolution of the global crisis?

This chapter argues that China's current account surplus was caused by the country's high corporate saving rate, resulting from its dual-track reform strategy, and by the relocation of the labor-intensive tradables sectors of East Asian economies to China in the 1980s, which accelerated after China's accession to the World Trade Organization in 2001.

China's dual-track reform strategy led to high corporate savings

China's large current account surplus reflects a high ratio of savings to investments. Saving and investment rates have both been extremely high in recent years. With a current account surplus equivalent to more than 0.5 percent of global GDP since 2005, China has accumulated more foreign reserves than the combined reserves of all industrial countries. While household savings are high, however, at about 20 percent of GDP they are not much higher than in India and some other Asian countries. China's corporate saving rate is substantially higher than that of other Asian countries and other emerging market economies, however.[1] At about 20 percent of GDP – double the share of corporate savings in the United States and France – retained earnings finance more than a half of enterprise investment. What explains China's high corporate saving rate?

[1] Servén (2011).

The main reason is China's dual-track reform strategy. China did not introduce its reforms all at once, as proposed by the Washington consensus. Instead, China continues to provide transitory supports and protections to old large state-owned firms in capital-intensive sectors so as to maintain stability and liberalizes new entries to labor-intensive light manufacturing sectors in order to achieve dynamic growth in the transition process. In sectors in which reforms were delayed to protect state-owned enterprises (SOEs), market distortions led to a concentration of wealth in large state and private-owned enterprises. This skewed income distribution is an important factor behind China's high saving rate.[2]

Income disparity has been increasing in China since the 1990s (Figure 5.1).[3] Even as China made great progress against poverty (poverty shrank from 53 percent of the population in 1981 to 8 percent in 2001),[4] income inequality increased – though not continuously. Because the marginal propensity to consume is higher among low-income people than among high-income people, savings rise along with wealth concentration. The concentration of wealth in large enterprises further increases savings.

Before 2004 China's total savings as a share of GDP stood at less than 40 percent (Figure 5.2). Household savings were high, but not out of line with those in India and some East Asian economies. After 2004, however, savings rose rapidly, driven mainly by a rise in corporate savings.[5] How did this happen? Four components of China's economic structure led to the increase in income disparity and the concentration of wealth in large corporations: fiscal policy, the financial sector, the resource sector, and monopolies in the telecommunications and financial sectors.

Tax policy favors large state-owned enterprises

Large SOEs have been able to retain their profits untaxed.[6] When taxes were reformed in 1994 SOE profits were excluded from taxation for an unspecified period. This decision was a natural extension of the SOE reforms of the 1980s and early 1990s, which stressed the

---

[2] Lin (2012a); Lin, Dinh, and Im (2010).   [3] Ravallion and Chen (2007).
[4] Ravallion and Chen (2007).   [5] Prasad (2011).
[6] Kuijs, Mako, and Zhang (2005).

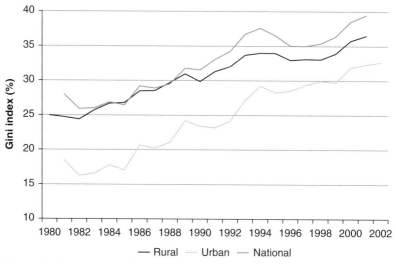

Figure 5.1 Income inequality in China
Source: Ravallion and Chen (2007).

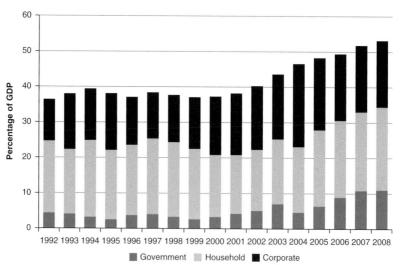

Figure 5.2 Chinese corporate, government, and household savings (percent of GDP)
Source: National Bureau of Statistics of China (1998, 1999, 2000, 2001, 2002, 2003, 2004, 2005, 2006, 2007, 2008, 2009).

independence of SOEs from the government by emphasizing managerial autonomy. Taxing SOE profits would be moving in the opposite direction. In addition, until SOEs were corporatized and corporate governance improved, determining appropriate tax rates on profits would require negotiating with the management of each SOE. Finally, SOEs were in shaky financial conditions in the early 1990s and were in urgent need of large capital injections. With the total profits of industrial SOEs standing at just 1.8 percent of GDP in 1994, the government would have been able to collect little in the way of taxes.

High concentration in the financial sector

China's financial structure is dominated by four large state-owned banks that serve only large state-owned and private enterprises. Labor-intensive small and medium-sized enterprises have no access to financial services.[7] China has an abundance of labor, but the development of labor-intensive small and medium-sized enterprises is repressed by the lack of access to financial services. This situation has implications for income distribution, since labor is the primary source of income for poor people. With fewer job opportunities, wages remain depressed.

A 2004 World Bank survey of Chinese enterprises offers further evidence of lending concentration.[8] Of the firms surveyed, 65 percent of large firms had received a loan from a bank or financial institution, but only 32 percent of medium-sized firms and 20 percent of small firms had. Many private firms had to resort to the informal lending market.

In addition, the highly concentrated financial structure artificially lowers the cost of credit and capital to enterprises that have access to financial services, effectively subsidizing them (Table 5.1). The subsidy is financed mainly by people who have deposits at financial institutions but who cannot borrow from them – the relatively poor. Poor people are thus subsidizing the investments of wealthy people and large corporations, concentrating even more income in large corporations and further skewing income distribution.

---

[7] Lardy (2007). [8] World Bank (2004).

Table 5.1 *Chinese interest rates on debt to state-owned and private enterprises*

Sector	2001	2002	2003	2004	2005
State-owned enterprises	2.46	2.23	2.67	2.86	2.61
Private enterprises	4.84	4.64	4.61	3.81	4.57
Difference	−2.38	−2.41	−1.94	−0.95	−1.96

Source: Ferri and Liu (2009).

Natural resources policies keep royalty rates low

Although China has few natural resources, and their prices are correspondingly high, royalties remain very low. Petroleum companies, both domestic and foreign, pay no royalties on crude oil production below 7 million barrels and just 4 to 12.5 percent for production above this threshold. Royalty rates are lower still on natural gas, with no royalties for production of less than 2 billion cubic meters and rates of 1 to 3 percent for larger volumes.[9] To put this into perspective, royalties in the United States stand at 12.5 percent for onshore crude oil and natural gas and 16.7 percent for offshore production, regardless of amount.[10] The low royalties in China clearly benefit state-owned and private mining companies, and constitute yet another transfer of wealth from the nation to the wealthy few.

Monopoly power in financial and telecommunication industries

Finally, financial institutions and telecommunications firms are extremely profitable because of their monopoly power. For example, profits in the top five banks in China rose 536 percent from 2003 to 2010; profits stood at 545 billion yuan in 2010. China Mobile, the primary telecommunications company, with a 69 percent market share, saw profits rise twenty-fourfold over the past decade.[11] Since the beginning of the dual-track reforms, SOEs have not had to pay dividends to shareholders. As industrial profits soared to trillions of yuan, corporate savings rose in tandem (Figure 5.3).

---

[9] These rates are as stipulated by the Ministry of Finance (1995).
[10] American Petroleum Institute (2011).   [11] China Mobile Limited (2011).

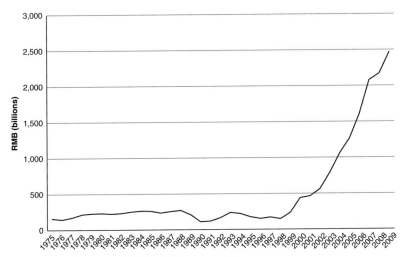

Figure 5.3 Chinese real industrial sector profits
Note: Industrial sector coverage is of enterprises with annual revenue of more than 5 million yuan.
Sources: CEIC's "China premium" database; OECD's "National accounts" data; UBS; and World Bank's "National accounts" data.

Lowering corporate savings by addressing the root causes

The only way to increase consumption and reduce excess savings and China's large current account surplus is by addressing the root causes of income disparity and corporate savings, primarily through three policy reforms.[12]

- Strengthening corporate governance and reviewing dividend policies with a view to lowering retained earnings. Requiring SOEs to issue dividends would reduce retained earnings and could increase household consumption.
- Making more credit available to small and medium-sized enterprises by developing small and medium-sized local banks and introducing more competition in the banking system, possibly by strengthening banking supervision, requiring large banks to allocate a set share of

[12] Kuijs (2006).

loans to small and medium-sized enterprises, and making it easier for new small banks to enter the market.

• Boosting royalties for coal, gas, and other mining companies, whose earnings are extremely high.

Relocation of labor-intensive production from East Asia to China

The current account balance reflects a country's savings–investment balance, as described above for China. The growing trade imbalance between China and the United States, however, results mainly from relocation of the production of many low value added labor-intensive products from East Asian economies to China. The United States has long had a trade deficit with East Asia because of its imports of labor-intensive products. The relocation of this production to China concentrates East Asia's trade surplus with the United States on China, as can be observed in the changing patterns of the US trade deficit with China and Japan from 1985 to 2009 (Figure 5.4).

Combined with regional integration through production networks, this relocation also explains China's trade deficit with East Asian

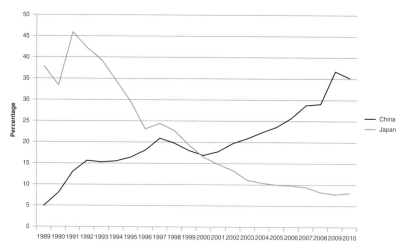

Figure 5.4 Share of US–Japan and US–China trade deficits in total US trade deficit

Source: United Nations' "Commodity trade statistics" database: http://comtrade.un.org/db.

economies. China's trade balance with these economies deteriorated as China imported more raw materials and semifinished products from them. Many product subcomponents are produced in developed countries and simply assembled in China. For example, China's share of value added at the firm gate for iPhones assembled in China is only 3.6 percent; components from Germany, Japan, South Korea, the United States, and the rest of the world account for the other 96.4 percent.

Conclusions

The financial crisis of 2008–9 led to the greatest recession in the global economy since the Great Depression. Although the coordinated efforts of the G20 countries have averted an even worse scenario, the world economy remains fragile, with high unemployment and large excess capacity in advanced economies and high sovereign debt and a weak recovery in the Eurozone. Many policymakers thought previously, however, that the global economy had reached a new era of "Great Moderation," with high growth and low unemployment. What made such a calamity possible?

At the core of the crisis was the bursting of the housing bubble in the United States, largely as a result of US domestic policy. The loose monetary policy stance after the dot-com bubble burst in 2001, magnified by financial deregulation and the spread of complex, innovative financial instruments, resulted in an exuberant boom in the US housing market. The wealth effect from the housing boom and the financial innovation that allowed households to capitalize those gains led to overconsumption and overindebtedness. The large US current account deficit, made possible by the US dollar's status as the major reserve currency, stemmed both from household overconsumption and from the rise in public debt to finance the Iraq and Afghanistan wars.

Some observers have blamed the global financial crisis on the export-oriented policies of other countries, the accumulation of reserves for self-insurance in East Asia, and especially the alleged undervaluation of the Chinese currency. But these accumulations of external surpluses through strong and rising exports were possible only because of excess demand in the United States. Had US domestic consumption not been maintained at artificially high levels by loose monetary and fiscal policies and expansionary housing policies, East Asian countries could not have sustained their export performance. Moreover, a detailed analysis of the global savings glut shows that it cannot explain the low interest rates and financial innovations.

In fact, it was US policymakers who, under the influence of the domestic financial industry, drove the financial deregulation and liberalization that created space for the unfettered innovations in the financial sector. These innovations transmitted the effects of the collapse of key financial sector institutions to the global economy and caused output disruptions from which many countries have yet to recover. The origins of the Eurozone sovereign debt crisis are similar.

The crisis demonstrates the risks emanating from uncontrolled financial deregulation and a lack of supervision, which led to the subprime mortgage crisis and the collapse of the shadow banking system. Developing countries must adopt appropriate levels of banking supervision to prevent a recurrence. Most fundamentally, financial instruments and how they interact need to be fully understood and regulated before they are adopted and closely supervised thereafter.

PART II

A Win-Win Path to Recovery

Without structural reforms to enhance competitiveness, the debt-ridden countries in southern Europe are likely to require repeated and increasingly large rescue packages. And, without structural reforms in Japan and the United States, they will continue their loose monetary policies to keep interest rates low in order to support the financial system, help indebted households, and reduce the cost of public debt. The likely outcome is that the Eurozone, Japan, and the United States will all be trapped in a protracted "new normal" of slow growth, high risks, and low returns on financial investment.[1] Low interest rates will also encourage short-term speculative capital flows to international commodity markets (resulting in volatile prices) and to emerging economies (resulting in asset bubbles, currency appreciation, and difficulties in macroeconomic management).

The problem is that structural reform is contractionary and may cut more deeply into jobs, economic growth, and government revenues, at least in the short run. Thus structural reforms are not politically feasible in many countries. And, even if implemented, such reforms might not reduce the fiscal deficit, because social spending generally increases in response to rising unemployment and fiscal revenue shrinks when growth slows. The market will respond negatively to the rising public debt.

The standard recommendation has long been to offset the contractionary effects of structural reforms by devaluing the currency to increase demand for a country's exports. But any attempt at currency devaluation in the Eurozone, Japan, or the United States could trigger a currency war and competitive devaluations. Instead, high-income countries need to stimulate demand to create space for structural reforms. Public or private debt restructuring and fiscal consolidation should not be the priority.

---

[1] Clarida (2010).

Fiscal policies should be countercyclical and focus on projects that create jobs now and enhance productivity in the future, especially in infrastructure, green sectors, and education. Monetary policy should accommodate fiscal needs. Productivity-enhancing investment opportunities in advanced economies are limited and may not be large enough to pull the countries out of crisis. Opportunities for productivity-enhancing infrastructure[2] investments abound in developing countries, however, and will generate demand for the exports of high-income countries, with an effect similar to that of a currency devaluation.

The funds for investment should come from both reserve-issuing and reserve-rich countries. In today's global economy, infrastructure projects are good investments for private sector funds, including pension funds, and sovereign wealth funds. Multilateral development banks and governments could help make infrastructure projects attractive to private investors through innovative arrangements that leverage private funds.

---

[2] "Infrastructure" refers to hard infrastructure, such as highways, telecommunications networks, port facilities, and power supplies, but not to soft infrastructure, such as institutions, regulations, social capital, value systems, and other social and economic arrangements.

6 | *Infrastructure investments – beyond Keynesianism*

Investing in infrastructure is a win-win strategy for developed and developing countries alike – for today and tomorrow. Such investments can create space for structural reforms and help developed countries avoid a protracted "new normal" of low growth, high risks, and high debts, replacing it with a "new new normal" of a return to precrisis growth rates in developed countries and enhanced growth in developing countries.

Infrastructure investments in advanced economies: solid but limited options

More than three years after the start of the recent recession, manufacturing in the United States and Europe – with the exception of Germany – has not rebounded to precrisis levels. Unemployment remains high in the United States and is still rising in the Eurozone, straining national as well as household budgets. In the United States, unemployment assistance increased fourfold from 2007 to 2009, climbing from 0.24 percent of GDP to nearly 1 percent. In Spain, government spending on social benefits rose from 15.1 percent of GDP in 2008 to 18.1 percent in 2010. High unemployment rates have also been devastating household incomes in many countries, weakening demand and eroding the tax base. With tax revenues falling and social expenditures rising in the United States and Europe, governments responded to the crisis by recapitalizing failing financial institutions and stimulating demand. In the process, sovereign debt has reached levels that raise concerns about financial stability.

At the same time, private investment has been falling. In countries with high unemployment rates, housing prices plummeted, weakening household balance sheets even more. The effect was particularly severe in the United States, where the bursting of the housing bubble in 2008 triggered a vicious cycle of foreclosures, sinking housing prices, and reduced household spending. Private investment fell steeply, driven largely by the decline in residential investments, while persistent excess capacity in other sectors led to a softening of nonresidential investment. Private investment declined sharply in Europe as well. Good private investment opportunities are hard to find when factories have massive spare capacity and office buildings remain vacant.

Limited policy options

Unemployment rates and debt levels cannot fall without strong growth. Private investment is likely to remain subdued as long as excess capacity persists and investment risks are high, while household consumption will not recover as long as unemployment rates are high and households are deleveraging. How can governments boost growth without adding to already high debt levels, especially when large excess capacity makes many macroeconomic tools less effective?[1]

Monetary policy has limited traction in countries caught in a liquidity trap, with close-to-zero short-term interest rates and aggregate demand far short of productive capacity.[2] In a liquidity trap, monetary expansion works mainly by affecting inflationary expectations. Even big changes in the monetary base will have little effect on the real economy, however, if people do not believe that the expansion marks a policy shift that will persist after the economy has recovered.[3] Even worse, fears of inflation could prompt some high-income countries to tighten their monetary policy instead, which could lead to further financial stress. Interest rates and refinancing costs could rise, and banks and businesses could find their balance sheets under renewed pressure as hidden vulnerabilities are exposed.[4]

Other policies to nudge the economy back onto a growth path also face constraints. Structural reforms to remove barriers to investment, competition, and job creation can boost growth but are unlikely to improve jobs and growth as long as aggregate demand remains weak. Most other structural reforms – reducing pensions, unemployment

---

[1] For an insightful discussion of the role of the government in balance sheet recessions, see Koo (2009).
[2] Krugman (1999).   [3] Woodford (2011).   [4] World Bank (2011b).

benefits, public employment, wages, and financial institution leverage – are contractionary. Governments could also resort to protectionism to support industries whose exports have flagged. The *Global Monitoring Report 2009* notes that "a pattern is beginning to emerge of increases in import licensing, import tariffs and surcharges, and trade remedies to support industries facing difficulties early on in the crisis."[5] So far, however, unlike during the Great Depression, the recent recession has not triggered a round of beggar-thy-neighbor policies.

In several advanced economies, high debt levels have made fiscal consolidation a political priority, despite the risk of depressing growth. Fiscal consolidation of just 1 percent of GDP could reduce real private consumption 0.75 percent and real GDP 0.62 percent over the next two years.[6] Large-scale fiscal consolidation that relies on cuts in spending is contractionary even in economies with a high perceived risk of sovereign debt default. The resulting weaker growth and higher unemployment then put upward pressure on debt and can breed social unrest (as in Greece) and political instability (as shown in the election outcomes in several European countries).

Raising government spending instead could boost demand and reduce unemployment, but concerns about debt levels would likely dictate that the spending be matched by revenue gains. For this approach to work, governments need to invest in areas with a strong growth impact that can eventually become self-financing (such as education, green technology, and infrastructure), thus adding little to government debt service. And they should embed the investments in a fiscal framework that also reduces long-term fiscal pressures. Governments could also use public resources to leverage private sector investment, as discussed below.

Infrastructure projects are particularly promising

Under current economic conditions, investing in infrastructure projects may be particularly promising – if they are carefully chosen. First, infrastructure investments can directly generate a large number of jobs in the short term in sectors hurt most by the crisis, such as construction and manufacturing. Infrastructure projects also generate indirect employment in related industries (for example, the use of capital

[5] World Bank and IMF (2009: 147).   [6] Guajardo, Leigh, and Pescatori (2011).

goods such as turbines and excavators generates manufacturing jobs). These new direct and indirect jobs boost household income and consumption, inducing further employment gains. Every $1 billion invested in the United States in infrastructure for energy, transportation, public schools, and water systems creates an estimated 18,000 direct and indirect jobs, about 40 percent of them in construction.[7] The total employment impact of infrastructure investment is likely to differ by sector,[8] technology, percentage of imports (estimated at about 12 to 22 percent of manufacturing supplies for energy, transportation, school building, and water infrastructure), and possible substitution effects.[9] Even so, these estimates suggest a large employment impact.

Second, in advanced economies, manufacturing jobs are important for sustaining a strong middle class, which has been in steady decline in many countries.[10] The manufacturing sector in advanced economies provides employment opportunities in capital-intensive sectors with high labor productivity whose wages are aligned with income levels.

Third, many advanced economies have major infrastructure gaps. In the United Kingdom at least 20 percent of London's main water lines are more than 150 years old. In the United States the median age of coal power stations is more than forty years. The European Commission, stressing the importance of continuing to invest in infrastructure, estimates that the European Union alone needs $2.1 trillion to $2.8 trillion in infrastructure investments from 2011 to 2020 to remain competitive.[11] The American Society of Civil Engineers estimates that the

---

[7] Infrastructure investments refer to investments in new projects and maintenance. For example, Heintz, Pollin, and Garrett-Peltier (2009) assume that about 43 percent of public investment in roads goes to expand the system and 57 percent to maintenance. Estimates from the US Department of Transportation Federal Highway Administration (2008) are even higher: every $1 billion in road construction generates 27,840 new jobs, 6,055 of them on-site and 7,790 related to equipment manufacturing. This implies that about 14,000 jobs would be created through multiplier effects.

[8] Heintz, Pollin, and Garrett-Peltier (2009) estimate that a $1 billion infrastructure investment would create 16,763 new jobs in the energy sector, 18,930 in transportation, 19,262 in school construction, and 19,769 in the water sector. Investments in mass transit systems have the highest direct and indirect employment impacts.

[9] For a detailed discussion, see Schwartz, Andres, and Dragoiu (2009).

[10] Lin (2011b); Spence (2011).

[11] European Commission (2011). The OECD estimates that annual global investment in telecommunications, land transport, water, and electricity will

United States needs $2.2 trillion in infrastructure investments over the next five years, more than half of which ($1.18 trillion) has not been budgeted.[12] While this could be an upper-bound estimate, many US government agencies confirm the need for extensive infrastructure repairs and upgrades.[13] In the World Economic Forum's *Global Competitiveness Report 2011–12*, the United States ranks sixteenth on the quality of its infrastructure and fifth in competitiveness, down from first place in 2005.[14]

Investing in infrastructure to boost economic growth in advanced economies with high debt levels will mean doing more with less.[15] First, governments should identify infrastructure projects with the largest economic impact – projects that will release economic bottlenecks. These types of investments are not necessarily shovel-ready, so governments will have to make tough choices between speedy disbursements that inject funds into the economy immediately and a longer investment horizon that optimizes impact. Japan's lost decades tell a cautionary tale. Japan experienced many years of sluggish growth following the bursting of financial and real estate bubbles at the beginning of the 1990s. The government's stimulus packages included building roads and bridges and cutting interest rates to near zero by 1995. But the programs did not produce large economic returns, investment multipliers were low, and growth remained subdued because many types of infrastructure were already near the saturation point.[16] Maximizing economic impact may require combining infrastructure investments with investments in human capital, for a stronger productivity impact. It may also require coordinating projects across levels of government, since many infrastructure projects are financed and implemented at the subnational level.[17]

Second, governments could give priority to bottleneck-releasing infrastructure projects that earn revenues through user fees and thus

average 3.5 percent of GDP, or approximately $2 trillion in 2009 prices, for OECD countries (OECD 2006).

[12] American Society of Civil Engineers (2009).

[13] For example, see US Environmental Protection Agency (2002) on water infrastructure gaps and US Department of Transportation Federal Highway Administration (2008) on roads.

[14] World Economic Forum (2011b).

[15] Governments should also embed stimulus packages in a medium-term budget framework that sets debt trajectories on a sustainable path.

[16] Krugman (2009b).   [17] OECD (2011b).

can be paid off more quickly.[18] These include bridge and highway construction projects.

Third, governments could employ innovative financing mechanisms to leverage private sector financing for long-term infrastructure investments. Economic uncertainty has driven many long-term private investors – such as pension funds and life insurers – to reduce their risk exposure and move into liquid assets. In addition, private sector involvement in infrastructure is concentrated in a few areas, such as telecommunications. The government could encourage more private financing in infrastructure, especially in areas in which this type of investment has been limited. The administration of Barack Obama, for example, has proposed establishing a National Infrastructure Reinvestment Bank,[19] which would issue infrastructure bonds, subsidize qualified projects, and provide loan guarantees to state or local governments. Loans would be matched by private investments, and each project would generate its own revenue stream to facilitate repayment.[20] The European Union is considering a new Europe 2020 Project bond initiative that would use public guarantees to leverage private financing from nontraditional investors, such as pension funds, investing €1.5 to €2 trillion from 2011 to 2020.[21]

The empirical evidence favors infrastructure investments

Critics may argue that fiscal stimulus with an investment focus has been tried and found wanting. The empirical evidence on fiscal multipliers is mixed. Most studies ignore the state of the economy and do not distinguish between investment and consumption spending. Studies of temporary, deficit-financed government spending in the United States estimate multipliers of 0.5 to 2.0.[22] Taking the state of the economy into account can lead to very different results, however, because multipliers

---

[18] For Brazil, Ferreira and Araujo (2008) find that a debt-financed increase in the infrastructure stock equivalent to 1 percent of GDP would pay for itself through tax revenues after twenty years. Of course, this result is very sensitive to changes in key assumptions, such as the interest rate on government debt, the tax collection rate, and depreciation of the infrastructure stock.

[19] For more information, see http://govtrack.us/congress/bill.xpd?bill=112-3259.

[20] See www.whitehouse.gov/blog/2011/11/03/five-facts-about-national-infrastructure-bank.

[21] European Commission (2011).   [22] Ramey (2011).

are likely to be larger in a recession.[23] Fiscal multipliers can be 3.0 or higher when the interest rate is held constant, such as at a zero lower bound in a model with sticky prices.[24] Multipliers have been found to have a higher cumulative impact over five years during recessions (1 to 1.5) than during booms (0 to 0.5).[25]

Few empirical studies estimating fiscal multipliers distinguish types of government spending. One study using a neoclassical model found dramatic effects of public investment on output.[26] If public capital raises the marginal product of private inputs, the output multiplier ranges from 4 to 13 in the long run. A study of US government spending during the New Deal found the highest multiplier (1.7) for public works.[27] In general, however, there are few studies of government spending multipliers in recessions or for different types of spending. Analyzing these questions could be a promising direction for theoretical and empirical research.[28]

There is strong empirical evidence that sound infrastructure enhances economic growth, however. Comprehensive literature reviews show that, while some studies found negative or zero returns, many found a high impact on growth.[29] A review of studies of the relationship between public capital and economic growth found that many of the studies focused on high-income countries; the elasticity of output to public capital was 0.1 to 0.2.[30] The effects differ considerably across countries, regions, and sectors, however. A meta-analysis of forty-nine studies of OECD countries reported an output elasticity of public capital of 0.14.[31] There is empirical evidence of particularly high returns on infrastructure investments in advanced economies when the investments complement an already fairly developed network.[32]

---

[23] Parker (2011).

[24] Christiano, Eichenbaum, and Rebelo (2011); DeLong and Summers (2012).

[25] Auerbach and Gorodnichenko (2010) use a nonlinear vector autoregression structure to distinguish multipliers during recessions and booms.

[26] Baxter and King (1993).   [27] Fishback and Kachanovskaya (2010).

[28] See Ramey (2011) and Parker (2011) for insightful and comprehensive discussions.

[29] In general, studies using physical indicators of infrastructure stock find a positive long-run effect of infrastructure on output, productivity, and growth; results are more mixed among studies using measures of public capital stock or infrastructure spending flows (Straub 2008; Calderón and Servén 2010a, 2010b).

[30] Romp and de Haan (2005).   [31] Ligthart and Martin Suarez (2011).

[32] See Roller and Waverman (2001) for a discussion on telecommunications in twenty-one OECD countries and Fernald (1999) for a discussion on roads in the United States.

Critics will point to the "Ricardian trap" and argue that fiscal stimulus spending crowds out private spending and that the scarce empirical evidence finds that fiscal stimulus is likely to have larger economic benefits if spent on projects with high economic returns that lead to permanently higher productivity than on projects that consist of, say, digging a hole and then filling it.[33] This is not to say that Ricardian equivalence (households increase savings in anticipation of future higher taxes levied to pay for debt-financed government spending, thus offsetting the short-run benefits of expansionary fiscal policies) is a good approximation of reality in the first place. There is a vast literature on the theoretical conditions under which Ricardian equivalence may fail,[34] and the empirical evidence supporting it is thin. One study argues that it is likely that no more than a half of current changes in public savings are offset by changes in private savings.[35]

The main impediment, however, is that opportunities for bottleneck-releasing infrastructure investments are likely to be comparatively limited in advanced economies, since their infrastructure capital stock is already well developed. Moreover, since growth in the global economy is increasingly driven by developing countries, any infrastructure initiatives should include them. Infrastructure investments in developing countries can be transformative. In 1919 it took the young Lieutenant Colonel Dwight Eisenhower fifty-six days to drive a Motor Transport Corps convoy the 3,250 miles from Washington, DC, to Oakland, California. He reported that the convoy had destroyed bridges, that trucks got stuck when it rained, and that some roads could not accommodate quick and easy travel.[36] Later, as president, Eisenhower promoted the Federal Aid Highway Act of 1956, envisioning that "its impact on the American economy – the jobs that it would produce in manufacturing and construction, the rural areas it would open up – was beyond calculation."[37] Such opportunities to transform economies through infrastructure investments still abound in developing countries – to the potential benefit of developing and advanced economies alike.

---

[33] See, for example, Barro (2009, 2010).
[34] It may happen, for example, if the life of individuals in infinite-horizon economies is finite or if idiosyncratic risks exist that cannot be insured.
[35] Solow (2005).   [36] Eisenhower (1919).   [37] Eisenhower (1963: 548–9).

Infrastructure investments in developing countries: abundant opportunities

Infrastructure shortfalls are pervasive in developing countries. Roughly 1.4 billion people have no electricity, some 880 million people are without access to safe drinking water, and 2.6 billion people are without access to basic sanitation.[38] An estimated 1 billion rural dwellers worldwide live more than two kilometers from an all-weather road.[39]

Demand for infrastructure is growing

Missing infrastructure not only reduces the quality of life for billions of people but also discourages enterprise start-ups and makes firms less competitive, by increasing transaction costs and lowering productivity and output quality. Nowhere is this more apparent than in sub-Saharan Africa, where per capita electricity consumption (excluding South Africa) averages 124 kilowatt-hours a year, barely enough to power one light bulb per person for six hours a day.[40] With electricity services sparse and unreliable, many firms generate their own electricity,[41] at an average of more than three times the cost of electricity from the grid.[42] Energy accounts for more than 10 percent of total costs for firms in Benin, Burkina Faso, The Gambia, Madagascar, Mozambique, Niger, and Senegal, for example, compared with just 3 percent for firms in China. Losses from power failure alone amounted to 10 percent of sales for the median Tanzanian firm but just 1 percent for the median Chinese firm.[43] Many sub-Saharan Africans are also cut off from domestic and global markets.[44] Although about two-thirds of people live in rural areas and many countries are landlocked, sub-Saharan Africa has the lowest road density in the world. Not surprisingly, transport costs are high, at about 16 percent of firms' indirect costs.[45]

Going forward, the demand for infrastructure services is likely to increase rapidly in developing countries, whose per capita GDP is

---

[38] World Bank (2010). [39] International Road Federation (2010).
[40] Foster and Briceño-Garmendia (2010).
[41] This is particularly common for firms in sectors that are not electricity-intensive and that experience frequent and extended power outages (Alby, Dethier, and Straub 2011).
[42] Foster and Steinbuks (2009). [43] Eifert, Gelb, and Ramachandran (2005).
[44] World Bank (2009b). [45] Iarossi (2009).

projected to grow at more than 5 percent a year over the medium term.[46] And, with the world population forecast to approach 9 billion by 2050 and greater numbers of people living in cities, the world's building stock is projected to double by 2050.[47]

Infrastructure is a driver of economic development

Infrastructure, a by-product of growth, is also an important driver of economic development. Economic development is a process of continuous technological innovation, industrial upgrading and diversification, and structural transformation. At the agrarian stage of development, much of the production is for the producer's own consumption, so the need for infrastructure services is limited. As countries industrialize, production moves to manufacturing, economies of scale become larger, and producers produce mostly for others. As market range expands, sound infrastructure is essential for getting products and services to markets in a secure and timely way and for enabling workers to travel to the most suitable jobs.[48] Sound infrastructure can also support sustainable development, minimize vulnerability to natural disasters, and promote reliance on public transportation, all of which are important for adapting to global climate change and the ever more intense natural disasters accompanying it.

Improving infrastructure affects a country's output through multiple channels. During construction, infrastructure investment can create jobs and growth in the local economy. After completion, infrastructure enhances productivity, increases private capital formation (by raising expected returns on private investments as the marginal productivity of inputs increases or transaction costs decline), and facilitates the exploitation of agglomeration economies. Infrastructure can also improve health and education outcomes.[49] In Morocco, girls' school attendance rose from 28 percent to 68 percent between 1985 and 1995 with the construction of all-weather roads, which greatly reduced the time women and girls had to spend on tasks such as collecting firewood.[50]

---

[46] IMF (2011e).   [47] World Bank (2011c).   [48] Lin (2011b).

[49] Agenor and Moreno-Dodson (2006).

[50] Before the road improvements, women had to spend an average of two hours a day collecting and carrying wood for fuel. Butane gas, used extensively in urban areas, did not reach rural areas because of the high transport and distribution costs. Initially, a bottle of butane cost 20 dirhams. Following road improvements,

Health indicators also improved, as the number of visits to hospitals and health centers doubled.[51]

Cross-country studies confirm that infrastructure investment has a large impact on growth in developing countries. One study estimated that infrastructure investments boosted annual growth in developing countries an average of 1.6 percent between 1991–5 and 2001–5 – and as much as 2.7 percent a year in South Asia.[52] The same study found that, if sub-Saharan African economies halved their infrastructure gap with India and Pakistan, growth would average 2.2 percentage points higher in Central African low-income countries and 1.6 percentage points higher in East and West African countries. Similarly, if every Latin American country raised its infrastructure to the average level in other middle-income countries (such as Bulgaria and Turkey), growth would average 2 percentage points higher a year.

China's experience demonstrates the benefits of infrastructure investments. Between 1990 and 2005 China invested $600 billion to upgrade its road system. The centerpiece investment was the national expressway network, which spans 41,000 kilometers and will eventually connect all cities with more than 200,000 inhabitants.[53] Only the US interstate highway system, at 79,000 kilometers, spans a similar distance. Aggregate real income was some 6 percent higher in 2007 than it would have been without the expressway.[54] The output elasticity of infrastructure investment in China is estimated at 0.2 to 0.4 percent, based on data for 1975 to 2007.[55] China's infrastructure investment strategy succeeded because it was embedded in an economic policy that focused on enhancing private sector investment and human capital formation, as well improving infrastructure.

the price dropped to as low as 11 dirhams, making it affordable for many more families (World Bank 1996).
[51] World Bank (1996).   [52] Calderón and Servén (2010a).
[53] The length had reached 84,900 kilometers by 2011 (National Bureau of Statistics of China 2012).
[54] Roberts *et al.* (2010).   [55] Sahoo, Dash, and Nataraj (2010).

7 | *A massive global infrastructure initiative*

The gap between infrastructure demand and supply is so large in developing countries mainly because of the difficulty raising the long-term financing required. Putting a price tag on this gap requires some heroic assumptions about missing data.[1] A 2011 study estimated annual infrastructure needs in developing countries for 2013 at $1,250 billion to $1,500 billion (in 2008 dollars) under various scenarios.[2] The study estimated the financing available for infrastructure projects in developing countries at about $850 billion. If the same amount continues to be available in the medium term, the estimated infrastructure financing gap would be $400 billion to $650 billion a year.

A global infrastructure initiative to finance bottleneck-releasing infrastructure projects would create much-needed jobs in developed and developing countries. It would generate a demand boost and create space for implementing necessary structural reforms in Eurozone and other high-income countries. And a concerted push for a global infrastructure initiative could contribute to a sustained global recovery from the current crises. It is a global win-win for developed and developing countries alike, today and into the future.[3]

Benefiting developed countries, developing countries, and the global economy

How would closing this financing gap affect exports in advanced economies? For each additional $1 spent on infrastructure, imports

---

[1] See Fay *et al.* (2011) for a detailed discussion. To overcome this data constraint, the Multilateral Development Banks (MDB) Working Group on Infrastructure has proposed that the G20 launch an infrastructure benchmarking initiative for regularly collecting data on key infrastructure variables that can be compared across countries and over time (MDB Working Group on Infrastructure 2011).
[2] Fay *et al.* (2011).   [3] Lin (2009); Sachs (2009).

rise $0.50.[4] In 2009 about 70 percent of traded capital goods in low- and middle-income countries were sourced from high-income countries (Table 7.1), so a $1 increase in infrastructure investment in developing countries would lead to a $0.35 increase in exports from high-income countries. If the entire infrastructure gap in the developing world, of about $500 billion annually, were closed, the associated demand for capital goods imports worldwide for infrastructure investment alone would be some $250 billion, $175 billion of it sourced from high-income countries. This corresponds to about 7 percent of total capital goods exports from high-income countries in 2010.

Estimates vary on the manufacturing exports required to generate one new job in advanced economies. For the United States, the Department of Commerce estimates that $165,000 in manufacturing exports would have supported one job in 2008.[5] The OECD estimates that, on average, $60,975 in manufacturing exports would generate one job.[6] These estimates suggest that closing the infrastructure gap in developing countries could create between 1.1 million and 2.9 million jobs in advanced economies. Although the numbers may seem small given total unemployment in those economies, the new jobs would constitute a substantial increase in manufacturing employment. In the United States, exports currently support 2.7 million manufacturing jobs, and President Obama's National Export Initiative aims at creating 2 million new jobs over the next five years by increasing exports.[7] The proposed global infrastructure investment initiative could help reach this goal.[8]

These calculations are based on simple correlations. The actual effect of infrastructure investments on exports and employment will vary across countries and sectors depending on the technology used, any substitution effects, and changes in global trade patterns. Capital goods, for example, are increasingly produced in developing countries,

---

[4] Based on 2008 trade data from the United Nations' "Commodity trade statistics" database: http://comtrade.un.org/db.

[5] Tschetter (2010).   [6] OECD data.

[7] The National Export Initiative was created on March 11, 2010, by an executive order issued by President Obama.

[8] Of course, infrastructure investments will also create jobs in the developing countries where these investments take place. Schwartz, Andres, and Dragoiu (2009) find that energy investments tend to have low short-term impact on employment, creating sometimes no more than 1,000 jobs per $1 billion spent. By contrast, water and sanitation projects can create up to 100,000 annual direct and indirect jobs, and road maintenance projects more than 250,000.

Table 7.1 *Sources of capital goods imports to developing countries, 2009 (percent)*

| Exporters → | High-income economies | | | | Low- and middle-income economies | | | | | | | |
Importers ↓	All	Europe	United States	Other	All	East Asia	China	Europe and Central Asia	Latin America	Middle East and North Africa	South Asia	Sub-Saharan Africa
Low- and middle-income	69	29	21	19	29	24	18	2	2	0	0	0
Least developed	51	32	11	7	49	37	31	2	1	0	0	8
East Asia	74	22	15	37	26	25	12	0	0	0	0	0
Europe and Central Asia	62	53	5	5	28	19	18	9	0	0	0	0
Latin America	73	16	50	7	27	20	18	0	7	0	0	0
Middle East and North Africa	69	56	6	7	29	22	21	6	0	1	0	0
South Asia	50	28	10	12	48	45	40	2	1	0	0	0
Sub-Saharan Africa	62	44	11	7	36	27	24	1	2	0	0	6

Notes: Capital goods imports exclude transportation equipment. 'Europe' consists of Belgium, Cyprus, Denmark, Finland, France, Germany, Greece, Ireland, Italy, Luxembourg, Portugal, Slovenia, Sweden, and the United Kingdom.
Source: Based on data from the United Nations' "Commodity trade statistics" database: http://comtrade.un.org/db.

particularly China. With wages in China rising and technology improving, Chinese exporters are moving up the value chain. China's market share of construction equipment exports has more than doubled in recent years, from 4.4 percent in 2005 to 10.2 percent in 2010. China is likely to have overtaken Germany and Japan in terms of construction equipment exports in 2011.[9] Most of the crane, tractor, and steam turbine exports from China go to developing countries. Developing countries tend to import as much in capital goods from other developing countries, in particular from China, as from high-income countries (see Table 7.1).

A good example is power generation, a highly capital-intensive infrastructure investment. Estimates for India indicate that 60 to 90 percent of the cost of turnkey power plants and substations is related to a few key mechanical devices, such as turbines and compressors, which are imported.[10] Turbines for larger power plants are generally produced in the United States and Europe, but 40 to 50 percent of capital equipment for substations is imported from emerging market economies, such as China and India. Low-income countries import more power-generating equipment from China than from the United States (Table 7.2). In a connected world, the growth in China and India will in turn generate import demand from the United States, Europe, and other high-income economies.

Simulations confirm that infrastructure investments in developing countries can contribute to a global recovery and improve the trade balance in advanced economies.[11] Contrast the results of a permanent increase in public infrastructure investment in developing countries of 1 percent of global GDP with an equivalent increase in current spending on goods and services (Figure 7.1). A rise in current spending leads to only a small increase in output, which dissipates over time because a larger stock of government debt is a drag on the economy. By contrast, a rise in infrastructure investment leads to a 7 percent rise in GDP in developing countries and a 2 percent rise in world GDP by 2022. Because infrastructure spending boosts private returns to capital in emerging market economies, more capital flows into these economies

---

[9] Economist Intelligence Unit (2011).   [10] Pauschert (2009).
[11] Calderón, Moral-Benito, and Servén (2011). The simulations used a multicountry, multisector, intertemporal general equilibrium model of the world economy based on panel data for eighty-eight countries. The study found that output rises 0.8 percent for each 10 percent increase in infrastructure stock.

Table 7.2 *Imports of power-generating equipment, 2010 (percent)*

Exporters →	High-income economies				Low- and middle-income economies							
Importers ↓	All	Europe	United States	Other	All	East Asia	China	Europe and Central Asia	Latin America	Middle East and North Africa	South Asia	Sub-Saharan Africa
Low- and middle-income	76	34	17	25	20	12	10	5	3	0	0	0
Least developed	64	44	6	13	35	28	24	2	1	1	0	4
East Asia	81	23	9	49	16	14	9	2	1	0	0	0
Europe and Central Asia	64	51	5	7	23	7	6	16	1	0	0	0
Latin America	83	24	47	12	16	5	4	1	9	0	0	0
Middle East and North Africa	83	62	7	14	16	8	8	5	0	2	0	0
South Asia	60	32	7	20	39	31	29	7	1	0	0	0
Sub-Saharan Africa	74	52	7	15	25	19	18	1	2	1	0	3

Notes: Power-generating equipment corresponds to Standard International Trade Classification Revision 4 code 71, which includes steam boilers, steam turbines, internal combustion piston engines, various other nonelectric engines and motors, rotating electric plants, and other power-generating machinery and parts thereof not elsewhere specified. 'Europe' consists of Austria, Belgium, Cyprus, Denmark, Finland, France, Germany, Greece, Ireland, Italy, Luxembourg, the Netherlands, Portugal, Slovenia, Spain, Sweden, and the United Kingdom.
Source: Based on data from the United Nations' "Commodity trade statistics" database: http://comtrade.un.org/db.

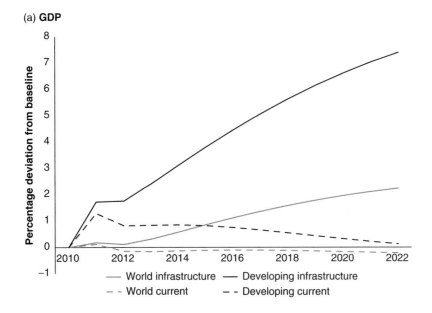

(a) **GDP**

Percentage deviation from baseline

— World infrastructure — Developing infrastructure
– – World current – – Developing current

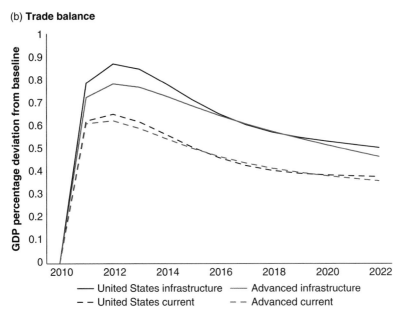

(b) **Trade balance**

GDP percentage deviation from baseline

— United States infrastructure — Advanced infrastructure
– – United States current – – Advanced current

Figure 7.1 Simulated growth and rebalancing implications of an increase in developing country spending on infrastructure and current spending of 1 percent of global GDP

Note: Simulations with a G-cubed model. All results are expressed as percentage deviations from baseline.

Source: McKibbin, Stoeckel, and Lu (2011).

to finance not just the government but also the private sector. As a result, the trade balance of advanced economies improves by more than it does when the spending is on goods and services.

Thus, if carried out properly, a global infrastructure initiative could raise exports and reduce unemployment in high-income countries while reducing poverty and boosting growth in developing countries. Demand would rise for capital goods from capital-goods-exporting countries, mostly advanced economies, raising their exports, employment, GDP, and, ultimately, their fiscal revenues. Infrastructure investments would also help diversify the export base of some capital-goods-exporting emerging economies, such as China, reducing their dependence on demand from a few high-income countries. As incomes rise in developing countries, so will their demand for products produced around the world. Boosting exports in advanced economies would not only reduce unemployment and speed growth there but also reduce external borrowing needs, with the potential to unleash more surplus global savings in support of investment and growth in developing countries, leading in turn to more investment opportunities and new markets. Ultimately, this could create a virtuous cycle of global growth, with surplus global savings flowing to support investment and growth in developing countries, generating more import demand, supporting recovery from the global crisis, and helping the world economy become more inclusive and stable.

To get the most out of existing resources, countries will need to implement the right bottleneck-releasing projects cost-effectively, and developing countries will need to raise the funds to close the infrastructure financing gap. As the scope for increasing government spending may be limited in many developing countries, and as official development assistance flows are unlikely to increase in the near future, developing countries will need to look for innovative financing mechanisms. They could follow the example of recent infrastructure financing initiatives in advanced economies, such as the National Infrastructure Reinvestment Bank in the United States and the Europe 2020 Project bond initiative, which leverage existing resources by attracting additional private sector financing. Moreover, governments will need to reduce the risk borne by private investors. The international community could help countries overcome these constraints by providing targeted financial resources and technical assistance.

Identifying bottleneck-releasing infrastructure projects

Infrastructure projects can be transformational in developing countries. But selecting the right bottleneck-releasing projects requires specific know-how that is not always available in developing countries, particularly project appraisal and selection capacities.[12] Cross-country empirical evidence confirms that the quality of project selection and implementation affects the return on investment and, ultimately, its growth dividend.[13]

Identifying bottleneck-releasing projects with high economic returns can be challenging. First, the institutional context can affect the returns to different types of infrastructure projects. Second, government decentralization in many developing countries has pushed revenue and expenditure assignments for infrastructure to lower levels of government, requiring fiscal responsibility and accountability to be aligned with coordination on project selection. Third, regional integration could greatly reduce infrastructure costs and improve access to regional and global markets by exploiting economies of scale in port, airport, and power generation and transmission projects.[14] In Africa, for example, regional power trading could lower energy costs by $2 billion and carbon emissions by 70 million tons annually.[15] Fourth, the long-term growth impact of infrastructure investments may shrink if the investments result in extensive environmental damage. Emissions from energy generation using fossil fuels, for example, can contribute to acid rain and global warming. Irrigation works can lead to the overuse of water, land degradation, and water pollution. Supporting environmentally sustainable infrastructure investment could greatly reduce the environmental costs associated with infrastructure investments, estimated at 4 to 8 percent of GDP for some developing countries.[16]

Not surprisingly, identifying the right projects often entails high project selection and preparation costs, including an array of institutional, legal, social, environmental, financial, regulatory, and engineering studies. For example, the Nam Theun 2 hydropower project in Laos, with a total investment cost of $1.4 billion, had project preparation costs of $124 million, or almost 9 percent of investment costs.[17] By one

---

[12] Dabla-Norris *et al.* (2011).   [13] Esfahani and Ramirez (2003).
[14] World Bank (2009b).   [15] Foster and Briceño-Garmendia (2010).
[16] World Bank (2007).   [17] World Bank (2011c).

estimate, bringing Africa's key transformational infrastructure projects to a stage at which they can attract investors (public or private) would require some $500 million.[18] Generally, however, the public and private sectors are both reluctant to allocate substantial resources upfront for project preparation.

Some new initiatives to address these shortcomings are already under way. In November 2010 the World Bank Group launched the Infrastructure Finance Center of Excellence, which aims to leverage Singapore's expertise in urban development and financing and the World Bank's global development knowledge and operational experience to attract more private capital for public infrastructure projects in Asia. The center provides tailored technical assistance to governments on project identification, preparation, and marketing and helps governments secure project preparation funds through third-party facilities.[19] In addition, the G20 Multilateral Development Bank Working Group on Infrastructure has developed an action plan detailing steps to improve infrastructure project preparation, develop regional projects, and increase spending efficiencies.[20]

Closing the financing gap

Public infrastructure projects in developing countries can be financed through taxes, bilateral and multilateral concessional loans (official development assistance), and private investment, with the type of financing depending largely on the country's stage of development. Investment financing through multilateral and bilateral concessional loans is particularly important for low-income countries, in which it accounts for about 35 percent of new capital spending (Figure 7.2). In middle-income countries, infrastructure investments are financed mainly by the public sector through taxes. Reliable data on tax-financed spending are very limited, however, reflecting the large share of infrastructure spending that occurs off-budget.[21]

---

[18] Foster and Briceño-Garmendia (2010).   [19] World Bank (2011b).
[20] MDB Working Group on Infrastructure (2011).
[21] In Africa, more than 60 percent of infrastructure spending occurs off-budget (Briceño-Garmendia, Smits, and Foster 2008).

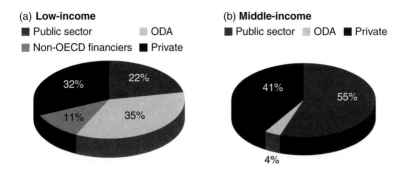

Figure 7.2 Infrastructure spending in developing countries by type of financing (annualized flows)
Note: ODA is official development assistance.
Source: Foster and Briceño-Garmendia (2010).

Tax financing

Increasing tax-financed infrastructure investments is unlikely to close the infrastructure gap in the short run, especially if growth remains sluggish. In many developing countries the tax base is small, tax administration is weak, and tax increases can be highly distortionary. In sub-Saharan Africa, each dollar raised by the government has a marginal cost of public funds of almost 20 percent.[22] Moreover, if infrastructure financing crowds out private investment, whether through high tax rates or high interest rates, its growth impact will diminish. In addition, the fiscal space to invest in infrastructure has contracted for some emerging market economies in the wake of the financial crisis. Even so, governments could narrow the infrastructure gap by spending their resources more efficiently. An estimated 11 percent of electricity and 24 to 50 percent of water is unaccounted for in developing countries.[23] In Africa, as much as $17 billion of the overall investment need of $93 billion could be met by increasing maintenance, improving the performance of utilities and other service providers, mending deficiencies in public expenditure frameworks, and modernizing administrative and regulatory frameworks.[24]

[22] Foster and Briceño-Garmendia (2010).   [23] World Bank (2011b).
[24] Foster and Briceño-Garmendia (2010).

Traditional donor financing

The scope for increasing infrastructure financing from traditional donors also seems limited under current economic conditions. Infrastructure aid doubled between 2006 and 2009, as multilateral creditors sought to dampen the impact of the financial crisis on developing countries. The World Bank Group and other international financial institutions (IFIs) increased their infrastructure financing from around $20 billion annually from 2006 to 2008 to $50 billion in 2009, when the former provided record support of $26 billion (Figure 7.3).[25] Because several donor countries suffered from the effects of the 2008–9 crisis, however, aid flows are likely to decline in the coming years. Past banking crises in donor countries have been found to be associated with a 20 to 25 percent decline in aid flows, with flows languishing for a decade after the start of the crisis.[26] Extending well beyond any income-related effects, the declines could have resulted from the reduced fiscal space and higher debt levels after the crises.

Nontraditional donors and sovereign wealth funds

Several nontraditional bilateral donors, such as Brazil, China, India, and the Arab countries, have emerged as major financiers of infrastructure projects in Africa. Infrastructure resources provided to Africa by economic agencies in these countries jumped from $1 billion a year in the early 2000s to about $8 billion in 2006.[27] These investments are often directed to resource-rich economies.

Sovereign wealth funds, with an estimated $3.2 trillion in financial assets at the end of 2008, have also begun to invest in infrastructure in developing countries.[28] The Emerging Markets Private Equity

---

[25] World Bank Group lending for infrastructure was even greater in 2010, but it is projected to decline going forward.

[26] Dang, Knack, and Rogers (2009) used panel data for the period from 1977 to 2007 to analyze the changes in aid flows following banking crises.

[27] Foster and Briceño-Garmendia (2010).

[28] Klitzing *et al.* (2010). Examples include the China–Africa Development Fund, an equity fund that invests in Chinese enterprises with operations in Africa, which reportedly invested nearly $540 million in twenty-seven projects in Africa that were expected to lead to total investments of $3.6 billion in 2010. The Qatar Investment Authority plans to invest $400 million in infrastructure in South Africa.

(a) **Change over time**

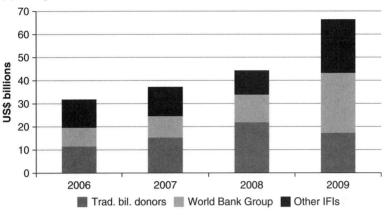

Trad. bil. donors　World Bank Group　Other IFIs

(b) **By creditor, 2009**

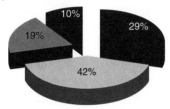

Africa　Asia　Latin America and the Caribbean　Europe

Figure 7.3 Aid flows for infrastructure from traditional bilateral donors and international financial institutions
Source: Based on OECD's "International development statistics" database.

Association estimates that sovereign wealth funds allocated just 18 percent of their portfolio to nondomestic emerging market investments, but only a small portion of that was for infrastructure. In the current economic turmoil, investment opportunities once deemed safe and attractive are losing their appeal, which could make infrastructure investments in developing countries more attractive to long-term investors. In addition, many developing countries are reducing the risks associated with long-term investments by implementing sound macroeconomic policies, improving regulatory frameworks, and strengthening their capacity for project identification and preparation.

Domestic savings

Developing country governments could also make more effective use of domestic savings to finance infrastructure investment. Domestic funding for infrastructure investment is still limited and costly, and domestic savings are generally low. Local capital markets tend to be illiquid and shallow, with limited secondary market activity, and the narrow range of their short-term instruments makes them ill-suited to infrastructure investments. Local banks, the major investors, prefer short maturities to match their liability structure. Institutional investors such as pension funds and insurance companies, which hold longer-term liabilities, are often underdeveloped. Governments in low-income countries could strengthen domestic capital markets by keeping inflation rates low and stable, developing a well-established yield curve for government bonds as a benchmark for the corporate sector, and enhancing the institutional investor base. Improving the domestic capital market would have benefits beyond infrastructure investment.

In several emerging market economies, local bond markets have sprung up to support longer-term issuances for infrastructure development. In other countries, bank loans play an important role. In China public banks provide long-term financing for infrastructure. In Brazil the publicly owned National Bank for Economic and Social Development (BNDES), which lent some $25 billion for infrastructure projects in 2009, lends to companies investing in infrastructure and guarantees and buys infrastructure bonds issued by some corporations.[29] BNDES is financed through retained earnings, foreign funding (including from bilateral and multilateral lenders), and government resources.

International financial markets

Developing countries are also tapping into international financial markets to finance infrastructure projects.[30] International bond issuances are attractive for infrastructure investments because they enable countries to augment domestic savings and broaden the investor base and

[29] Walsh, Park, and Yu (2011).
[30] Senegal and Sri Lanka, for example, issue bonds for infrastructure projects.

because they have a back-loaded repayment profile. But they also entail considerable risks, including exchange rate exposure, high refinancing needs, potentially large costs-of-carry, and the possibility of a reversal in international investor confidence.

Public–private partnerships

The private sector also invests in infrastructure through public–private partnerships, established through long-term contracts with the government that cover both investment and service provision. The private investor (usually a group of investors) finances and manages construction and operates and maintains the project over the life of the contract (generally twenty to thirty years). It then transfers the assets to the government. During operation, the investor receives a stream of payments as compensation.[31]

Interest in public–private partnerships for infrastructure investment is growing in developing countries. The World Bank's "Private participation in infrastructure" database provides information on infrastructure investment commitments in which private parties assume operating risks.[32] These commitments reached a high of $170 billion in 2010, but they are heavily concentrated in telecommunications and in just a few countries. India has been the top recipient of private sector flows in infrastructure since 2006 (Figure 7.4).

Excluding the top five recipients of private sector investments in infrastructure (Brazil, China, India, the Russian Federation, and Turkey), private investment commitments fell around 30 percent between 2007 and 2010 as a result of the financial crisis. The number of countries attracting private sector involvement reached its lowest level since the early 1990s. As investors became more risk-averse, they sought lower debt–equity ratios, shorter tenors, and higher expected rates of return.[33]

Public–private partnerships for infrastructure investment entail considerable risk, because infrastructure assets are illiquid, upfront capital financing requirements are large, and repayments are often made over decades. Risks include higher-than-projected costs, revenue shortfalls if

[31] Engel, Fischer, and Galetovic (2010).   [32] See http://ppi.worldbank.org.
[33] Izaguirre (2010).

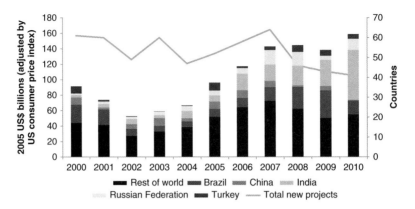

Figure 7.4 Investment in public–private partnership projects in developing countries
Source: World Bank's "Private participation in infrastructure" database: http://ppi.worldbank.org.

demand is lower than projected, exchange rate risks if infrastructure financing is in foreign currency but user fees are paid in domestic currency, force majeure, and political and regulatory risks.

Diversifying some of these risks could make investments in developing countries more attractive. Government guarantees can insure against project-related risks, such as a demand shortfall,[34] but guarantees are unlikely to lessen investors' concerns about governmental risk, such as policy reversal, regulatory failure, and government default. Multilateral institutions and bilateral donors are likely to be better positioned to assume these risks. The World Bank Group has increasingly used guarantees to catalyze private finance by reducing the risk of government default. Since the early 1990s the World Bank Group has approved thirty-six guarantees in twenty-eight countries, with a cumulative guarantee amount of $3.8 billion.[35] The Multilateral Investment Guarantee Agency, the arm of the World Bank Group that provides political risk insurance for foreign investments, recently adapted its

---

[34] In several low-income countries, demand for infrastructure services may not be high enough to attract private investors. In sub-Saharan Africa, for example, where population density is low, private investment in power, water, and rail has been very limited (Foster and Briceño-Garmendia 2010).

[35] Russell (2009).

products and guarantees in order to facilitate the underwriting of infrastructure projects.

Even more promising than diversifying risks through guarantees is reducing risk by strengthening the regulatory framework and implementing sound macroeconomic policy. When country risk is high, infrastructure investors often demand real returns on equity of 20 percent or higher and a country risk premium of up to 5 percent on debt.[36] Regulatory risks to investments in Latin America can add up to 6 percent to the cost of capital.[37] Projects in countries with a strong legal framework have lower funding costs and tighter interest rate spreads.[38] Macroeconomic stability is a key to earning an investment-grade rating, which is essential to tap the large savings of institutional investors at attractive prices. Multilateral institutions and bilateral agencies could work with countries to reduce risk by supporting improvements in these areas.

Public–private partnerships can help governments overcome temporary budget constraints, but they do not necessarily provide additional financial resources. Public–private partnerships can change the timing of government disbursements and revenues, but they have little impact on the government's intertemporal budget constraint,[39] unless they increase the efficiency of the investment.[40] While there is some empirical evidence that private management has been more efficient than public management,[41] the cost can be much higher under public–private partnerships than under pure public provision.[42]

In addition, public–private partnerships can impose substantial fiscal risks if not managed carefully. Such arrangements often include contingent liabilities, including minimum revenue guarantees, foreign exchange guarantees, and government commitments to offset any shortfall in demand.[43] Clear accounting standards are often lacking for these arrangements, and infrastructure spending related to public–private partnerships is often moved off-budget and the related debt is

---

[36] Klein (2005).   [37] Guasch (2004).   [38] Dailami and Hauswald (2003).
[39] With a public–private partnership, the current government can forgo the investment outlays, which can be large on infrastructure projects, but then relinquish the user fees or tax revenues in the future.
[40] Engel, Fischer, and Galetovic (2010).
[41] Guasch (2004); Foster and Briceño-Garmendia (2010).
[42] Engel, Fischer, and Galetovic (2010).   [43] Calderón and Servén (2010b).

moved off the government's balance sheet.[44] The associated costs can be considerable. In Colombia, government guarantees resulted in fiscal costs that were 50 percent higher than the investment supplied by the private sector.[45] Keeping such costs in check requires credible hard-budget constraints on service providers, a comprehensive regulatory framework, and independent regulatory and supervisory bodies, all of which are hard to come by in many low-income countries.

Countries can reduce the impact of infrastructure investments on public debt levels by choosing infrastructure investments with high economic returns and reducing contingent liabilities. But there are other factors to keep in mind. First, if infrastructure financing crowds out private investment and puts upward pressure on debt levels, its growth impact shrinks. Second, the government's ability to capture at least part of the marginal product of infrastructure projects, through taxes or user fees, will determine how the investment affects fiscal sustainability. If tax administration is weak and fiscal revenues capture only a small fraction of the extra income, even projects with high growth impacts will weaken government finances. Collecting user fees may also pose challenges, especially in countries in which most people are poor and administrative capacities are weak. Third, government finances will also be affected by the cost of borrowing, which depends on the type of financing, the government's debt level, and investors' risk perceptions. Prudent macroeconomic policies, a stable political environment, and good debt management could lower the costs of borrowing.

Designing the global infrastructure initiative

The G20, now focused largely on securing resources so that the IMF can help countries avoid an impending debt crisis, should also provide support for a global infrastructure initiative. IMF lending to countries in debt crisis will ease their pain temporarily but will not increase their competitiveness and growth potential, so the same problems will recur. Pledges to stabilize the Eurozone are needed, but they are not an exit strategy. Only well-designed structural reforms can extricate countries from repeat crises. But most structural reforms are contractionary, at least initially. Without growth they can be difficult to

---

[44] Engel, Fischer, and Galetovic (2010).   [45] Calderón and Servén (2010b).

implement, as Japan's experience since its bubble burst in the early 1990s demonstrates. The proposed global infrastructure initiative, by investing in bottleneck-releasing projects, will boost demand and growth and create space for structural reforms in the Eurozone, Japan, and the United States. If growth is rekindled, there will be less need for firewalls.

The proposed global infrastructure initiative should incorporate several important design features. First, the initiative should encompass infrastructure needs in developed and developing countries. The European Commission estimates that the European Union needs to invest some $2.8 trillion in infrastructure over the next decade. The American Society of Civil Engineers calculates that the United States needs to spend $2.2 trillion in infrastructure over the next five years. The World Bank estimates the infrastructure needs of developing countries at $1.5 trillion a year. Some estimates are even higher. India alone requires $1 trillion between 2012 and 2017.[46] Demand for electricity is expected to double in Latin America by 2030, generating investment demand of some $430 billion.[47] The Asian Development Bank estimates infrastructure investment needs of $750 billion a year in Asia.[48] And McKinsey projects that $8 trillion will be committed to infrastructure projects in Asia over the next decade to address persistent underinvestment, rising demand from a growing population, faster urbanization, and the impacts of climate change.[49] If all these demands for infrastructure investment in developed and developing countries are met, global demand and growth will leap ahead, creating space for structural reforms in the Eurozone and other high-income economies.

Second, the global infrastructure initiative should focus on bottle-necks to growth and projects that are self-financing, so as to avoid creating an unsustainable public debt burden. Therefore, the initiative

---

[46] Consulate General of India, New York (2010).
[47] Yepez-García, Johnson, and Andrés (2010).
[48] The World Bank "guess-timates" the financing gap at $175 to $700 billion. For many countries, however, lack of financing does not seem to be the major constraint. The Asian Development Bank's analysis of infrastructure need focuses on implementation capacity, intermediation, the development of project financing, the financing of regional projects, and similar topics rather than on the financing gap.
[49] Tahilyani, Tamhane, and Tan (2011).

should be implemented through institutions that have the capacity to select, design, implement, and manage bottleneck-releasing infrastructure projects. Funds should be channeled through existing multilateral development banks and regional development banks and new multilateral development banks, such as the proposed BRICS Bank, put forward in the Delhi Declaration in March 2012.[50]

Third, funds for the initiative should come from reserve-issuing and reserve-rich countries. Public funds could be used to leverage private investment funds. If they are well chosen and well managed, infrastructure projects should generate attractive long-term returns. Under the current economic conditions of low interest rates and high risks, infrastructure projects could be particularly interesting to sovereign wealth fund and pension fund investors, especially if suitable arrangements can be made, such as giving private investors seniority.[51] Sovereign wealth funds had an estimated $3.2 trillion in financial assets at the end of 2008; Asia's sovereign wealth funds alone manage more than $1.2 trillion in assets. Government pension assets exceed $1.9 trillion.[52] Despite their large size, these financing sources provide little funding for infrastructure projects. Asian savings are heavily invested in low-yielding securities in developed countries, such as US Treasury bills.

Moving from the "new normal" to the "new new normal"

The Eurozone and the United States face the possibility of a protracted "new normal" of decades of sluggish growth accompanied by a rapid accumulation of unsustainable public debt, as Japan has experienced in its "lost decades." There is a better alternative, however. Promoting bottleneck-releasing infrastructure investment in developing and

---

[50] The Delhi Declaration was issued by the leaders of Brazil, the Russian Federation, India, China, and South Africa (the BRICS countries) at their fourth summit, held in New Delhi on March 29, 2012. The text of the declaration is available at www.cfr.org/brazil/brics-summit-delhi-declaration/p27805.

[51] As proposed by the Europe 2020 Project bond initiative (European Commission 2011).

[52] The estimated assets of government pension funds are $1,414 billion for the Japan Pension Bureau, $240 billion for the Korea National Pension Service, $140 billion for the China Hong Kong Monetary Authority, $114 billion for the China National Security Fund, and $16 billion for the Thailand Government Pension Fund.

developed countries could pave the way for a "new new normal" of solid growth in developed countries and stronger growth in developing countries. Infrastructure investment has accounted for two-thirds of the increase in growth in East Asia and about half the increase in Africa in recent years.[53]

China's experience during the East Asian financial crisis of 1997–8 shows that a "new new normal" is possible. Facing economic conditions similar to those of the recent global downturn, China focused its fiscal stimulus investments on highways, railroads, port facilities, and electricity – areas that were bottlenecks to China's growth. China's highway network expanded from 4,700 kilometers in 1997 to 25,100 kilometers in 2002. And China's annual growth rate rose from an average of 9.6 percent between 1979 and 2002 to 10.9 percent between 2003 and 2010, without the two-digit inflation that had previously accompanied rapid growth. Meanwhile, as growth accelerated, public debt fell from more than 30 percent of GDP in the early 2000s to 23 percent in 2008.[54]

Low-income countries need to seize the opportunity presented by the coming transition of China and other middle-income growth poles from low-skilled manufacturing jobs by fostering structural transformation. This is feasible if policymakers can tap into the potential advantages of being a latecomer and help their economy develop industries according to the country's comparative advantage. The Growth Identification and Facilitation Framework, an implementation tool for the new structural economics, can help policymakers in developing countries identify industries with latent comparative advantage[55] and facilitate competitive private sector development, as elaborated in Part III.

In 2010 the G20 announced the goal to "boost and sustain global demand, foster job creation, contribute to global rebalancing, and increase the potential for growth" through investment in infrastructure to address bottlenecks and enhance growth potential.[56] It is time to

---

[53] Zoellick (2010b).   [54] National Bureau of Statistics of China (2012).

[55] An industry is counted as a country's latent comparative advantage if the factor costs of production in the industry are competitive internationally but the industry is yet to become competitive because of high transaction costs as a result of inadequate infrastructure.

[56] This goal was included in the declaration issued by the G20 leaders at the summit held at Seoul on November 11 and 12, 2010. The text of the declaration is available at www.g20.utoronto.ca/2010/g20seoul.html.

make this happen, by launching a global infrastructure initiative that brings together governments, development banks, and the private sector to remove obstacles to sustained global recovery and growth. This could be the last opportunity for the world to avoid a protracted "new normal" of low growth and high debt, replacing it with a "new new normal" of a return to precrisis growth rates in advanced countries and enhanced growth in developing countries.

PART III

How Poor Countries Can Catch Up: Flying Geese and Leading Dragons

A global push for infrastructure investments in developing countries, as proposed in Part II, will work only if developing countries can grow dynamically in the coming decades. But do they have the space to do so in today's uncertain, stressful global economy? And, if so, how do they seize the opportunity and then sustain their growth?

Development thinking has focused on what developing countries do not have and that developed countries do (capital-intensive industries in structuralism), and on what developing countries cannot do well and developed countries can (governance and business environment in the Washington consensus). Guided by this development thinking, developing countries after World War II adopted import substitution strategies in order to develop capital-intensive industries that defied their comparative advantage. For protecting nonviable firms in priority sectors, the strategies created distortions, and led to rent-seeking, political captures, stagnation, and frequent crises. The Washington consensus attempted to correct the distortions that resulted from previous import substitution strategies, but it neglected the government's role in overcoming coordination and externality issues in the process of structural transformation. The new structural economics focuses on what developing countries have (their endowments) and what they can do well based on their (latent) comparative advantage (as determined by their endowments), to start them on the road to dynamic structural change.

For low-income countries the news is heartening: in a globalized world, opportunities for economic transformation abound. The emergence of new growth poles (a multipolar world) gives even the least developed economies the opportunity to enter a new age of rapid industrialization and structural transformation. If developing countries

99

follow their comparative advantage and tap the potential of the latecomer's advantage in adopting or adapting new technologies, they can transform their economic structure and grow dynamically for decades, advancing from low-income to middle-income, or even high-income, economies in just a generation or two. Successful economies in the West and in East Asia took this approach by following a "flying geese" pattern.[1]

In coming years, as China, with some 85 million labor-intensive manufacturing jobs, absorbs its surplus labor, wages in China will rise and its economy will move up the industrial ladder from low-skilled, low-wage sectors into more capital- and technology-intensive industries. This will free up an enormous reservoir of employment possibilities that low-income countries can tap to start their own dynamic industrialization – the "leading dragon" pattern of development.[2] If Brazil, India, Indonesia, and other large middle-income countries maintain their current pace of growth, a similar pattern of structural change will emerge in other regions.

Low-income countries can grow at 8 percent or more a year for several decades if their governments follow the new structural economics' recommendations to establish a policy framework that nurtures private sector development on the basis of each country's comparative advantages and taps into the potential left by the leading dragons. Their dynamic transformation will require huge infrastructure investments to release growth bottlenecks, as described in Part II. The new structural economics and its implementation strategy (the Growth Identification Facilitation Framework; see Chapter 11) advise governments on how to facilitate this development.[3] If they succeed, the global crisis can be turned into an opportunity for achieving a win-win outcome for developing countries and developed countries alike, for today and tomorrow.

---

[1] Akamatsu ([1932] 1962: 11); Gerschenkron (1962); Ozawa (2011).
[2] Lin (2011a).
[3] The new structural economics proposes the application of a neoclassical approach to study the determination of economic structure and the mechanism of its evolution in an economy. It is called new structural economics rather than structural economics to distinguish it from the structuralism that prevailed in the early years of development economics. See Lin (2011b, 2012b).

8 | *The mystery of the great divergence*

Before the eighteenth century all countries were poor, stagnant, and agrarian. The Industrial Revolution in Britain marked the start of a new era. In the first eight decades of the eighteenth century economic growth in Britain, the world's leading country, accelerated to an average of 0.7 to 0.8 percent a year. In the nineteenth century growth quickened even more, averaging 2.8 percent a year from 1781 to 1913.[1] More remarkably, output per employee doubled from 1840 to 1911. Several other advanced economies – notably the western European countries, the United States, and other Western offshoots – followed in Britain's footsteps, and their growth also accelerated. During the past century a few economies in Asia – notably Japan and the East Asian "tigers," including Hong Kong SAR, China; South Korea; Singapore; and Taiwan, China – also achieved sustained growth that propelled them into the ranks of high-income economies. Most countries, however, failed to advance in the same way.[2] Why?

The great divergence

Between 1950 and 2008 only twenty-eight economies reduced their per capita income gap with the United States by 10 percentage points or more (Table 8.1). Only twelve of the economies were not western European or not oil or diamond producers. The remaining 180 or so countries have remained trapped in their middle- or low-income status. As a result, incomes have diverged widely across countries (Figure 8.1). From an insignificant difference at the beginning of the eighteenth century, per capita income in the developed countries of western

---

[1] Gerschenkron (1955).
[2] Of the 192 member states of the United Nations, only fifty-two are currently classified as high-income economies. In other words, 140 countries (73 percent) are still considered developing economies.

Table 8.1 *Economies that reduced their per capita income gap with the United States by at least 10 percentage points from 1950 to 2008 (percentage of US per capita income)*

Economy	1950	1980	2008	Percentage point change 1950–2008
Hong Kong SAR, China	23	57	102	78
Singapore	23	49	90	67
Equatorial Guinea	6	8	71	65
Taiwan, China	10	28	67	58
South Korea	9	22	63	54
Ireland	36	46	89	53
Japan	20	72	73	53
Spain	23	50	63	40
Austria	39	74	77	39
Norway	57	81	91	35
Finland	44	70	78	34
Greece	20	48	52	32
Trinidad and Tobago	38	67	68	30
Israel	29	59	58	28
Italy	37	71	64	27
Germany	41	76	67	26
Puerto Rico	22	44	48	26
Portugal	22	43	46	24
Mauritius	26	24	47	21
Oman	7	22	27	20
Thailand	9	14	28	20
Belgium	57	78	76	19
France	54	79	71	17
China	5	6	22	17
Malaysia	16	20	33	17
Netherlands	63	79	79	16
Bulgaria	17	33	29	12
Botswana	4	9	15	11

Source: Based on data from Maddison (2010).

Europe and its offshoots rose to more than twenty times that of the developing countries by the end of the twentieth century.

This diverging performance on the part of world economies is puzzling, and has been studied by development economists for many

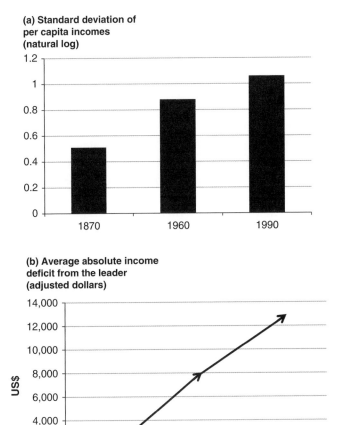

Figure 8.1 Diverging incomes among countries
Source: Based on data from Pritchett (1997).

decades. Yet there is an important clue. Before the eighteenth century it took about 1,400 years for the Western world to double its income. In the nineteenth century the same process took about seventy years, and in the twentieth century it took only thirty-five years.[3] This dramatic acceleration in growth rates came about with the rapid technological

[3] Maddison (1995).

innovation following the Industrial Revolution and the transformation of agrarian economies into modern industrialized societies, with agriculture's share of employment declining from more than 80 percent to less than 10 percent. This intriguing trend led to the recognition that the industrialization, technological innovation, and industrial upgrading and diversification that characterize ongoing structural change are essential features of rapid, sustained growth.

If the West took 300 years to innovate and industrialize, Japan less than 100, and the East Asian "tigers" only forty, however, development economists have to find the secrets of successful catching-up strategies. More recently other emerging economies, such as Brazil, China, and India, have also been growing dynamically. But other low-income countries, with more than one-sixth of humanity – the "bottom billion" people, a term coined by Oxford economist Paul Collier – continue to be trapped in poverty.[4] The mystery of diverging country performances, especially during the second half of the twentieth century, persists.

Flying geese and leading dragons to the rescue

The flying geese and leading dragon metaphors referenced in the title to Part III sum up the main messages. Economic development is a process of continuing industrial and technological upgrading in which any country, regardless of its level of development, can succeed if it develops industries consistent with its comparative advantage, as determined by its endowment structure. The secret to a winning performance is for developing countries to exploit the latecomer advantage by building up industries that are growing dynamically in more advanced countries with endowment structures similar to theirs. By following carefully selected lead countries, latecomers can emulate the flying geese pattern, which has enabled trailing economies to catch up quickly since the eighteenth century.

The emergence of large middle-income countries (such as Brazil, China, and India) as new growth poles in the world economy, with their dynamic growth and scaling of the industrial ladder, offers an unprecedented opportunity to low-income developing economies – including those in sub-Saharan Africa. China, having itself been a "follower goose," is on the verge of graduating from low-skilled

---

[4] Collier (2007).

manufacturing to a "leading dragon" in more capital- and technology-intensive industries. That will free up nearly 100 million labor-intensive manufacturing jobs, enough to more than quadruple manufacturing employment in low-income countries. A similar trend is emerging in other middle-income growth poles. The lower-income countries that can formulate and implement a viable strategy to capture these new industrialization opportunities will set out on a dynamic path of structural change that can reduce poverty and increase prosperity.

9 | The mechanics and benefits of structural change

The Roman emperor Marcus Aurelius famously observed that "the universe is transformation; our life is what our thoughts make it." He thus outlined the essentially voluntary nature of success. Writing two millennia later, biologist Charles Darwin brought scientific reasoning to Aurelius's observation and took it to another level by emphasizing the inevitability of transformation. In studying what he called "the struggle for existence," Darwin conjectured:[1]

> More individuals are born than can possibly survive. A grain in the balance will determine which individual shall live and which shall die, ... which variety or species shall increase in number, and which shall decrease, or finally become extinct. [...] The slightest advantage in one being, at any age or during any season, over those with which it comes into competition, or better adaptation in however slight degree to the surrounding physical conditions, will turn the balance.

Economists concerned with the development of poor countries have not pronounced such a stark diagnosis. Economics typically is not a zero-sum game, and even the most egregious policy failures rarely cause a country to disappear from the face of the earth.[2] After all, few national economies perish simply because of natural selection. But the basic

---

[1] Darwin ([1859] 1964: 467–8).

[2] Krugman (1996: 5–6) observes that "the idea that a country's economic fortunes are largely determined by its success on world markets is a hypothesis, not necessary truth; and as a practical, empirical matter, that hypothesis is flatly wrong. That is, it is simply not the case that the world's leading nations are to any important degree in economic competition with each other, or that any of the major economic problems can be attributed to failures to compete on world markets. [...] The bottom line for a corporation is literally its bottom line: if a corporation cannot afford to pay its workers, suppliers, and bondholders, it will go out of business. So when we say that a corporation is uncompetitive, we mean that its market position is unsustainable – that unless it improves its performance,

insight that underlies Aurelius's and Darwin's intuitions applies to economic development: long-term growth depends on continuing structural transformation.

It is possible to analyze what characterizes the evolution of successful economies from low-income, agrarian economies to urban industrial economies with a much higher per capita income. This analysis shows that countries that have failed to achieve the structural transformation of their economy away from their agrarian past have remained poor. While researchers have studied that crucial dynamic and documented some stylized facts about it, it has been more challenging to conceptualize positive structural change and fashion a clear framework for policymakers in developing countries. The new structural economics, which takes into account lessons from world economic history and advances in economic theory, provides a pragmatic approach for facilitating structural change and sustained growth in developing countries.

Early insights about leader–follower dynamics

Structural transformation, broadly defined as the interrelated processes of structural change that accompany economic development, has been a subject of active research since the beginning of the period of modern growth.[3] Within this rather broad characterization, various interpretations have been offered. The most common relates to the relative importance of economic sectors in production and factor use. From this perspective, the main changes in structure studied by early development economists were the acceleration of technological innovation, the increased rate of capital accumulation, and the shifts in the sectoral composition of growth, often with changes in the main location of economic activity (urbanization).

Simon Kuznets sought to understand and document long-run transformation through a series of stylized facts, though he was reluctant to offer a theory of development. His empirical studies identified four features of modern economic growth.[4] First, the sectoral composition of the economy changes as the nonagricultural shares rise and the

---

it will cease to exist. Countries, on the other hand, do not go out of business. They may be happy or unhappy with their economic performance, but they have no well-defined bottom line. As a result, the concept of national competitiveness is elusive."

[3] Syrquin (1988).   [4] Kuznets (1966, 1971).

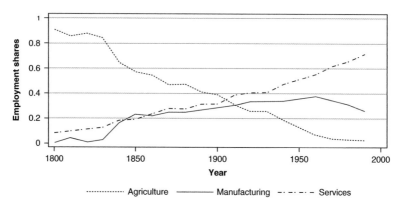

Figure 9.1 An illustration of Kuznets's stylized facts: sectoral shares of US employment
Source: Adapted from Kuznets (1966: ch. 3) author's calculation.

agricultural share falls (Figure 9.1). Second, this sectoral shift is mirrored in employment (Figure 9.2). Third, the population is redistributed from rural to urban areas. Fourth, the capital–labor ratio in the non-agricultural sectors of the economy rises.

Based on these observations, Kuznets concludes that "*some* structural changes, not only in economic but also in social institutions and beliefs, are required, without which modern economic growth would be impossible."[5] This view has been corroborated by Hollis Chenery, who defines economic development as "a set of interrelated changes in the structure of an economy that are required for its continued growth,"[6] and by Moses Abramowitz, who notes that "sectoral redistribution of output and employment is both a necessary condition and a concomitant of productivity growth."[7]

Industrialization in particular is recognized as one of the main engines of economic growth, especially in the early stages of development.[8] Its essential characteristics include an increase in the proportion of

[5] Kuznets (1971: 348, emphasis in original).   [6] Chenery (1979: xvi).
[7] Abramowitz (1983: 85). Matthews, Feinstein, and Odling-Smee (1982: 250) express a more nuanced view when they write that "neither structural change nor growth in GDP is an exogenous variable; both result from a complex of interacting causes on the supply side and demand side."
[8] Analyses of the process for the 1950s and 1960s found that manufacturing in particular tends to play a larger role in total output in richer countries and that

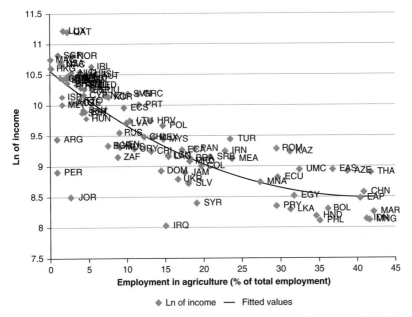

Figure 9.2 Agriculture and development: agricultural employment and GDP, 2007
Note: Income in 2005 PPP dollars.
Source: Based on data from World Bank's "World development indicators" database: http://data.worldbank.org/data-catalog/world-development-indicators.

national income derived from manufacturing and secondary industry in general, except perhaps during cyclical interruptions; a rising trend in the proportion of the working population engaged in manufacturing; and an associated increase in per capita income.[9] Few countries have achieved economic success without industrializing. Only countries with an extraordinary abundance of natural resources or land have been able to do so.[10] This is confirmed by the strong positive correlation between the growth of value added in the manufacturing sector and the change in GDP per capita from 1993 to 2007. The correlation is stronger in sub-Saharan Africa than in the rest of the world (Figure 9.3).

higher incomes are associated with a substantially bigger role for transport and machinery sectors (see Datta 1952 and Kuznets 1966).
[9] Bagchi (1990).
[10] UNIDO (United Nations Industrial Development Organization) (2009).

(a) **World**

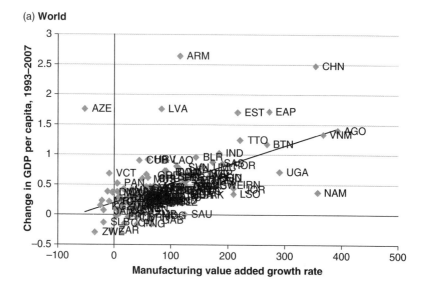

(b) **Africa**

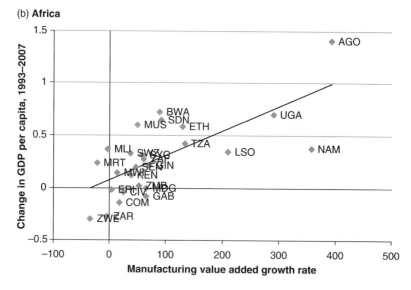

Figure 9.3 Industrialization as an engine of growth: manufacturing and income growth
Source: Based on data from World Bank's "World development indicators" database: http://data.worldbank.org/data-catalog/world-development-indicators.

Looking at these facts, early development economists embarked on a search for a theory of structural change. Walt Rostow advanced one of the most widely discussed theories of structural transformation, the theory of stages of development, which posits that the takeoff phase features two key elements: a sharp increase in the rate of capital accumulation, and the emergence of a leading sector that fosters the change in the production structure.[11] Rostow proposed a unique path to development and the need for a country to meet certain prerequisites before taking off. Despite his great insight about leading sectors that suggested the ideas of agglomeration and clustering, his theory has generated a lot of criticism.[12]

Alexander Gerschenkron developed a framework that focused on structural transformation, pointing out that growth prerequisites are substitutable. Analyzing the catching-up process among European countries after the Industrial Revolution, he observed that rapid industrialization started from different levels of "economic backwardness" and that capital accumulation was not a precondition for success. In fact, "the more backward a country's economy, the greater was the part played by special institutional factors (government agencies, banks) designed to increase the supply of capital to the nascent industries."[13]

[11] Rostow (1960).

[12] From the point of view of the new structural economics, any economy can start on a dynamic growth path if the government can help the private sector reduce its transaction costs to facilitate the development of industries that are consistent with the economy's comparative advantage as determined by its endowment structure. As a result, a sharp increase in capital accumulation is not a necessary condition. Capital will accumulate if the economy starts growing dynamically. Therefore, capital accumulation is a consequence of dynamic growth rather than a precondition. For other comments on Rostow's theory, see Hoselitz (1960).

[13] Gerschenkron (1962: 354). From the point of view of the new structural economics, the targeted industries for catching up should be consistent with a latecomer country's latent comparative advantage. Thus, the state's role is limited to facilitating the private sector's entry into the new industry by overcoming coordination problems and externalities, which are beset with market failures. Industries in the most advanced country will not be a catching-up country's latent comparative advantage if the gap between the two countries' levels of development is too large. Private firms in those industries will not be viable in open, competitive markets. Their initial investments will depend on capital mobilization by the government, and their continued operations will require government subsidies and protection. Trying to develop industries too far ahead of a country's level of development and using the government's interventions through various distortions to overcome the viability issue of firms in priority

An obvious limitation of Gerschenkron's work was that he studied only the path followed by relatively high-income Western countries to catch up with Britain.[14] Kaname Akamatsu's work on Japan, a country starting from a much lower income position than the Western countries, is of greater interest for developing countries. In a seminal paper published in 1932 but translated into English only in the 1960s, he documented what he called the "wild geese flying pattern" in economic development, noting that "wild geese fly in orderly ranks forming an inverse V."[15] His observation is illustrated in Figure 9.4, from a note prepared by the National Graduate Institute for Policy Studies (GRIPS) for the GRIPS Development Forum in 2002.[16]

The flying geese pattern describes the sequential order of industrialization by latecomer economies. It focuses on three dimensions: (a) the intraindustry dimension; (b) the interindustry dimension; and (c) the international division of labor. The intraindustry dimension views the product cycle from the perspective of a particular country that initially imports the good, then moves to production combined with imports, and finally moves to exports. The interindustry dimension concerns the sequential appearance and development of industries in a particular developing country, with industries diversifying and upgrading from consumer goods to capital goods or from simple to more sophisticated products. The international division of labor dimension concerns the relocation of industries from advanced to developing economies, as the developing economies begin to converge with advanced economies.

Are the Asian geese still flying?

This sequential pattern of industrialization by latecomer economies appears to have persisted in Asia over the past two decades. For example, in the early 1990s China was already a dominant player in some light manufactures such as footwear and toys (Table 9.1). Japan continued to

sectors are the root causes of the failure of many governments' industrial policies. Gerschenkron failed to recognize firms' viability issues' and as a result there are problems in his argument for using special institutional arrangements to develop advanced industries in backward countries.

[14] According to estimates by Maddison (2010), the per capita incomes of Germany, France, and the United States were about 60 to 75 percent of Britain's in 1870.

[15] Akamatsu (1962: 11).

[16] The GRIPS note draws on Kojima (2000) and Schroeppel and Mariko (2002). See www.grips.ac.jp/module/prsp/FGeese.htm.

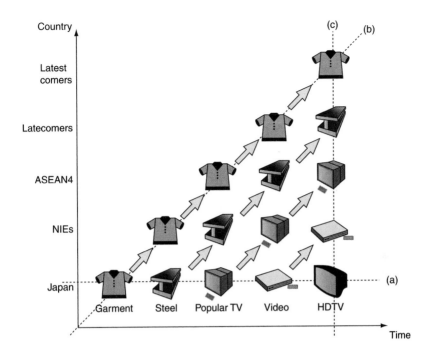

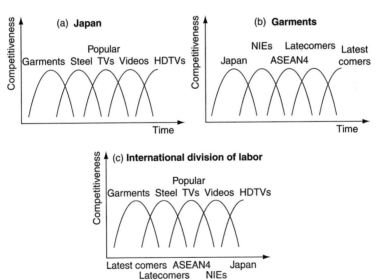

Figure 9.4 The "wild geese flying" pattern in Asia
Notes: ASEAN4 = Indonesia, Malaysia, the Philippines, and Thailand. NIEs = newly industrialized economies: Hong Kong SAR, China; Singapore; South Korea; and Taiwan, China.
Source: GRIPS: www.grips.ac.jp/module/prsp/FGeese.htm (figure reproduced with permission).

Table 9.1 *Asian geese: country rankings in selected industries*

Country	Live animals		Pharmaceuticals		Footwear		Iron and steel	
	1992	2008	1992	2008	1992	2008	1992	2008
China	1	1	2	3	1	1	3	1
India	5	4	3	1	4	2	4	4
Japan	3	3	1	2	5	5	1	2
South Korea	2	5	4	4	2	4	2	3
Thailand	4	2	5	5	3	3	5	5

Country	Plastics		Electrical machinery, parts		Television receivers		Toys	
	1992	2008	1992	2008	1992	2008	1992	2008
China	3	1	3	1	3	1	1	1
India	5	5	5	5	5	5	5	5
Japan	1	2	1	2	1	2	2	2
South Korea	2	3	2	3	2	3	3	4
Thailand	4	4	4	4	4	4	4	3

Note: Rankings established from data at the two-digit International Standard Industrial Classification (ISIC) level for exports.
Source: United Nations' "Commodity trade statistics" database: http://comtrade.un. org/db.

be a dominant player in toys but was clearly moving up the technology ladder to more sophisticated games, such as Nintendo[®] and Sony PlayStation.[®] As a low-income country in the 1990s, China exported live animals on a large scale. In the 2000s it was able to move up the product ladder to more sophisticated manufactures and overtake Japan in terms of world export shares in plastics, television receivers, and electrical machinery and parts. South Korea was a major exporter of live animals in the early 1990s but has since moved out of that primary sector. India lags in market shares but has gradually moved up in footwear.

The international division of labor and production offers another angle for examining the flying-geese pattern. Historical trade statistics for footwear, which reveal comparative advantage indexes for lead countries and latecomers, add credibility to the flying geese hypothesis (Table 9.2). Japan revealed comparative advantage in footwear in the

Table 9.2 *Flying geese and the international division of production: Asian economies with a revealed comparative advantage in footwear*

1962	1965	1970	1975	1980	1985	1990	1995	2000
Japan	Japan							
China	China	China	China	China	China	China	China	China
	Taiwan, Ch.	Taiwan, Ch.	Taiwan, Ch.	Taiwan, Ch.	Taiwan, Ch.	Taiwan, Ch.		
	South Korea	South Korea	South Korea	South Korea	South Korea	South Korea		
		Pakistan						
				Philippines	Philippines	Philippines		
					Thailand	Thailand	Thailand	Thailand
						Indonesia	Indonesia	Indonesia
						India	India	India
							Vietnam	Vietnam
							Sri Lanka	Sri Lanka
								Myanmar
								Bangladesh
								Fiji
								Cambodia

Note: Revealed comparative advantage is calculated as the share of footwear in the economy's exports divided by the share of footwear in global exports. The comparative advantage of a particular economy is "revealed" when this ratio is greater than 1. All economies except China are ranked by income level.

Source: United Nations' "Commodity trade statistics" database: http://comtrade.un.org/db.

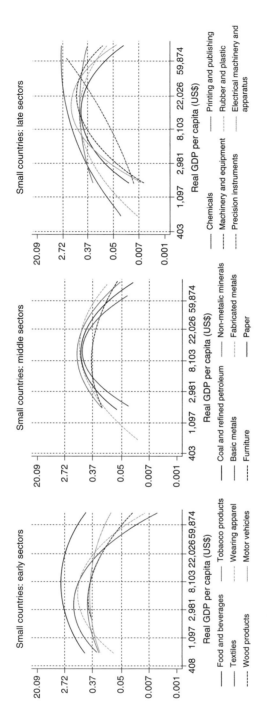

Figure 9.5 The flying geese pattern in 148 small countries: value-added shares of 18 industries and real GDP per capita, 1963–2006

Notes: Industries are at the two-digit ISIC level. Real GDP per capita is measured in 2005 US dollars.

Source: Haraguchi and Rezonja (2010) (figure reproduced with permission).

early 1960s, during the light manufacturing phase of its development. Later, other countries began to take over larger shares of global production. The pattern does not conform precisely to the dynamics of flying geese. Real-world data always involve some noise because products of differing sophistication and capital and technology intensities may be grouped in the same category. And government interventions may cause the industrial structure to deviate slightly from the optimal one determined by the country's comparative advantage. Even so, the general picture is consistent with the theory.

Across countries with different per capita incomes, the pattern of change in the share of manufacturing industries in GDP is also consistent with the flying geese hypothesis. The value-added share for each industry follows an inverse V, first increasing with real GDP per capita and then declining (Figure 9.5).[17] The pattern of change is similar for large countries.

Stylized facts – and unexplained failures of transformation

The empirical literature on catching up has gathered considerable evidence for economic development as a process of structural change and for the patterns associated with that change.[18] It has established that low-income countries look very similar in some fundamental ways. They have a large share of their population living in rural areas and employed in agriculture. And much of that agricultural activity is confined to subsistence agriculture. The basic starting point is, therefore, a transformation out of agricultural activities in rural areas.

The same evolution is clear whether looking at a cross-section of countries by per capita income or at the pattern of production of a single country over time. Higher-income countries have a lower share of the population living in rural areas, a lower share of production in agriculture, and a lower share of employment in agriculture (Figure 9.6). The advanced economies and the economies that have caught up with them have experienced dramatic structural changes in the composition of employment and value added in primary, secondary, and tertiary industries. By contrast, low-income countries have failed to achieve similar structural changes.

---

[17] Haraguchi and Rezonja (2010).
[18] See, for example, Syrquin (1986), Syrquin and Chenery (1986), Fei and Ranis (1964), and Haraguchi and Rezonja (2009, 2010).

(a) Rural share of population

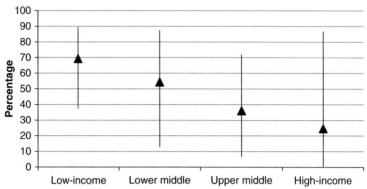

(b) Agriculture's share of GDP

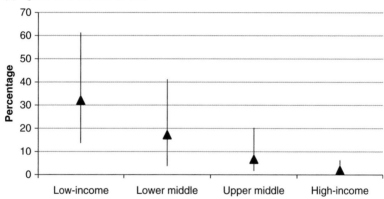

Figure 9.6 Observed patterns of structural change across country income groups

Notes: Data for rural population and GDP shares are for 2008. Data for employment shares are for 2000 for low-income countries (because of limited data availability) and for 2006 for other country groups. Some small island states with very high rural population shares were removed as outliers from the high-income and upper middle-income groups. The lines represent the range of values within each country group, and the triangles represent the average.

Source: World Bank's "World development indicators" database: http://data.worldbank.org/data-catalog/world-development-indicators (figure reproduced with permission).

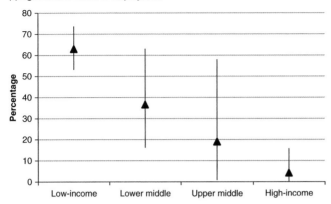

(c) **Agriculture's share of employment**

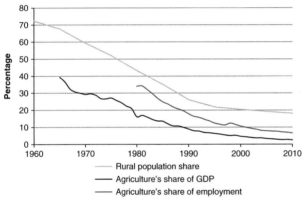

(d) **The case of South Korea**

- - - - - Rural population share
——— Agriculture's share of GDP
——— Agriculture's share of employment

Figure 9.6 (cont.)

Why have development strategies failed to deliver sustained growth and structural transformation in so many developing countries, especially in Latin America and Africa? A recent assessment that decomposes productivity growth into its sectoral and structural change components is illustrative.[19] It shows that the variation in the

---

[19] McMillan and Rodrik (2011) construct a simple index based on the idea that productivity differentials exist both between broad sectors of the economy and within modern manufacturing activities. These gaps are indicative of the allocative inefficiencies that reduce overall labor productivity. But they can

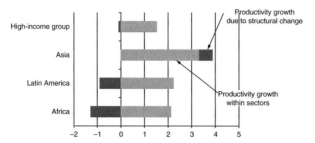

Figure 9.7 Decomposing productivity growth, by country group, 1990–2005
Source: McMillan and Rodrik (2011) (figure reproduced with permission).

contribution of structural change to overall labor productivity explains
most of the difference between the recent rapid growth in Asian countries and the slow growth in Latin American and African countries
(Figure 9.7).

African economies, which constitute the core of the development
challenge today, exhibit many signs of limited structural transformation
that help explain why progress has remained slow since their independence. In 1965 agriculture contributed 22 percent of sub-Saharan
GDP, services 47 percent, and industry 31 percent (manufacturing
17.5 percent). In 2005 agriculture contributed 15 percent of GDP,
services 52 percent, and industry 33 percent (manufacturing less than
15 percent; Figure 9.8).

The decline in the agricultural labor force that usually accompanies
economic development has not taken place in sub-Saharan Africa.
The region's economies were overwhelmingly rural in 1960, with the
agricultural labor force accounting for 85 percent of the total. Although
this share has fallen steadily over the past four decades, it is still high
(63 percent in 2009, slightly above the average for other developing
countries in 1960). With high population growth, the small change
meant that rural population density increased substantially, putting
pressure on arable land per capita.

In a closed economy, a decline in the agricultural share of the labor
force can be sustained only if labor productivity in agriculture increases

potentially be an important engine of growth. When labor and other resources
move from less productive to more productive activities, the economy grows even
if there is no productivity growth within sectors. This kind of structural change
can be an important contributor to overall economic growth.

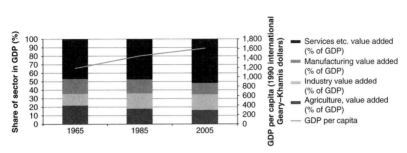

Figure 9.8 Sub-Saharan Africa: sectoral contributions to GDP (left axis) and real GDP per capita (right axis), 1965–2005
Sources: World Bank's "World development indicators" database: http://data. worldbank.org/data-catalog/world-development-indicators for sectoral GDP; Maddison (2010) for GDP per capita.

rapidly enough to feed a growing urban population. In an open economy, food can be imported, but agricultural productivity remains a key determinant of agricultural household income and overall living standards and an essential source of foreign exchange for importing capital goods. But there is little evidence that the modest observed shift out of agriculture in Africa was driven by advances in rural labor productivity. From 1960 to 2000 agricultural value added per worker rose at a trend rate of 0.5 percent a year in sub-Saharan Africa, less than a third of the prevailing rate in other developing regions.[20]

Growth in real GDP per worker in sub-Saharan Africa has been driven by the contributions of physical and human capital accumulation per worker; total factor productivity (regarded as accounting for technological progress) has generally been nil or negative.[21] Not surprisingly, manufacturing development has remained very slow in many African economies. Indeed, twenty-one of thirty-one sub-Saharan countries for which data are available deindustrialized between 1993 and 2007.

Economic diversification has also been limited in sub-Saharan Africa, as evidenced by the region's vulnerability to shocks and the volatility of

[20] According to Ndulu *et al.* (2007), cereal yields did only slightly better, rising at 0.74 percent a year, compared with 2.4 percent in the rest of the world. They also note that relative food prices show little evidence of a systemic food crisis. The answer may lie in rising food imports: the ratio of net imports of food to GDP rose by 1.4 percentage points a decade in sub-Saharan Africa, eight times more rapidly than in the rest of the world.

[21] Hall and Jones (1999); Ndulu *et al.* (2007).

its annual growth rates, both of which are much higher than in other developing regions. Many small African economies rely primarily on exports. Yet exports have remained concentrated in a narrow band of primary commodities with volatile prices,[22] and in many cases exports have become more concentrated over time through the exploitation of mineral resources.[23] Thus, while Asian economies have been broadly successful in transforming their export sectors toward high-technology, high-value-added goods, African countries have remained exporters of commodities or low-technology goods.

Africa's failure to upgrade its industrial structure and to diversify is particularly disturbing. Unlike other developing regions, sub-Saharan Africa has benefited only slightly from the deindustrialization in high-income countries. The transition toward a service-dominated economic structure in Japan, the European Union, and the United States – often stimulated by innovation and technological upgrading – has been accompanied by retreating industrial sectors. Globalization and the quest for competitiveness and profitability have led many firms to relocate their labor-intensive manufacturing production to middle- and low-income countries – as shown by the evolution of foreign direct investment flows in recent years. So far, sub-Saharan countries, excluding South Africa, have received only a small amount of those investment flows.

---

[22] Monga (2006).
[23] Gersovitz and Paxson (1990); Berthelemy and Söderling (2001).

10 | *Lessons from the failures and successes of structural transformation*

The insights of early development thinkers such as Akamatsu,[1] Gerschenkron,[2] and Kuznets[3] enriched development knowledge. But they did not answer many of the most burning questions facing policymakers in developing countries.

Arthur Lewis, observing that "the central problem in the theory of economic development is to understand how a community that was previously saving and investing 4 or 5 percent of its national income or less converts itself into an economy where voluntary saving is running at about 12 to 15 percent of national income or more," concludes that "the central fact of economic development is that the distribution of incomes is altered in favor of the saving class."[4] His analysis assumed that saving is a prerequisite to sustained growth. This is not necessarily so. But, even assuming that it is, a key question for structural transformation remains how to foster capital accumulation in poor countries.

Besides the saving constraint, some researchers have introduced foreign exchange requirements or human capital as additional limitations to economic growth.[5] Again, taking these assumptions as true, the question of how to overcome such obstacles remains unanswered.

Other important questions for the structural change agenda concern how to facilitate enterprise clustering to produce economies of scale and how to facilitate the emergence of "leading sectors" that can propagate growth and links to other industries. Even in resource-rich countries there have been many instances of fast growth based on the exploitation

---

[1] Akamatsu (1962).   [2] Gerschenkron (1962).   [3] Kuznets (1966, 1971).
[4] Lewis (1954: 155, 156).
[5] See, for example, Chenery and Bruno (1962) and Chenery and Strout (1966).

of natural resources that did not lead to structural transformation –
notably when employment in the industrial sector did not expand
rapidly enough to absorb a growing labor force. Well-known cases
include mineral-rich African countries such as Chad, the Republic of
Congo, the Democratic Republic of Congo, Gabon, Guinea, Niger, and
Sudan.

Seeking answers to these puzzling questions, the recent literature on
structural transformation has expanded its inquiry to economic diversification, export composition, and industrial and technological
upgrading. Economic diversification reduces vulnerability to shocks
and reflects the pace at which low-income economies reallocate their
resources to take advantage of emerging opportunities. Empirical
research suggests that growth rates tend to be lower in economies that
fail to engage in this process and that technological progress is faster in
more sophisticated sectors.[6] In early stages of development, sectoral
diversification is accompanied by geographic agglomeration.[7] In later
stages, however, sectoral *concentration* is accompanied by geographic
deagglomeration.

Export composition also seems to matter for sustained growth and
structural transformation. But a recent study concludes that *how* a
country exports may matter even more.[8] One of the main observations
is that externalities and rents are not equally associated with all goods,
justifying government interventions to encourage the development of
certain goods beyond what the market would do naturally.[9]

Other recent approaches to structural transformation have emphasized the determinants of technological upgrading and innovation,
essential for long-run productivity growth. In low-income countries,
where budgets for research and development are scarce and industries
are far from the technological frontier, technological upgrading and
innovation typically take the form of adapting and adopting known
technologies rather than introducing new ones.[10]

---

[6] Hulten and Isaksson (2007).   [7] Imbs and Wacziarg (2003).
[8] Lederman and Maloney (forthcoming).
[9] Lederman and Maloney (forthcoming) also note how difficult it is to measure
    which goods have more potential for rents or externalities, which leads them to
    caution.
[10] Libecap and Thursby (2008); Aghion (2006); Aghion *et al.* (2005).

Looking more closely at industrialization – and deindustrialization

Despite the importance of these issues, mainstream development economics in the Washington consensus era has given only limited attention to the role of industrialization in structural transformation. The pervasive failures of government interventions guided by structuralism after World War II – in Africa, Latin America, South Asia, and the former socialist countries – have discredited policies aimed at "picking winners" for creating unsustainable and socially costly distortions. The dominant view is that the private sector is better at identifying new industries.

While industrial policies have succeeded in some countries – mainly in East Asia – the economic literature remains skeptical. A critical review of rationales for industrial policy objects that civil servants would need to be omniscient to be successful in designing and implementing government interventions.[11] But much of the literature fails to distinguish policies supporting new industries that are inconsistent with the economy's comparative advantage or protecting old industries that have lost comparative advantage from policies facilitating the development of new industries that are consistent with the economy's comparative advantage. The first set of policies generally fails; the second often succeeds.

Establishing the empirical regularities of the changing patterns of industrial structure and technological upgrading across the world is not straightforward, however. Industrialization has been a key to lifting countries out of poverty, but the recent trend in advanced economies has been toward deindustrialization – a decline in manufacturing employment as a share of the total in parallel with a decline in the share of manufacturing value added in GDP. This trend has been observed not only in the United States and Europe but also in the newly industrialized East Asian economies (Hong Kong SAR, China; South Korea; Singapore; and Taiwan, China). By contrast, the share of employment in services has increased steadily in both high- and low-income economies.

Deindustrialization in advanced and successful developing economies might at first glance suggest that domestic spending on

[11] Pack and Saggi (2006).

manufactured goods has declined while spending on services has increased. But empirical analyses and country studies reveal another picture. Measured in real terms, the share of domestic expenditure on manufactured goods has been broadly stable for decades.[12] Thus, deindustrialization reflects higher productivity in manufacturing than in services, with the patterns of trade specialization among the advanced economies explaining why the trend is faster in some countries. Deindustrialization is therefore a feature of successful economic development.

Justified skepticism about applied industrial policy

These observations justify much of the skepticism among economists about government interventions in economic development. Yet they also underline the need for a clear intellectual framework for understanding the dynamics of structural change and its potential benefits for low-income economies.

Understanding why the ambitious policy objectives set by developing country leaders in the 1950s and 1960s led to poorly designed strategies requires a return to the starting point of long-term macroeconomic analysis: a review of the key characteristics of endowment structure. In developing countries, which typically have a relative abundance of natural resources and unskilled labor and a scarcity of human and physical capital, only labor-intensive and resource-intensive industries will have a comparative advantage in open, competitive markets. By contrast, in advanced economies, with abundant capital and relatively scarce labor, capital-intensive industries will be the most competitive.[13]

Acknowledging this basic truth should be the cornerstone of any viable development strategy. Yet most developing countries in the 1950s and 1960s followed structuralism, the dominant development paradigm of the day, which advocated developing the same advanced industries as in high-income industrialized countries. Developing

---

[12] According to Rowthorn and Ramaswamy (1997), expenditure on services in current prices has increased in the advanced economies. But this growth can be accounted for by the fact that labor productivity has grown more slowly in services than in manufacturing, pushing up the relative price of services and making manufactured goods cheaper in comparison.

[13] See Heckscher and Ohlin (1991) and Lin (2003).

country leaders often had big dreams for their countries, wanting them to compete on the global technological frontier as quickly as possible.

The strategy was fatally flawed for developing countries, though. The structuralist paradigm was a comparative-advantage-defying strategy that advised countries to develop capital-intensive heavy industries even though capital was scarce.[14] The strategy implied very high production costs compared with countries with similar industries that followed their comparative advantage. Firms facing high production costs could not survive in an open, competitive market. Thus, governments have provided strong protection through subsidies and tax incentives.

Indonesia launched a ship construction industry in the 1960s, when its GDP per capita was only 10 percent of that of its main competitor. Similarly, the Democratic Republic of Congo (then Zaire) attempted to build an automobile industry in the 1970s when its GDP per capita was only 5 percent of that of the industry leader (Table 10.1). The common denominator of these strategies was the targeting of industries in countries whose per capita income was far higher than their own. Unable to produce the goods at a cost advantage, developing countries could not compete in these industries.

To implement the comparative-advantage-defying strategy, developing country governments had to protect numerous nonviable enterprises through measures to reduce their investment and operation costs. These included granting a market monopoly, suppressing interest rates, overvaluing the domestic currency, and controlling raw material prices. Such interventions caused widespread shortages in funds, foreign exchange, and raw materials. Consequently, governments also had to allocate resources directly to these enterprises through administrative channels, including national planning in the socialist countries and credit rationing and investment and entry licensing in other developing countries. For ease of implementation, many countries also relied on state-owned enterprises to develop the targeted industries.

Protection also led to other costs. The domestic prices of imports and of import-substituting goods rose relative to the world price, pushing the economy to consume the wrong mix of goods from an economic efficiency perspective. Markets fragmented as economies produced too many small-scale goods, again resulting in efficiency losses. Protection

[14] Lin (2009).

Table 10.1 *The development economics of unrealistic ambitions*

Industry	Time	Latecomer country	Main producer country at the time	Real GDP per capita of latecomer country	Real GDP per capita of leading country	Income ratio of follower to leader (percent)
Automobile	1950s	China	United States	577	10,897	5
Automobile	1970s	Congo, Dem. Rep.	United States	761	16,284	5
Automobile	1950s	India	United States	676	10,897	6
Automobile	1950s	Turkey	United States	2,093	10,897	19
Automobile	1970s	Zambia	United States	1,041	16,284	6
Iron, steel, chemicals	1950s	Egypt	United States	885	10,897	8
Shipping	1960s	Indonesia	Netherlands	983	9,798	10
Trucks	1960s	Senegal	United States	1,511	13,419	11

Source: Calculated on the basis of data from Maddison (1995).

also lessened competition from foreign firms and encouraged monopoly power among domestic firms whose owners were politically connected. It also created opportunities for rents and corruption, raising input and transaction costs.

In some countries (mainly the socialist countries in eastern Europe and the former Soviet Union), the comparative-advantage-defying industrialization strategy appeared to be successful initially, because large-scale investment through massive state mobilization of resources increased the growth rate and improved productivity indicators. But firms in the capital-intensive sectors could survive only as long as government subsidies and protection continued. When the state could no longer mobilize investment resources, economies stagnated. And because investments in the capital-intensive sectors generated little employment, the labor force remained predominantly rural.

Drawing the wrong conclusions

The failure of the old structuralist policies to deliver structural transformation, economic growth, and prosperity was interpreted to mean that government economic interventions were bound to fail because of the inevitable price and incentive distortions and the resulting misallocation of resources. These conclusions prompted a shift in development thinking toward a free market approach that promoted economic liberalization, privatization, and rigorous stabilization programs, which came to be referred to as the Washington consensus. The results of these policies for growth and employment were at best controversial, however.[15] The Washington consensus was soon viewed as a set of neoliberal policies imposed on hapless developing countries by the Washington-based international financial institutions that led to crisis and misery.[16]

Why did the Washington consensus, which attempted to correct the mistakes of the old structuralist approach, also fail to foster structural transformation and sustained growth in low-income countries? The simple answer: it focused on the government failures without fully considering the externalities and the crucial market failures of coordination inherent in industrial upgrading and diversification.

[15] Easterly (2001, 2005); World Bank (2005a). [16] Williamson (2002).

Upgrading industrial structures

To reach the income levels of advanced economies, developing econo-mies need to have the same labor productivity, which requires them to upgrade their industrial structure to the same relative capital intensity. But upgrading that is consistent with factor endowments cannot rely solely on market mechanisms. For example, even if the targeted industry is consistent with the economy's comparative advantage as determined by its factor endowment, starting a new industry may be difficult because complementary intermediate inputs and infrastructure are lack-ing. Private firms may not be able to internalize in their upgrading or diversification decisions the investments to produce the intermediate inputs or provide the infrastructure. Therefore, the government has an important role in providing or coordinating these investments.

In addition, innovation, which underlies industrial upgrading and diversification, is risky because of the first-mover problem. Failing and succeeding as a first mover both create externalities. When first movers fail, they pay the cost of the failure while producing valuable informa-tion for other firms. When they succeed, that experience also provides valuable information to other market participants about the type of industries that can be profitable in the country. If many new firms enter, that may eliminate any rents that the first mover enjoys. In an advanced economy a successful first mover is generally rewarded with a patent and can enjoy the administratively created rents. But a patent may not be an option in a developing country, because industries new to devel-oping countries are likely to have already existed in high-income countries.

Thus, while the successes and failures of first movers all generate useful information for other firms, there is an asymmetry between the losses of failure and the gains of success. Firms will have little incentive to be first movers unless the government provides some compensation for the information externality they generate. And, without first movers, an economy will not enjoy industrial upgrading and diversification and the dynamic growth that results.

Assembling the puzzle: the new structural economics

Asked about enduring life lessons, American humorist Arnold Glasgow replied: "Success is simple. Do what's right, the right way, at the right time." This is difficult advice to put into practice, as developing country policymakers who struggled for decades to come up with effective economic development strategies could tell you. The first difficulty in doing the right thing is knowing what is right.

The historical and empirical evidence discussed previously suggests looking closely at structural change and its corollary, industrial upgrading and diversification, and imitating (not replicating) the successful approaches that have allowed a small group of countries to move from low- to high-income status is right. What propelled into prosperity countries as diverse as England (catching up with and surpassing the Netherlands in the sixteenth century), the United States, Germany and France (catching up with Great Britain in the nineteenth century), Japan after the Meiji Restoration, and a few other newly industrialized economies throughout the twentieth century? The new structural economics proposes a framework for structural change that complements earlier approaches to economic development, while taking several principles into account.[17]

First, the structure of an economy's factor endowment, which determines comparative advantage, is specific to its level of development, so an economy's optimal industrial structure also differs with its level of development. Different industrial structures imply differences in the capital intensity of industries, in optimal firm size, in the scale of production, in market range, in transaction complexity, and in risk. As a result, each industrial structure requires corresponding hard and soft infrastructure to facilitate its operations. Hard infrastructure includes power, transport, and telecommunications systems. Soft infrastructure includes the financial system and regulation, the education system, the legal framework, social networks, values, and other intangible structures in an economy. The optimal industrial structure determines the economy's production frontier, and whether production locates on the frontier depends in part on the adequacy of the infrastructure, both hard and soft.

Second, each level of economic development is a point on a continuum from low-income agrarian to high-income industrialized, not a dichotomy of two stages: poor or rich, developing or industrialized. Given the endogeneity of industrial structure at each level of

---

[17] The new structural economics is outlined in some of my previous work; see, for example, Lin (2011b, 2012b, 2012c).

development, the targets of industrial and infrastructure upgrading would not necessarily be the same in developing countries as in high-income countries.

Third, following comparative advantage to build up industries is the best way for a developing country to sustain industrial upgrading and economic growth and to become competitive domestically and internationally. Capital will accumulate at the fastest rate possible because the country will generate the highest possible surplus for its level of development, investment will have the highest possible return, and thus the incentives to save and invest will be the greatest. The country's endowment structure will thus evolve rapidly from fairly resource- or labor-abundant to more capital-abundant, and its comparative advantage to more capital-intensive. Latecomers to industrial upgrading can benefit from the advantage of backwardness, as Gerschenkron explained, by borrowing technology from more advanced economies, and as Kuznets observed in his analysis of the leader–follower relationship and Akamatsu highlighted in his analysis of the flying geese pattern.[18] This means that latecomers have the potential to grow much more rapidly than forerunners.

Fourth, the market is a necessary mechanism for development. Only through market competition will relative prices reflect the relative abundance of factors and induce firms to develop industries according to the economy's comparative advantage. Because market failures are inherent in industrial upgrading and diversification, however, government facilitation is required to help firms overcome coordination and externality obstacles as the economy moves from one level of development to another.

This approach to development is not just theoretical. Historical evidence shows how latecomers in development can exploit their backwardness. It also provides a practical economic strategy for countries willing to follow the flying geese pattern, which has successfully helped so many countries catch up. This experience is all the more relevant today, as new growth poles have emerged with the spectacular progress of large economies such as Brazil, China, and India, and as globalization has opened up new economic space and new possibilities for low-income countries.

---

[18] Kuznets (1966, 1971); Akamatsu (1962).

11 | *Unique opportunities for poor countries*

As policymakers in poor countries contemplate the challenges facing their countries after decades of misguided strategies, they should respond with optimism rather than despair. Many opportunities lie ahead in an increasingly globalized world.

In the aftermath of the recent global recession, former World Bank president Robert Zoellick described the new economic landscape:[1]

We are now in a new, fast-evolving multipolar world economy – in which some developing countries are emerging as economic powers; others are moving toward becoming additional poles of growth; and some are struggling to attain their potential within this new system – where North and South, East and West, are now points on a compass, not economic destinies. [...] We are witnessing a move toward multiple poles of growth as middle classes grow in developing countries, billions of people join the world economy, and new patterns of integration combine regional intensification with global openness.

These words herald the opening of important opportunities for low-income countries in today's rapidly evolving world economy. During this century a burst of convergence has occurred as developing countries have grown more quickly than high-income countries and emerging market economies have become the new growth poles. In the 1980s and 1990s, except for China, the top five contributors to global growth were the advanced economies of the G7. But from 2000 to 2009, except for the United States, all the top contributors were emerging market economies, and China was the top contributor (Figure 11.1). This trend is being reinforced in the aftermath of the 2007–9 global crisis, with developing countries as a group growing more than twice as rapidly as high-income countries.

---

[1] Zoellick (2010a: 1).

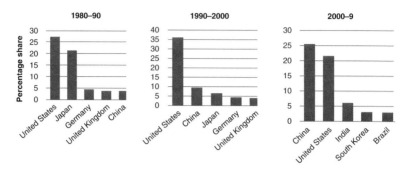

Figure 11.1 Top five contributors to global economic growth, by decade (percent)
Source: Based on data from World Bank's "World development indicators" database: http://data.worldbank.org/data-catalog/world-development-indicators.

The world economy should feel this shift in economic weight as positive effects for high-income and developing countries alike. For high-income countries, the growth of emerging economies will expand the markets for their exports of capital goods and intermediate goods. For many developing countries that are still major commodity producers, higher consumption and production in the new growth pole economies will support adequate prices for their commodity exports. In addition, firms and governments in emerging market economies will provide funds for infrastructure and natural resource investments in low-income developing countries.

These benefits are already here – and more are emerging. Propelled by domestic demand for raw materials, Brazil has rapidly expanded investment and trade with Africa, with imports from the continent rising from $3 billion in 2000 to $18.5 billion in 2008.[2] Similarly, bilateral trade between China and Africa increased from $10 billion in 2000 to $91 billion in 2009, and China's investment in Africa jumped from $490 million in 2003 to $9.3 billion in 2009.[3] Chinese finance has a

[2] See Lapper (2010). In Mozambique, Brazilian companies are developing coal reserves, building a power station, and constructing rail and port infrastructure to bring the coal to export markets. In Angola, a Brazilian firm has become the largest private sector employer, with food and ethanol production, offices, factories, supermarkets, and more.
[3] State Council (2010).

growing role in Africa, the developing region facing the greatest constraints on access to finance.[4] Meanwhile, India's government – observing that five of the world's twelve fastest-growing economies are in sub-Saharan Africa, a continent richly endowed with natural resources – plans to invest $1.5 trillion in infrastructure development in Africa in the next decade.[5]

More important than these beneficial trade and financial flows are the golden opportunities for industrialization in lower-income countries presented by the dynamic growth in the new growth poles. China, because of its size and income, is of particular interest. After three decades of sustained growth (at 9.9 percent annually in real terms), the Chinese economy is at a crossroads, with wages rising rapidly and surplus labor disappearing. These are the common challenges of economic success over time. To maintain dynamic growth, China will need to upgrade its industrial structure from its labor-intensive industries and become a producer of more technologically advanced and more capital-intensive products. As China moves into more sophisticated product markets, it will clear market space for other developing countries to enter the more labor-intensive industries.

A tectonic shift ahead – with opportunities

The early 1980s marked the beginning of a new era in economic development, with China emerging as a powerhouse. It is hard to remember that, only thirty years ago, China was much poorer than most sub-Saharan countries; its GDP per capita (measured in purchasing power parity) in 1980 was less than a third of the sub-Saharan average. Today China is an upper middle-income country, with a per capita income of $5,400 in 2011 – more than four times the sub-Saharan average. Its share of world GDP is nearing 10 percent, and its economy ranks as the world's second largest, next to the United States. Without oil, cocoa, coffee, cotton, timber, diamonds, or uranium to export, China, a country of 1.3 billion people, has made spectacular progress.

China achieved this success over three decades through the disciplined implementation of a realistic economic strategy that was

---

[4] Wang (2009).
[5] Statement by Indian minister of commerce and industry Anand Sharma, reported by *Leadership* (Abuja, Nigeria), January 15, 2010.

consistent with the country's endowment structure and its comparative advantage in labor-intensive industries. It followed a two-part strategy. First, it achieved both stability and dynamic transformation by adopting a dual-track approach to reforms: giving transitional protection to old comparative-advantage-defying, capital-intensive sectors and liberalizing entry to comparative-advantage-following, labor-intensive sectors. Second, as a latecomer, China chose an economic development strategy that tapped the potential of backwardness along the lines of the flying geese pattern, borrowing technology from more advanced economies to accelerate its development.[6] Looking forward, China can still rely on the advantage of backwardness, and it has the potential to maintain dynamic growth for another twenty years or more.[7]

Propelling China's growth over the past three decades has been a dramatic structural transformation – in particular, rapid industrialization and urbanization. At the start of the 1979 economic reforms China was still an agrarian economy. Even in 1990 74 percent of its population lived in rural areas, and primary products accounted for 27 percent of GDP. In 2009 these shares had plunged to 49 percent and 10 percent, respectively. A similar change occurred in China's exports. In 1990 primary products made up a large share of merchandise exports. In 2009 almost all China's exports were manufactures (Figure 11.2).

China is unquestionably the leading dragon in the global marketplace for low-technology products today. In the four product categories in which it has the highest global market concentration, China's share of global exports exceeds 35 percent; in travel goods and handbags, it is close to 50 percent (Table 11.1). Most impressive is the rate at which its shares have grown. For travel goods and handbags, for example, China's share in 1976 was only 1.6 percent.

---

[6] For further discussion of these two points, see Lin (2012a).

[7] Estimates by Maddison (2010) show that China's per capita income in 2008 was 21 percent of US per capita income (measured in purchasing power parity). This income gap indicates that there is still a large technological gap between China and the industrialized countries and that China can continue to enjoy the advantage of backwardness before closing the gap. China's current status relative to the United States is similar to that of Japan in 1951, Singapore in 1967, Taiwan, China, in 1975, and South Korea in 1977. Annual GDP growth was 9.2 percent in Japan from 1951 to 1971, 8.6 percent in Singapore from 1967 to 1987, 8.3 percent in Taiwan, China, from 1975 to 1995, and 7.6 percent in South Korea from 1977 to 1997. China's development strategy after the 1979 reforms is similar to that of these four economies (Lin 2012a).

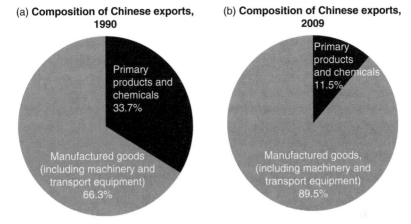

(a) **Composition of Chinese exports, 1990**

Primary products and chemicals 33.7%

Manufactured goods (including machinery and transport equipment) 66.3%

(b) **Composition of Chinese exports, 2009**

Primary products and chemicals 11.5%

Manufactured goods, (including machinery and transport equipment) 89.5%

Figure 11.2 Structural transformation of China's exports
Source: United Nations' "Commodity trade statistics" database: http://comtrade.un.org/db (figure reproduced with permission).

Table 11.1 *The leading dragon in the global marketplace for low-technology products: China's growing share of labor-intensive exports*

SITC code	Product	1976	1980	1990	2000	2005	2009
83	Travel goods and handbags	1.6	2.8	5.6	31.7	38.2	47.5
75	Office machinery and automatic data-processing equipment	0.0	0.0	0.3	5.2	25.1	40.4
85	Footwear	1.4	1.7	7.4	25.9	32.8	39.0
84	Articles of apparel and clothing accessories	2.1	4.2	9.3	18.5	27.0	35.9

Note: Data are at the two-digit Standard International Trade Classification level.
Source: United Nations' "Commodity trade statistics" database: http://comtrade.un.org/db.

An important consequence of China's rapid rise to dominance as a global exporter of labor-intensive products has been the absorption of its vast reserves of unskilled labor, especially in rural areas. Some labor economists still predict that China will remain a labor surplus economy until 2014. But the growing demand for service sector employees and the reluctance of some workers to leave rural areas will gradually stretch China's job market, particularly at the lower end.[8] So too will China's shift from labor-intensive industries toward a more advanced industrial structure – the flying geese pattern of development – with machinery increasingly dominating manufactured exports.

Labor productivity is a key driver of wage dynamics. As industrial upgrading continues in the context of burgeoning global demand for labor-intensive products, rising wages will erode China's competitive edge in such products. Manufacturing wages rose from $150 a month in 2005 to around $350 a month in 2010.[9] The wage gap between China and some upper middle-income countries is closing – a trend that is almost certain to continue over the coming decade.

China's Twelfth Five-Year Plan projects that the economy will grow 7 percent a year on average from 2011 to 2015 and, for the first time, predicts that real wages will grow at least as quickly as GDP. Both growth rates are likely to be achieved, implying a doubling of real monthly wages over the next decade, to around $700 a month. Adding in the effects of China's likely continuing currency appreciation, real wages could approach $1,000 a month within a decade, the level in such upper middle-income countries as Brazil and Turkey today – and $2,000 a month by 2030, the level in South Korea and Taiwan, China, today.

To continue growing dynamically against the background of declining wage competitiveness, China will have to follow the path of the earlier Asian "geese" – Japan in the 1960s; and Hong Kong SAR, China; South Korea; Singapore; and Taiwan, China, in the 1980s – and begin relocating its labor-intensive industries to low-income countries.[10] Indeed, this is already happening. A large share of China's outward foreign direct investment in Africa, which had reached $9.3 billion by the end of 2009, has gone to manufacturing (22 percent), second only to mining (29 percent). And China is building six economic and trade cooperation zones in Egypt, Ethiopia, Mauritius, Nigeria, and Zambia.[11] More such initiatives are likely.

---

[8] McMillan (2011).   [9] Data from Oxford Analytica, March 28, 2011.
[10] Estimates by Maddison (2010) indicate that China's per capita income (measured in PPP terms) was $6,725 in 2008, the same level as in Japan in 1966, South Korea in 1986, and Taiwan, China, in 1983. These economies started to relocate their labor-intensive manufacturing industries at that income level – Japan to the East Asian "tigers" and South Korea and Taiwan, China, to mainland China.
[11] State Council (2010).

How large are the benefits?

As China moves ahead, there will be a major difference from previous patterns of industrial upgrading; its economy is substantially larger than the economies that led the first round of structural transformation in Asia (Table 11.2). China has an estimated 85 million workers in manufacturing, most of them in labor-intensive sectors. Their reallocation to more sophisticated, higher-value-added products and tasks will open great opportunities for labor-abundant, lower-income countries to produce the labor-intensive manufacturing goods that China leaves behind. As a result, China will not be a *goose* in the traditional leader–follower pattern of industrialization for a few lower income countries – it will be a leading *dragon*.

Without detailed data on manufacturing employment in African countries, the potential gains for the region can only be conjectured. But even back-of-the-envelope calculations suggest that the benefits would be enormous. In just one year, 2009, China exported $107 billion in apparel worldwide, compared with $2 billion for sub-Saharan Africa. If rising wages shift just 1 percent of China's apparel production to lower wage African countries, that alone would boost African production and exports of apparel by 47 percent, all things equal. A 5 percent shift could translate into $5.4 billion in additional sub-Saharan exports – a 233 percent increase.

Even rough estimates of the potential opportunities for Africa's labor-intensive economies, which today export mostly natural resources, are enormous. Africa's population (north and south of the Sahara) is 1 billion, slightly less than India's 1.15 billion. In 2009 manufacturing value added stood at 16 percent of GDP in India, 13 percent in sub-Saharan countries, and 16 percent in North African countries such as Egypt, Morocco, and Tunisia.[12] India's employment in manufacturing was 8.7 million in 2009. It is reasonable to assume, therefore, that total manufacturing employment in Africa is at most 10 million. This suggests that relocating even a small share of China's 85 million labor-intensive manufacturing jobs would go a long way

---

[12] Data from World Bank's "World development indicators" database: http://data. worldbank.org/data-catalog/world-development-indicators.

Table 11.2 *Manufacturing in China, Japan, and South Korea at similar levels of development*

| Country | Year | GDP per capita (constant US dollars) | | Manufacturing | | |
		2000	2005 (PPP)	Share of value added (percent)	Share of labor (percent)	Employment (millions)
China	2009	2,206	6,200	43	17.7	85
Japan	1960	5,493	6,976	35	20.0	9.7
South Korea	1982	3,709	6,123	25	14.6	2.3

Sources: Data from the World Bank's "World development indicators" database: http://data.worldbank.org/data-catalog/world-development-indicators; the International Labour Office's "LABORSTA" database of labor statistics: http://laborsta.ilo.org; and National Bureau of Statistics of China (2010).

toward creating opportunities for employment and sustained growth in Africa.[13]

The story is similar for low-income countries elsewhere. In other low-income economies in 2009, with a total population of 846 million and 13 percent of their GDP coming from manufacturing, manufacturing employment likely amounted to no more than 10 million. So China's industrial upgrading could provide a golden opportunity for dynamic manufacturing-led growth in these countries as well as in Africa. The dynamic growth of other middle-income growth poles, such as Brazil, India, and Indonesia, will provide the same opportunities as China's growth for industrialization in other low-income countries.

For developing countries everywhere, however, the ability to benefit from the opportunities provided by China and other middle-income countries depends on the timely formulation and implementation of credible economic development strategies consistent with their comparative advantage and the flying geese paradigm.

A roadmap for seizing the moment: the Growth Identification and Facilitation Framework

The coming transition of China and other middle-income growth pole economies from low-skilled manufacturing jobs provides an opportunity for poor countries, including those in sub-Saharan Africa (home to thirty-seven of the fifty-one low-income countries).[14] African countries

---

[13] The creation of manufacturing jobs, especially through foreign direct investment, generally leads to the creation of jobs in other sectors through backward and forward linkages (UNCTAD [United Nations Conference on Trade and Development] 2006) and through multiplier effects as additional employment raises income levels. Backward linkages tend to be weaker in developing countries, because it is often difficult to source local products. But forward linkages can have a substantial effect on employment. In Lesotho, computable general equilibrium model simulations indicate that the employment of 56,000 workers in the garment sector, sustained by foreign direct investment flows, could have led to the creation of 77,000 additional nonmanufacturing jobs (World Bank 2005b). In India, it is estimated that creating 2.5 million jobs in the information technology sector could lead to 8.3 million additional jobs (NASSCOM [National Association of Software and Services Companies] 2011).

[14] All economies with a GDP per capita below $1,280 in 2010 are in sub-Saharan Africa except Afghanistan, Bangladesh, Cambodia, Haiti, Kyrgyzstan, Laos, Nepal, Nicaragua, Pakistan, Solomon Islands, Tajikistan, Timor-Leste, Uzbekistan, and Vietnam.

need to seize the opportunity provided by the industrial upgrading of China and other leading dragons by initiating structural transformation. This is feasible if policymakers can tap into the potential advantages of being a latecomer and help their economy develop industries according to their country's comparative advantage.

The Growth Identification and Facilitation Framework, an implementation tool for the new structural economics, can help policymakers in developing countries identify industries with latent comparative advantage and facilitate competitive private sector development by following these steps.

- Identify the dynamically growing tradable goods and services that fast-growing, lower middle-income countries such as China have successfully produced over the past two decades. These are likely to be new industries consistent with the country's latent comparative advantage.
- Among the industries, identify those in which domestic private firms are already active and pinpoint obstacles that may be preventing them from upgrading the quality of their products or barriers that may be discouraging other firms from entering. Value chain analysis or the growth diagnostics method can help.[15] The government can then implement policies to ease the constraints, carrying out randomized controlled experiments to test the effectiveness of the policies in eliminating the constraints before scaling them up nationally.
- In industries on the list that are new to domestic firms, encourage investment by those firms in China or other higher-income countries that want to reduce their labor costs by relocating production to lower-income countries. The government could also set up incubation programs to encourage start-ups in these industries.
- Take advantage of unexpected opportunities arising from the country's unique endowments or from new technological breakthroughs around the world. The government should pay close attention to successful discoveries and engagement in new business niches by private domestic enterprises and provide support to scale up those industries.
- In a country with poor infrastructure and an unfriendly business environment, set up special economic zones or industrial parks to

---

[15] Hausmann, Rodrik, and Velasco (2005).

help firms and foreign investors scale entry barriers. These zones can create preferential business environments and infrastructure that most governments, constrained by budgets and implementation capacity, are unable to improve quickly economywide. Establishing industrial parks or zones can also facilitate the formation of industrial clusters.

- To compensate for the externalities created by first movers and encourage firms to form clusters, grant pioneer firms in the identified industries time-limited tax incentives, investment co-financing, or access to foreign exchange. Because the identified industries are consistent with the country's latent comparative advantage, the incentives should be limited in financial cost and duration. To prevent rent-seeking and political capture, governments should avoid incentives that create monopoly rents, high tariffs, or other distortions.

While the emphasis here has been on structural transformation and dynamic growth through industrialization, technological innovation and structural change within agriculture must not be overlooked. In low-income countries, in which most people depend on agriculture for their livelihood, improving agricultural productivity is important for reducing poverty and generating economic surpluses to support industrialization. Agricultural development also requires structural transformation in technology, a good product mix, and improved infrastructure. Governments should facilitate technological innovation and extension and improve the infrastructure for agricultural production and commercialization. Finally, resource-abundant developing countries, besides ensuring good management of the wealth generated from natural resources, should invest part of that wealth in infrastructure and human capital. This will facilitate the economy's diversification into nonresource sectors, creating jobs and promoting inclusive growth – and transforming resources from a curse to a blessing.

PART IV

Toward a Brave New World Monetary System

The global financial crisis of 2008–9 originated in the international monetary system. Part I argued that global imbalances arose from the wealth effect of the excess liquidity created by US financial deregulation and monetary policy. These imbalances could be as large as they were and last as long as they did because the US dollar was the major reserve currency. The United States creates reserves through its current account deficit and capital outflows.

The financial crisis highlighted major deficiencies in the international monetary system. Although the system weathered the initial shock, it remains fragile. Before World War II the global economy had been rocked by periodic payments crises. After the war industrial economies focused on reconstruction, and, with the memory of the prewar depression still fresh, policymakers created new institutions to oversee international transactions. Referred to as the Bretton Woods system, these new institutions were designed to promote growth and stability in international trade and finance. For nearly two decades the system relied on fixed exchange rates based on gold. Since the early 1970s, however, when the United States stopped trading gold at the fixed price of $35 an ounce, global economic governance has been characterized as one of "benign neglect."[1] Countries follow their own monetary and exchange rate regimes, and the US dollar has established itself as the predominant international reserve currency.

Looking forward, however, there is mounting evidence that the world is moving toward a more diversified set of reserve currencies. Either gradually, as the weight of the US economy in the world economy declines, or through a sudden debilitating shock, the dollar's role as a reserve currency will diminish. In this new international monetary system, currencies from several large economies will compete for use in international transactions and as international reserves.

---

[1] Rogoff (1983).

This situation suggests three key questions.

- How will the evolution toward a multiple reserve currency system affect global monetary and economic stability? Will such a system be more or less stable than the current system?
- Are there better alternatives, such as the creation of a new international currency, to be used alongside national currencies for international transactions and reserves?
- Which alternative would be more favorable to the global economy and to developed and developing countries alike? A new international currency will be acceptable only if it is a win-win for both.

The international monetary system has been a major source of financial instability, and it is in need of reform. A reformed international monetary system should allow countries to run temporary surpluses and deficits on current account and accumulate net claims, a (rather mechanical) task accomplished by the current system. But it should also incorporate incentives to encourage countries to return to a balanced position. The failure to do this is the biggest deficiency of the current system.[2]

Some economists argue that the current international monetary system, while not perfect, showed resilience during the recent financial crisis and that the US dollar, by continuing to serve the global economy as a safe haven asset, has contributed to the stability of the global economic and financial system.[3] I take a far less sanguine view. The current system is responsible for highly volatile capital flows and exchange rates, large and persistent payments imbalances and exchange rate misalignments, and inadequate global adjustment mechanisms. It lacks a global oversight framework for cross-border capital flows and exerts little discipline on the macroeconomic policies of reserve currency countries. And it precipitated the Great Recession of 2008–9.

Would an international monetary system with multiple reserve currencies be more stable than the current system? Several economists believe that competition among major reserve currencies can be a disciplining mechanism to resolve the incentive incompatibility between domestic and global interests under the current system. If a reserve

---

[2] Major deficiencies of the current international monetary system are documented by IMF (2011c), Dorrucci and McKay (2011), and Angeloni *et al.* (2011).

[3] Dadush and Eidelman (2011).

currency country follows a monetary policy that caters only to domestic interests and that is irresponsible from a global perspective, reserve holders could switch to other reserve currencies, and the offending country's currency would lose the privilege of being a reserve currency.

This argument might be valid if all major reserve currency countries had strong and healthy economies. But it is more likely that each country has some intractable structural weaknesses. When a reserve currency country's structural weakness is exposed, it can trigger a large exodus of short-term funds to other reserve currencies, causing a sharp appreciation of one or all other reserve currencies, as recently happened to the Swiss franc and Japanese yen. Such appreciations weaken the real economy and exacerbate its structural weaknesses. The short-term funds may then move out of the next reserve currency with the most apparent structural weakness. As a result, a multiple reserve currency system may be less stable than the current one, to the detriment of reserve currency countries and nonreserve currency countries alike.

Stability could be achieved and the conflicts between national interests and global interests inherent in using national currencies as reserves could be resolved, however, if all countries agreed to adopt a single supranational reserve currency. Chapter 17 makes a bold proposal for creating a new global reserve currency, called paper gold ("p-gold"), to replace the current "nonsystem" of reserve currencies. P-gold would be issued by an international monetary authority according to Friedman's k percent rule.[4] Each central bank would hold p-gold as reserves and issue its domestic currency according to a fixed exchange rate. P-gold would also be used in international trade and capital flow transactions (as the US dollar is now). The international monetary authority could use the increase in p-gold each year – the global seigniorage – to finance its operating costs, and international development institutions could use it to finance global public goods. This system would avoid the fatal limitations of a gold standard (which cannot expand to meet the needs of a growing global economy) and of the use of national currencies as reserves (the inherent conflict between national and global interests). The p-gold system would have a disciplinary effect on national monetary authorities while avoiding the dilemma that Greece faces today – an inability to devalue the national currency.

---

[4] Friedman (1960).

The time is right for reforming the international monetary system. Past transitions have been marked by instability, and the ongoing transition from the system dominated by the US dollar to a multiple reserve currency system will probably be even more unstable. More technical work on the details and gradual policy experiments (such as greater use of Special Drawing Rights and inclusion of the currencies of the large and rapidly growing emerging economies) could help the system evolve and avoid serious financial crises. In the future, no major reserve currency is likely to be dominant. Rather, the US dollar, the euro, the yen, and eventually the yuan are expected to constitute a new multiple reserve currency system. Each currency will be associated with a substantial share of world output, trade, and financial flows and will serve as a monetary anchor for other currencies. Instability will then arise from speculative movements of capital from one reserve currency to another – induced partly by the inherent structural weakness in reserve currency countries and partly by excessive capital flows due to policy changes. Speculative movements, resulting in volatility in exchange rates and capital flows that hurts economic activity, have been occurring since the 2008–9 global crisis, especially following the Eurozone debt crisis.

Chapter 12 surveys the history of the international monetary system and the real economy and considers their likely future evolution. Chapters 13 and 14 explore challenges to the current system and the shortcomings of the emerging multiple reserve currency system. Chapters 15 and 16 review the thinking behind the main proposals for reform, as well as their benefits and drawbacks, and Chapter 17 lays out a notional design for a monetary system based on the new international currency I have outlined, offering suggestions for further research on the three key questions identified above. Chapter 18 concludes with a call for seizing the opportunity to reform the international monetary system.

12 | *The evolution of the international monetary system*

The international monetary system comprises the mechanisms and institutions that organize and regulate foreign exchange systems and cross-border monetary and financial exchanges and flows. An international currency serves as a store of value (allowing transactions to take place over time and across the world), a medium of exchange (substantially increasing efficiency over barter), and a unit of account (facilitating calculations of valuation and conversion).[1] As a store of value, an international currency facilitates official transactions and use as a reserve currency, while the other two functions underpin the use of the international currency in both domestic and international transactions. The distinction between "reserve" and "international" currencies has grown more important with the rapid expansion in the size and role of private flows in the world economy.

In antiquity, much of the trade between countries and regions was conducted as barter. As the volume and diversity of trade grew, however, people needed a convenient common commodity to settle transactions. Metals were an obvious choice, for their durability, innate value as a material for making things, and ability to be fashioned into easily portable coins. Archaeologists have documented the wide use of metal coins around the world during antiquity;[2] eventually, silver and gold became the bimetal choice.

Bimetallism prevailed during the Industrial Revolution and for several decades afterwards. While much debated, in general the bimetallic system was fairly stable over 1850–73,[3] despite the huge increase in the gold supply following the California Gold Rush of the 1850s.

---

[1] Kenen (1983).   [2] Williams (1997) provides a graphic history.
[3] See, for example, Fisher (1894), Friedman (1990), and Flandreau (2002), who argue that there is no inherent superiority of a single specie system over a bimetallic system. Diebolt and Parent (2008) provide evidence that policy coordination

Eventually, political and economic factors following the end of the Franco-Prussian War led to the demise of bimetallism in continental Europe.[4] Decades earlier, the United Kingdom had moved to the gold standard, discussed in more detail below.

The United States had no formal central bank during the bimetal period. States allowed banks to issue notes backed by state bonds during the "free banking" era from 1837 to 1863. During the American Civil War the US government created the inconvertible "greenback." In the "crime of 1873,"[5] the government returned to minting specie (paper notes), dropping the silver dollar and focusing solely on gold. Immediately thereafter the United States switched to a gold standard. The market price of gold rose sharply (including in terms of silver), leading to a strong deflationary trend over the following two decades.

The gold standard (1819–1914)

The United Kingdom established the gold standard in 1819. Other countries in continental Europe, as well as Japan and the United States, adopted it as the basis for their currency in the following decades. By 1880 most countries were on some form of the gold standard. China and India, which maintained a silver standard, were important exceptions.[6] Under the gold standard, a central bank's primary responsibility was to preserve the official parity between its currency and gold. To do that, the central bank had to own an adequate stock of gold. Any surplus or deficit in the balance of payments had to be financed through shipments of gold between central banks – from deficit countries to surplus countries.

---

between French and British central banks also may have helped stabilize bimetallism for decades before its collapse.

[4] Flandreau ([1995] 2004).

[5] The US Coinage Act of 1873 eliminated the free coinage of silver and cast the die for the gold standard (Friedman 1990). See Velde (2002) for a history of the move toward the gold standard. See Rolnick and Weber (1983, 1988) for a discussion of the "free banking" era.

[6] The impact of the changing relative price of gold and silver was particularly strong on silver-based economies. For a discussion of China's experience during the interwar period, when it abandoned the silver standard, see Kreps (1934) and Leavens (1936).

In many ways the period of the classical gold standard was remarkable in world history. Trade flourished. Empirical studies have estimated that the gold standard contributed positively (around 20 percent) to the growth of world trade from 1880 to 1910.[7] Exchange rates and prices were generally stable, and labor and capital moved freely across political boundaries. For the most part, the world was at peace. Nevertheless, the world economy suffered a major depression during the 1890s and a severe contraction in 1907, as well as a number of smaller recessions, largely as a result of the priority given to external balance over other goals, such as internal balance and full employment.

The interwar period (1914–39)

The gold standard broke down during World War I (1914–18) and then was briefly reinstated from 1925 to 1931 as the gold exchange standard.[8] To avoid the gold shortages that had plagued the system previously, the United States and the United Kingdom could hold only gold reserves under this system, but other countries could hold both gold and dollars or pounds sterling as reserves. The Great Depression hit in 1929 and was quickly followed by massive bank failures the world over. The United Kingdom was forced off the gold standard in 1931, when foreign holders of pounds sterling began converting their pounds into gold. As the depression continued, one country after another left the gold standard, allowing their currencies to float.

In the United States, a dramatic 33 percent reduction in the money supply between 1929 and 1933[9] helped transmute the financial shock into a full-blown depression. Scholars differ in explaining the monetary contraction, but there are two general views. One holds that the contraction was the result of the international monetary

---

[7] López-Córdova and Meissner (2003).
[8] According to Eichengreen and Temin (2010), the United States remained on the (fractional) gold standard during the war.
[9] The size of the decline is from Friedman and Schwartz (1971), as cited by Hsieh and Romer (2006).

system's adherence to the gold standard. The other holds that the contraction was caused by a monumental policy blunder: the failure of the United States to implement expansionary monetary policies.[10]

Under the gold standard, expansionary monetary policy, with its low interest rates, had the potential to spur a speculative attack on the currency and to force an adjustment in gold parity – or even a full-blown abandonment of gold convertibility. A study using data on forward exchange rates and cross-country interest differentials found that there had been no expectation of a devaluation in the United States, and thus concluded that monetary policy could have been more expansionary early in the downturn.[11]

The gold standard may have been more important in spreading the crisis internationally. During the 1930s most countries attempted to maintain the gold standard.[12] Based on the adjustment mechanism defined by a strict gold standard, countries initially tried to support the gold standard in the face of a decline in global trade by deflating their currency through contractionary monetary and fiscal policies. This classical adjustment mechanism did not work as quickly and painlessly as theorized.[13] In addition, countries used trade protection or controls on capital flows as stop-gap measures to preserve gold reserves – exacerbating the global depression.

---

[10] Hsieh and Romer (2006). The first view could be called the "golden fetters" view, as laid out by Eichengreen (1992a) and by Eichengreen and Temin (2010), while the policy blunder view was developed by Friedman and Schwartz, as cited by Hsieh and Romer (2006). The authors do not maintain that it was impossible to conduct expansionary monetary policy; they argue instead, however, that the "gold-standard *mentalité*" prevented policymakers from even considering this option.

[11] Hsieh and Romer (2006). Others have also found that monetary policy could have been more expansionary (Bordo and MacDonald 2003; Bordo, Choudhri, and Schwartz 2002). Almunia *et al.* (2010) find that growth was superior in countries that applied some form of stimulus.

[12] Eichengreen and Irwin (2009).

[13] Eichengreen and Sachs (1985) make the case that devaluations by groups of countries could have ended the Great Depression sooner, even if individual country depreciations had negative effects on other countries. Bernanke and Carey (1996) find evidence of substantial nominal wage rigidities during the Great Depression – a key limitation to a smooth classical price adjustment mechanism under a gold standard.

The Bretton Woods system (1946–73)

In 1944 representatives of the Allied nations, meeting in Bretton Woods, New Hampshire, agreed to create a new monetary system, and established two new international institutions: the International Monetary Fund and the World Bank. The new system, designed to avoid the destructive economic policies that had led to the Great Depression, set exchange rates against the US dollar, which in turn had a fixed price relative to gold of $35 an ounce. Member countries could hold most of their official reserves as gold or dollar-denominated assets and had the right to sell their dollars to the US Federal Reserve in exchange for gold at the official price. The IMF would provide support in cases of temporary balance of payments problems.

Fixed exchange rates, along with the dollar's fixed and convertible parity with gold, were viewed as a way to discipline monetary policy. Although each country's exchange rate was fixed to the dollar, the rate could be devalued or revalued provided that the IMF agreed that the country's balance of payments was in "fundamental disequilibrium." The IMF's articles of agreement called for "convertibility" only on current account transactions, not on capital accounts. Based on experience during the interwar period, policymakers viewed private capital movements as a key factor behind economic instability, and they feared that speculative movements of "hot money" would undermine free trade and the new fixed exchange system.[14]

While that was the system ultimately agreed on, more comprehensive proposals had also been made during the Bretton Woods conference. Representing the United Kingdom, John Maynard Keynes proposed an International Clearing Union, which would issue an international currency that he called the "bancor." The bancor would be tied to a basket of commodities, accepted as equivalent to the basket of commodities by the United States and the United Kingdom, and exchangeable with participating national currencies at fixed rates. The International Clearing Union would provide for extensive balance of payments financing, subject to strict conditionality, and substantial exchange

---

[14] Par exchange rate values could be changed by 10 percent or less to correct a "fundamental disequilibrium" without IMF approval. Larger changes required prior approval. Moreover, the articles of agreement allowed countries to control the movements of capital across borders. Both provisions were contrary to the US proposal (Krugman and Obstfeld 2002).

rate movement.[15] The proposal was eventually dropped in the face of US opposition. (See Box 12.1 for a discussion of the "exorbitant privilege" of the US dollar as reserve currency.) The decision on the final system was more political than economic:[16] countries, especially the United States, were not willing to sacrifice national policymaking autonomy.

The United States, as issuer of the reserve currency, was to keep the value of the dollar fixed at its gold parity and to guarantee the exchange of dollar reserves held by foreign central banks into gold at the agreed parity. In theory, this requirement imposed constraints on US monetary policy. By the middle of the 1960s, however, US macroeconomic policy turned expansionary because of the fiscal requirements of the Vietnam War and increased social spending under President Lyndon Johnson's "Great Society" agenda. As a result, there was a speculative attack on the monetary gold stock in 1968, and, after three volatile years, the Bretton Woods system collapsed.[17]

Box 12.1 The "exorbitant privilege" of the US dollar as a reserve currency

At the time of the Bretton Woods conference, proposals for a more radical international system were dismissed in favor of the US dollar as the reserve currency, for two main reasons: the position of the United States as the dominant economy, with more than 50 percent of global GDP; and its strong economic growth and fiscal position, which generated confidence in the US dollar.

Thus the United States assumed the "exorbitant privilege" of being the dominant reserve currency – an exorbitant privilege because, akin to seigniorage, the dominant reserve currency country does not have to earn foreign exchange to pay for its imports or other obligations. A certain amount of goods or services or assets could be

---

[15] Eichengreen (2010a).
[16] Boughton (2002). In 2009 the UN Commission on Financial Reforms led by Joseph Stiglitz proposed a system based on a greatly expanded Special Drawing Right, which is similar to the "bancor" system. See United Nations (2009).
[17] Bordo (1993) details the history of the Bretton Woods era and its collapse. Eichengreen (1992b) suggests that it was the interaction of US domestic policies and an inherent flaw – the Triffin dilemma – in the system that caused the demise; less expansionary policies might have delayed the collapse but not prevented it.

acquired simply by exchanging currency that foreigners wished to hold as a reserve asset. In the modern world, since reserves are held mainly in the reserve currency country's government bonds, exorbitant privilege includes the ability to borrow from abroad more cheaply than the reserve currency country lends. In addition, depreciation of the reserve currency improves the net foreign asset position of the reserve currency country, which creates space for depreciating (similar to inflating) the country's way out of global debt.

One estimate of the benefits and costs of the reserve currency status of the United States is $10 billion in annual benefits from pure seigniorage, $90 billion in lower borrowing costs, and –$30 to –$60 billion from exchange rate appreciation, for a net annual benefit of $40 to $70 billion (0.3 to 0.5 percent of GDP).[18] A World Bank estimate is similar: $15 billion a year in seigniorage since the early 1990s and $80 billion annual savings from lower interest costs.[19] Estimates of the reduction in interest rates range from fifty to ninety basis points.[20] These estimates thus put the annual benefits to the United States – during normal times – of the dollar's dominance as a reserve currency at $40 to $150 billion. During a regional or global crisis, these net annual benefits could be even larger, since dollar-denominated assets often act as a "safe haven" for foreign funds. Using the excess returns on net foreign assets approach yields an excess return of 330 basis points; applied as "savings" on the current US negative net foreign asset position of $2.5 trillion (2010), this yields annual savings of $82 billion.[21]

Since Bretton Woods (1973–present)

The adjustable peg system collapsed of its own internal contradictions. One of these was the so-called Triffin dilemma, which contended that the relative value of the dollar would necessarily erode because the United States, as the final provider of liquidity and reserve assets to a growing world economy, would need to increase the supply of dollars

---

[18] Dobbs *et al.* (2009).   [19] World Bank (2011a).
[20] Cited by Eichengreen (2011a); Dobbs *et al.* (2009); Warnock and Warnock (2006).
[21] Habib (2010), Hausmann and Sturzenegger (2006), Gourinchas and Rey (2005), and Lane and Milessi-Ferretti (2007, 2008) also provide estimates.

beyond what it could back by barely growing gold reserves.[22] Other explanations included differences between US and foreign monetary and fiscal policies, the failure of deficit countries to devalue, the failure of surplus countries to revalue, and a long-term decline in the international competitiveness of the US economy.[23] The proximate cause of the collapse, however, was the expansionary US macroeconomic policies. In February 1973 the Bretton Woods currency exchange markets closed, and by March 1976 all major currencies were floating.

During the attempts to save the Bretton Woods system, alternative reserve assets were proposed for replacing the US dollar. The Special Drawing Right (SDR) was created under the auspices of the IMF. To hold the dollar's peg against gold, the SDR was set at one to the dollar. After more than three decades the SDR still functions only as a unit of account. When members of the IMF "purchase" SDRs (borrow from the IMF), they receive disbursements in dollars or euros or yen, according to the borrower's preference. Another proposal called for creating "substitution accounts" at the IMF so that countries that wanted to convert their dollar reserves could replace them with SDRs.[24] A sticking point was the exchange rate risk to the IMF's balance sheet. If the dollar subsequently depreciated against the SDR, the IMF and its shareholders would suffer losses. In the early 1970s there were suggestions that the US government could guarantee or cover those losses, but no agreement was reached, and the substitution account proposal was never implemented.

One of the main flaws in the nonsystem that evolved in the post-Bretton-Woods period eventually led to the 2008–9 global crisis: the potential conflict of interest between US macroeconomic policy for domestic objectives and the dollar's role as a global reserve currency, as discussed in Chapter 3. Inevitably, national economic concerns guided US fiscal and monetary policies, at times in ways that were detrimental to global stability.[25]

As Chapter 11 discussed, developing countries have been growing more rapidly than high-income countries in the twenty-first century. High-income countries have experienced persistent economic difficulties that have diminished their chances for growth. Prospects may not recover even over the medium term if countries are unable to put their

---

[22] Triffin (1960).   [23] Eichengreen (1992b).   [24] IMF (2011a).
[25] IMF (2011f).

(a) **United States and China**

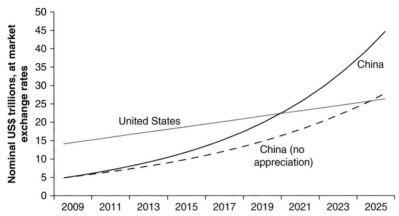

(b) **Japan, United Kingdom, and India**

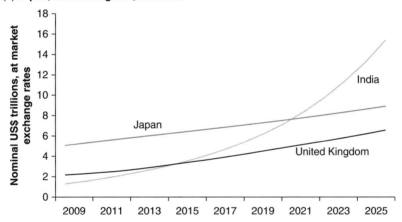

Figure 12.1 The global economy in 2025: major middle-income countries and reserve currency countries

Notes: Real GDP growth is based on forecasts from the baseline scenario of the World Bank (2011a). Inflation is assumed to remain constant at 0 percent for Japan, 2 percent for the United States, 4 percent for China and the United Kingdom, and 7 percent for India. Currency appreciation relative to the US dollar is assumed to be 2 percent for Japan and constant at 0 percent for China (no appreciation case) or 3 percent for China (appreciation case).

Source: World Bank (2011a); used with permission.

(a) **Percentage of world exports**

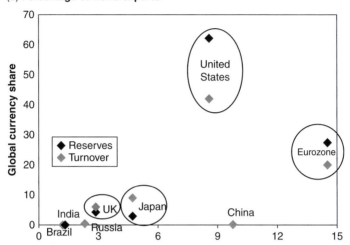

(b) **Percentage of world GDP**

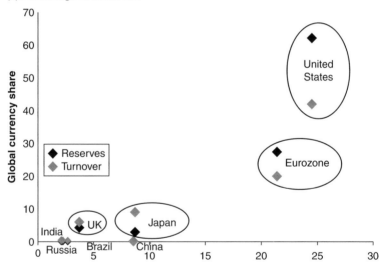

Figure 12.2 Currency composition of international reserves and economic indicators, 2009
Note: Currency turnover is for 2010.
Source: World Bank (2011a); used with permission.

large excess capacity in housing, construction, and some manufacturing sectors back into production and if structural reforms are not implemented in financial and labor markets in high-income countries, particularly in Europe.

With the high probability of slower economic demand growth than in the past in high-income countries, two processes are key to ensuring continuation of the "great convergence"[26] of developing economies with advanced economies of the past decade: developing countries sustaining their high growth rates by continuing their industrial upgrading and structural transformation; and developing countries broadening their interconnectedness by increasing the flows of goods, services, investments, and knowledge between themselves.

What does this mean for the international monetary system? High-income countries, particularly the reserve currency countries, are likely to see their share of world GDP continue to decline. In an optimistic case, this will result more from continuing strong growth in developing countries than from slow or stagnant growth in high-income countries. For Japan, the United Kingdom, and some Eurozone countries, zero or negative population growth, combined with an aging population, is one contributor. In the United States, fiscal retrenchment over the medium and longer terms may inhibit growth. The most likely scenario in coming decades is thus a shifting pattern of economic power, with China overtaking the United States in nominal GDP and India surpassing first the United Kingdom and then Japan by 2022 (Figure 12.1).[27]

The implication for the international monetary system is even greater misalignment in the currency composition of international reserves relative to countries' shares of the global economy (Figure 12.2). Unless a new reserve currency or an international substitute arises, the scenarios laid out above for economic growth imply that the misalignment, as well as volatility in asset prices and capital flows, will continue to grow over time.

---

[26] Martin Wolf (2011) coined this phrase. Nobel laureate Michael Spence (2011) has called it the "next convergence."
[27] World Bank (2011a).

13 | *Emerging pressures and policy challenges*

The first dozen or so years following the demise of the Bretton Woods system were tumultuous for the international monetary system. Two oil price shocks complicated national monetary policy, and inflation reached double digits in the United States and other major economies. From the middle of the 1980s, however, prices stabilized, as central banks in the major economies adopted inflation targeting, and GDP growth became less volatile – at least until 2007 – especially in reserve currency countries (referred to as "the Great Moderation").[1]

That said, the United States experienced a series of asset price bubbles, and the high-income countries are still staggering from the effects of the 2008–9 financial crisis. Although several leading economies experienced less growth volatility (as measured by the standard deviation of GDP growth) before the crisis, some newly industrialized countries suffered from high volatility (such as South Korea). Even some of the top-performing emerging economies were hurt by the crisis.

Part I argued that the crisis arose because of US financial deregulation combined with lax monetary policy facilitated by the dollar's role as an international reserve currency.[2] Is there an alternative to the dollar-dominant system?

Is there an alternative to the dominance of the US dollar?

On January 1, 1999, the eleven founding members of the European Monetary Union effectively surrendered their monetary policy to the newly established European Central Bank. From then on, only the new

---

[1] Stock and Watson (2003). The concept is not without controversy; see, for example, Smith and Summers (2009).

[2] Caballero (2006) and Eichengreen (2011a) have also noted a role in the crisis for the international monetary system and the dollar's prominence.

central bank could create money. Since then the euro has emerged as the most serious rival to the US dollar as an international currency. As of 2009 the euro accounted for 27 percent of global reserves and 20 percent of cross-border loans, and served as the currency anchor for twelve countries. More than 31 percent of international debt was denominated in the euro.[3] Divergent fiscal policies and emerging sovereign debt problems in some Eurozone countries have undermined the system once again, however.

Despite the euro's gains, the US dollar is still the dominant international currency. Consider these quantitative dimensions of reserve currency holdings. In 1965 nearly 60 percent of world reserves were denominated in US dollars. This share rose to 71 percent in 2000, and then, as the euro's share rose, the dollar's share fell back to 60 percent (Table 13.1). As of 2009 the dollar was used in more than 85 percent of foreign exchange transactions, most commodities were still priced in dollars, and nearly 75 percent of world trade transactions were denominated in dollars. The currencies of more than half the countries in the world were still linked to the US dollar in 2008 through dollarization, currency boards, pegging, and managed floating with the dollar as reference currency. By 2009 the dollar's share in international debt securities was about 50 percent, and its share in all outstanding public and private debt securities was nearly 40 percent.[4] The dollar's widespread use in pricing commodities such as oil and gold and in international trade transactions also contributed to its leading international role.

The US economy is likely to remain the world's largest economy for at least another five to ten years, but growing instability in the multipolar monetary system would be a strong motivation for reform. Recent developments in the United States, including Standard & Poor's August 2011 downgrade of US long-term sovereign debt (from AAA to AA+), presage such growing instability.

The continuing transition to a genuine multiple reserve currency system could be gradual, as has been the case since the euro began to challenge the dollar's dominance. To a large extent, the speed and nature of the transition will depend on the size, structure, and speed of change in the global economy. The historical precedent exists for the rise and fall of reserve currencies. Between 1931 and 1945 the dollar

[3] Dorrucci and McKay (2011).   [4] Goldberg (2010).

Table 13.1 *Currency distribution of foreign exchange market turnover, international bond issues, and cross-border lending (percentage share)*

Currency distribution	Currency	1980 Bretton Woods II	1992 After Plaza Accord	2002 Eurozone	2008–2010 Financial crisis
Global foreign exchange market turnover	US dollar		82	90	85
	Pound sterling		14	13	13
	Deutschemark		40		
	Euro			38	39
	Other		65	59	63
International bond issues (since 1993)	US dollar		40	52	37
	Pound sterling		7	7	8
	Euro		25	32	47
	Other		27	9	9
Cross-border lending	US dollar	64	52	50	40
	Pound sterling	3	4	6	7
	Euro	23	23	31	41
	Other	10	21	13	12

Notes: The European currency unit was used as the internal accounting unit for bond issues and lending in the European Community from 1979 to 1999, when it was replaced by the euro. For global foreign exchange market turnover, because two currencies are involved in each transaction, the sum of the percentage shares of individual currencies totals 200 percent instead of 100 percent.
Source: BIS (2010, 2011b).

overtook the pound sterling as the dominant reserve currency; the pound's final decline was precipitous, however, once it had reached a tipping point.[5] Policy coordination among the key actors will be essential for an orderly process of change. The current situation in some ways resembles that at the end of the Bretton Woods system I, just before its collapse.

Persistent payments imbalances and volatile capital flows

Following the widespread debt defaults caused by the Great Depression, international capital markets virtually disappeared, and in the interwar period capital movements consisted primarily of hot money. When the Bretton Woods institutions were being designed in 1944, negotiators assumed that the disappearance of private capital flows was permanent. In reality, foreign direct investment revived rapidly in the 1950s, and financial capital markets reemerged, soon swamping official assistance and lending. Financial flows consisted mainly of floating-interest bank loans rather than the fixed-interest bond finance prevalent before World War I.[6] In the following thirty years bank lending grew dramatically, some of it in the form of recycling petro-dollars following the oil price shocks of the 1970s.

International financial integration accelerated after the Asian financial crisis of 1997–8. Gross cross-border flows rose from 5 percent of world GDP in the middle of the 1990s to around 20 percent in 2007, and international financial openness (external assets plus liabilities) rose sharply from 150 percent of world GDP to 350 percent.[7]

Gross cross-border flows dwarfed net flows. For example, US cumulative current account deficits from 2002 to 2007 totaled $4.8 trillion; gross outflows were even larger, at more than $5.8 trillion (excluding outflows related to financial derivatives). But these outflows were financed by some $10 trillion in gross inflows. Financial innovation and development in both advanced and emerging economies accelerated global financial integration, along with financial institutions' rising share in cross-border ownership and their rising funding of international capital markets. As a result, the value of banks' external assets

---

[5] Eichengreen and Flandreau (2008) date the dollar's dominance as a reserve currency to the middle of the 1920s.
[6] Williamson (1987); Obstfeld and Taylor (2004).   [7] Padoan (2011).

and liabilities doubled as a share of GDP, from around 30 percent in the early 1990s to about 60 percent in 2007.[8] The rapid growth of world trade through increased trade credits and export insurance also contributed to global financial integration. International capital flows rose even more rapidly until the financial crisis of 2008–9, at about three times the rate of international trade, as a result of financial liberalization and innovation. During this rapid globalization, emerging markets increased their share in international capital markets from 7 percent in 2000 to 17 percent in 2007.

The 2008–9 crisis was preceded by massive increases in global capital flows. After fluctuating between 2 and 6 percent of world GDP during the 1980s and the first half of the 1990s, these flows rose to almost 15 percent of world GDP before the crisis. By 2007 global capital flows totaled nearly $8 trillion, more than three times their aggregate in 1995. By comparison, major global payment imbalances have been much smaller, at around 0.5 to 1 percent of world GDP.[9]

The global economic crisis, which began with the collapse of mortgage lending in the United States in 2007, quickly spread around the world. And, for the first time since the Great Depression, major international banking systems began to deleverage their external positions sharply in response to pressures on their funding and capital. As a result, gross cross-border flows plummeted from 20 percent of world GDP in 2007 to less than 1 percent in the second half of 2008.[10]

Since the crisis, advanced economies as a group have been running a smaller current account deficit (about $90 billion, or 0.2 percent of their combined GDP in 2010). Current account deficits in advanced countries and current account surpluses in developing countries mask massive differences across regions, however.

In 2010 Asian countries accounted for nearly 73 percent of the overall current account surplus in developing countries ($313 billion). Most other developing countries (except oil exporters) had deficits, which were financed by capital inflows and reserve drawdowns. International reserves held by emerging and developing economies rose to 66 percent of the $8.1 trillion global reserve stock at the end of 2010.[11] China alone accounted for almost half the massive stock of reserves held by emerging and developing economies. The changes in reserve holdings were far

---

[8] BIS (2010).   [9] OECD (2011a: table 1.3).
[10] Speller, Thwaites, and Wright (2011).   [11] World Bank (2011a).

smaller than the volume of capital flows, however. For example, in 2007, when total holdings of foreign reserves rose to $1.5 trillion, capital flows reached $8 trillion, mainly held by or originating from advanced economies and thus driven largely by their macroeconomic policies.

Among advanced economies, the United States continued to accumulate a large current account deficit, which, at $470 billion in 2010, amounted to 3.2 percent of its GDP. The expansionary fiscal and monetary policies of the United States both accounted for much of the deficit and helped start and sustain the global economic recovery. The Eurozone, Japan, and the other advanced economies all had large surpluses on their current account, amounting to some $380 billion in 2010.

These large current account deficits and surpluses have been matched by massive net capital flows across borders, supported by even bigger gross flows induced largely by the loose monetary policies in the reserve currency countries. According to the Bank for International Settlements, global capital markets reached $95 trillion in 2010, or 1.5 times world GDP. These large, persistent deficits and surpluses carry substantial risks of a disorderly adjustment, which could cause sizable movements in exchange rates, capital, and goods and services through their impacts on prices. In addition, massive trade imbalances can lead to protectionist policies in deficit countries. About 60 percent of 268 episodes of large foreign capital inflows ended in "sudden stops," and about one in ten episodes ended in a banking or currency crisis.[12] This experience is evidence of the major weaknesses in the current international monetary system, and the problems could be exacerbated in a multiple reserve currency system. And that is where the current system seems to be heading, particularly if the reserve currency countries fail to coordinate their macroeconomic policies closely.

The persistence of large balance of payments imbalances and the sharp increase in international transactions brought about by globalization and an expanding global economy have exposed the limitations of the current international monetary system and national policies designed for a far less financially integrated world. A well-designed international monetary system would allow countries to run temporary surpluses and deficits on current account and accumulate net claims, as the current system does. Unlike the current system, though, it would also encourage countries to return to a balanced position.

---

[12] Padoan (2011).

14 | *(In)stability of the emerging multiple reserve currency system*

Events in the global economy during 2008 to 2011 imply that a move to a multiple reserve currency system is inevitable. Without strong policy coordination and macroeconomic policy discipline among the reserve currency countries, however, this new system could prove unstable, to the detriment of economic activity and employment across the globe.

Moving forward, the international monetary system and the global economy face three possible outcomes.

- One is the continuation of the current nonsystem, with a future punctuated by occasional regional and global financial crises, as has been the case since the 1970s, and with the distinct possibility that the system will collapse.
- A more likely scenario is that the current international monetary system, centered on the US dollar, will evolve into a multiple reserve currency system supported by three major currencies – the US dollar, the euro, and the yuan – along with smaller currencies, such as the yen, sterling, and the Swiss franc, with the currencies of other large emerging economies (such as Brazil and India) possibly joining later.
- Alternatively, there could be a collective decision by major global economies to reform the international monetary system and move toward a new supranational currency along the lines of Keynes's bancor (see Chapter 15).

Moving toward a multipolar growth system

The world economy is moving toward a multipolar growth system, which has implications for the medium-term stability of the international monetary system. High-income economies, such as the United States, the Eurozone, and Japan, which are projected to grow more slowly than their trend growth and than the average for emerging economies, will likely see their share of global GDP continue to decline. At the end of 2011 growth in the advanced economies as a group was slowing, with parts of the Eurozone having entered another recession after an anemic recovery from the 2008–9 crisis. Worries about sovereign debt sustainability are now widespread, and long-term unemployment is a troubling concern in many countries. The strong headwinds of deleveraging in the financial and public sectors are further slowing economic growth.

Over the medium term, high debt levels and structural rigidities in the Eurozone and the United States are likely to hold growth and productivity gains below trend rates and keep unemployment rates from falling. These economies are likely to continue their loose monetary and fiscal policies for domestic reasons, causing further volatility in capital flows and exchange rates over the next few years. As a result, advanced economies as a group are expected to grow just 1.5 to 2 percent annually over the next few years – substantially below their average trend growth of 2.5 percent.[1] The emerging economies and other developing countries are projected to grow much more rapidly, at 5.5 to 6 percent a year.[2] This growth differential is likely to accelerate the economic rise of the emerging economies, solidifying the multipolar growth structure of the global economy.

All the key global players, including the reserve currency countries, pursue fiscal and monetary policies targeted primarily at the domestic economy, to the neglect of cross-border issues. And, not surprisingly, global imbalances are on the rise again, including large and volatile capital flows, exchange rate misalignments, and mounting reliance on cross-border liquidity. The likely outcome is extreme cycles and serious disruptions in the cross-border flow of funds.[3]

In light of the economic challenges, the preoccupation of policymakers in the major economies with weakening economic conditions, and the possibility of yet another global crisis, crucial questions arise. Is a multiple reserve currency system likely to emerge, and would such a system be less stable than the current one? The short answer to both questions is a conditional "Yes."

---

[1] Recent projections from both the IMF (2012b) and the World Bank (2012).
[2] World Bank (2012).   [3] IMF (2011f).

Prospects for the US dollar, euro, and yuan

Although the current international monetary system remains dollar-dominated, the US share of the global economy has been shrinking, from nearly 40 percent in the 1960s to about 20 percent in 2010. The United States is now in third place, behind China and Germany, in manufactured exports. And, in August 2011, Standard & Poor's downgraded the credit rating of US long-term sovereign debt, because of the perceived lack of a credible plan for fiscal consolidation to stabilize the government's medium-term debt dynamics. The projected slower pace of US economic growth over the medium term will only make conditions worse.[4]

Nevertheless, the dollar still dominates foreign exchange reserves and transactions, and the US economy remains the world's largest. Unless the United States commits a serious policy blunder that undermines its economic prospects and credit rating, the dollar can be expected to remain a key reserve currency for at least another decade. This is likely despite the continuing erosion of the US share of the global economy and of its capacity to provide needed liquidity for a growing global economy or to implement countercyclical policies at a global level.

The euro faces far more serious economic and political challenges, even though it has many of the attributes required of an international currency and its use as a reserve currency in both the private and official sectors has grown. As of 2009, only a decade after its creation, the euro accounted for almost 28 percent of official reserve holdings, close to 40 percent of global foreign exchange transactions, 47 percent of global bond issuance, and 40 percent of cross-border lending. Nearly fifty-five countries' national currencies are linked to the euro.

Despite this solid progress in establishing the euro as a true rival to the dollar as a reserve currency, countries in the Eurozone are beset by sovereign debt problems, a dysfunctional fiscal system, structural rigidities, and an aging population (see Chapter 5). Most forecasts point to a fairly long period of slow growth for the region and a massive rise in associated fiscal costs over the longer term. Although these problems are soluble, they are difficult politically and will take time. Obstacles include the amplified volatility of financial flows and asset prices and growing divergence in national economic situations, including market

---

[4] IMF (2012b); World Bank (2012); OECD (2011a).

forces that are setting the stronger European economies apart from the weaker ones. While the challenges are likely to be surmounted, and the euro is expected to remain an important international currency, it is unlikely to increase its share in global markets markedly for some time.

Prospects for the yuan as a reserve currency are mixed. Short- and medium-term prospects for the Chinese economy remain favorable, despite some slowdown in growth because of the sluggish European and US economies. In 2010 China overtook Japan as the second largest economy and overtook Germany as the largest exporter. China has the largest foreign exchange reserves in the world and is a leading investor in developed and developing countries alike. Nevertheless, the internationalization of the yuan is severely constrained by China's underdeveloped financial sector. In particular, the Chinese bond market is tiny – just 2 to 3 percent of Japan's and probably less than 1 percent of US and Eurozone bond markets.

If China decides that it wants the yuan to become an international currency, it will need to liberalize its economy gradually over the next few years, by making the yuan fully convertible, further developing the local government bond market, and opening its capital account.[5] An open capital account is a key requirement for any currency to become a reserve currency, but financial sector strengthening needs to come first.[6] To be acceptable to other countries as a currency for settling payments in international trade and financial accounts, the yuan needs to be fully tradable in international financial markets. China's target for internationalizing the yuan seems to be 2020,[7] which is also around the time when China's economy is projected to exceed that of the United States.[8]

The government is encouraging gradual internationalization of the yuan. Chinese firms and financial institutions are beginning to settle more of their cross-border transactions in yuan, and the yuan is expected to be used in a growing range of cross-border transactions in

---

[5] See Lin (2012a: ch. 12) for an overview of financial sector reforms moving forward, as well as other reforms for sustaining equitable growth in China.

[6] Subramanian (2011). Kenen (1983) lists the key requirements for an international currency, and Maziad *et al.* (2011) discuss the risks and rewards of internationalizing a national currency.

[7] Eichengreen (2010b).

[8] Calculations that estimate GDP in market exchange rates put the date between 2020 and 2030; those that use purchasing power parity put the date at 2016 (IMF 2011d).

the next two to three years – perhaps including limited capital account convertibility in the next five years.[9] A strategic next step will be when the central banks of key countries begin to hold part of their reserves in yuans. China is also expanding its role as lender of last resort by participating in the Chiang Mai initiative for multilateralization,[10] and it has signed bilateral swap arrangements in yuans with several countries, including some advanced economies. Although the yuan will be playing an increasingly important role in East Asia's and in China's own international trade and financial transactions, its ascendance to fully fledged reserve currency status must await substantial reform of its financial markets.[11]

How stable would the emerging multipolar international financial system be?

To be financially stable, the international monetary system must be capable of reducing the frequency, scope, and severity of crises. A multipolar system would require participating governments to be disciplined in their macroeconomic policies, to be strongly motivated to cooperate (by sharing some or all of the resulting seigniorage with international bodies to support global public goods, for example), and to take cross-border effects into account in setting policies. Participating governments would also need enough national policy autonomy to manage their domestic economies, as well as an arrangement for pooling reserves among themselves and with countries linked to their currencies. Finally, the system would need to control liquidity – avoiding

---

[9] Huang *et al.* (2011).

[10] This is an agreement reached in May 2000 at the ASEAN (Association of Southeast Asian Nations) Plus Three finance ministers' meeting in Chiang Mai, Thailand, on regional cooperative financing arrangements to supplement IMF resources. The agreement covered an expansion of swap facilities among ASEAN member countries and included bilateral swap arrangements with members of the "Plus Three" group (China, Japan, and South Korea).

[11] As argued by Lin, Sun, and Jiang (2009), an economy's optimal financial structure depends on its stage of development and the structures of its real economy and underlying factor endowments. So, in 2020 or 2025, China may be the world's largest economy, but it will still be a developing country and its financial market may not be deep enough for the yuan to become a global reserve currency.

both excessive liquidity, which can lead to asset bubbles, and inadequate liquidity, which can lead to deflation.

Even beyond these requirements, a key question is whether a multiple reserve currency system is stable enough in the absence of a powerful governance structure for adequate cooperation and policy coordination to avoid crises or mitigate their impacts. In theory, reserve currencies would become increasingly substitutable, which could reduce volatility in exchange rates and interest rates in the reserve currency countries as demand for these assets becomes more elastic – provided that this substitutability exerts sufficient discipline on macroeconomic policies and that the major economic powers coordinate their policies enough to prevent destabilizing capital flows.

Less stability likely, with more frequent financial shocks

In reality, however, the new system is likely to be less stable than the current arrangement, with more frequent financial shocks and fluctuations in asset prices. Each reserve currency country faces difficult macroeconomic and structural challenges that require politically arduous, multiyear policy responses. These challenges make it unlikely that countries will be able to achieve the tight policy coordination required. Making the challenges more difficult is the fact that the slow growth with limited reforms projected for these countries is likely to provoke expansionary monetary policies as a palliative measure. Without tight policy coordination, the increased substitutability of currencies could worsen volatility. Small changes in market perceptions of the riskiness of each asset (because of sudden changes in policies or other market fundamentals) would lead to large shifts in capital among the reserve currency countries, as capital flows out of the country with perceived higher risk and into the other countries in order to take advantage of more favorable market conditions. Large inflows of capital could lead to asset bubbles and an overvalued exchange rate, thus increasing weaknesses in the financial sector, reducing competitiveness in the real economy, and inducing capital to move to yet another reserve currency country.

This pattern is already being observed, as the fiscal and banking crises have led capital to flee from the euro into assets denominated in US dollars, yens, Swiss francs, and gold – and even yuans. Foreign exchange markets remained highly volatile in 2011, as the Eurozone crisis dominated the attention of markets and monetary authorities in the advanced economies and as emerging economies unexpectedly intervened to adjust the value of their currencies. When the euro did not decline in value as expected, market participants suffered. In the second half of 2011 expectations of further quantitative easing by the US Federal Reserve, the surprising move by the Swiss National Bank to weaken the Swiss franc, and interventions by the Japanese monetary authority to weaken the yen created volatility in foreign exchange markets, with spillover effects on financial markets and capital flows. In the fall of 2011 the Swiss National Bank set a floor on the franc–euro exchange rate following a surge in capital inflows, particularly hot portfolio flows (Figure 14.1, panels (a) and (b)). Emerging markets were hit hard as their currencies depreciated sharply – because of increased uncertainty and irrespective of domestic economic conditions and fundamentals, such as interest rates. For example, the Brazilian real appreciated against the dollar throughout 2010 as portfolio flows surged (Figure 14.1, panels (c) and (d)).

Capital flows from advanced economies to emerging economies rebounded strongly in the postcrisis period, with the largest recipients being emerging market economies in Asia and Latin America, as well as some other economies, such as South Africa and Turkey. In several emerging market economies net inflows approached record highs. Although gross inflows are still behind their precrisis peak, they reached 6 percent of GDP in less than a year following the crisis trough in 2009; it took three years to reach a similar level before the crisis.[12]

The recent episode is different from others, however, in being dominated by highly volatile portfolio inflows. Portfolio inflows now account for nearly half the inflows into emerging markets – a substantial increase. The global crisis and concerns about the economic and financial prospects of the Eurozone "have exposed balance sheet vulnerabilities in advanced economies and appear to have triggered a gradual shift in the portfolio allocation of institutional investors toward emerging economies, many of which are enjoying low debt, proven resilience to shocks, and improved ratings."[13]

---

[12] IMF's "International financial statistics" database: http://elibrary-data.imf.org/FindDataReports.aspx?d=330610e=169393.
[13] World Bank (2011d: 58).

(a) **Swiss net portfolio investment flows, quarterly**

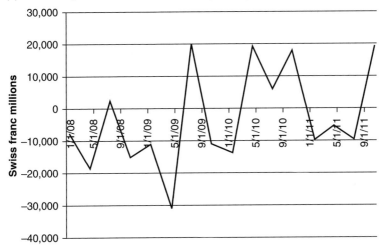

(b) **Swiss franc nominal exchange rate, monthly**

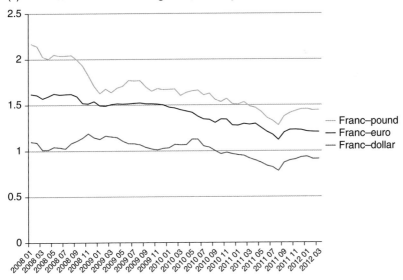

Figure 14.1 Portfolio flows and exchange rates for Switzerland and Brazil
Sources: Swiss National Bank (2012); Banco Central do Brasil's "Economic indicators" data, balance of payments table: www.bcb.gov.br/?INDECO.

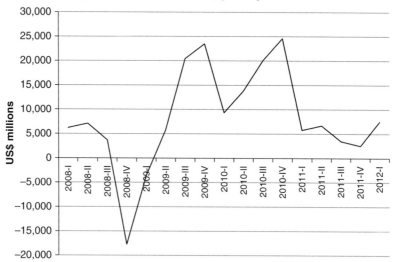

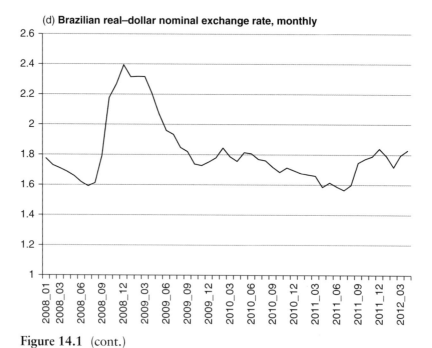

Figure 14.1 (cont.)

A key driver of these inflows is the loose monetary policy and low interest rates in advanced economies. The portfolio inflows tend to be quite volatile. In the past they have reversed themselves suddenly and en masse, leading to sharp currency depreciations and severe balance sheet dislocations. Thus another inherent instability in the current international system is the herdlike behavior of international investors, including mutual funds, pension funds, and hedge funds, which reinforces and even magnifies (rather than mitigates) the initial changes, causing massive capital flows and large fluctuations in exchange rates and interest rates. This phenomenon could cause frequent macroeconomic and financial crises, with potentially devastating consequences for the affected economies, and even globally through contagion effects, leading to a sudden contraction in the supply of safe assets. The financial crisis and rising concerns about the sustainability of sovereign debt in many advanced economies have "reinforced the notion that no asset can be viewed as truly safe."[14] In turn, global demand for safe assets has risen in response to this increased uncertainty and regulatory and policy responses to the crisis. The emerging supply and demand imbalance for safe assets can intensify global financial instability through "short-term volatility jumps, herding behavior, and runs on sovereign debt."[15]

It is quite likely, then, that, under a multipolar system without strong policy coordination and with the reserve currency countries facing macroeconomic and structural problems, exchange rate and interest rate volatility could sometimes be exacerbated. Moreover, given the various market forces and economic stagnation, exchange rate misalignment could become less sustainable and the likelihood of currency wars could rise, resulting in a loss of market share for exports.

Some shocks to the global economy are naturally occurring – such as natural disasters or major technological innovations – and some are driven by fundamental policy errors by major national governments. In addition, financial innovation can outpace regulators' capacity to establish and enforce rules that can prevent excessive leverage or risk-taking by globally connected financial institutions, as preceded the 2008–9 financial crisis.

There are two approaches to enforcing policy discipline on national governments to avoid the policy mistakes that lead to international financial instability: rules and competition. Economists favoring rules

---

[14] IMF (2012d: 81).   [15] IMF (2012d: 81).

have argued for maintaining a tightly fixed exchange rate with an open capital account, which implies no possibility for an independent monetary policy.[16] Another approach is to limit monetary policy to a fixed rule, such as Friedman's *k* percent rule or the Taylor rule.[17] International agreements can impose discipline (the gold standard is a clear example). Other economists believe that market competition can impose discipline. This idea is behind the argument that a multiple reserve currency system would be more stable than the current system: end the dollar's monopoly, and discipline will be restored as the market punishes extreme policies.[18] The main goal of a reserve currency country's monetary and fiscal policies is to maintain its own domestic economic stability, however, and, considering the structural problems in the major reserve currency countries, monetary policy is likely to remain accommodative to keep interest rates low. Large speculative capital flows may therefore occur periodically – a messy process that could involve considerable financial and economic volatility that would harm not only the reserve currency countries but also the rest of the world.

Global liquidity and the emerging multiple reserve currency system

If the macroeconomic policies of reserve currency countries are geared toward achieving global stability, the international monetary system can ensure adequate liquidity at the global level, which is one of its primary functions. The literature on international monetary relations refers to the "hegemonic stability" of the current unipolar system: the hegemon has an incentive to preserve the system by providing monetary stability.[19] US macroeconomic policies over the last forty years have been concerned mainly with domestic economic stability, however, and thus might not always have aligned with policies that would have preserved international stability.[20] And there is no reason to believe that, under a multipolar system, reserve currency countries would be

---

[16] Mundell (1995, 2005, 2011); McKinnon (2010).
[17] The Friedman *k* percent rule sets a constant *k* percent growth rate for the monetary aggregate (Friedman 1960). The Taylor rule allows for a countercyclical response, but according to a fixed rule (Taylor 1993).
[18] Dorrucci and McKay (2011); ECB (2010); Eichengreen (2012).
[19] Eichengreen (1987).   [20] See Rajan (2010) and Lin and Treichel (2012).

any more likely to change fundamentally how liquidity is provided absent close policy cooperation among the countries.

In addition to the inherent contradiction in US fiscal and monetary policies that need to be directed to ensure global stability but instead focus on internal stability, there is serious concern about the fiscal capacity of the United States to meet its massive debt obligations to the rest of the world. This problem is likely to worsen over the longer term, particularly if the rapid increases in US indebtedness are not reversed. In any case, over the next decade, as the relative weight of the United States in the world economy continues to decline gradually, it will likely play a less important role in providing liquidity to the global economy by issuing interest-bearing "safe assets," which currently constitute the bulk of dollar-denominated reserve assets held by other countries. And, as argued earlier, the euro's economic base is also bound to decline over the medium term relative to the size of the world economy, because of the slow growth projected for the region and the rapid aging of its population.

A priori, then, the new multipolar international monetary system could help resolve the potential liquidity shortage at the global level, by substantially increasing the supply of reserve assets without resorting to overexpansionary macroeconomic policy – assuming (perhaps unrealistically) that the reserve currency countries increase the supply of safe assets to match demand without any one country or group of countries resorting to unsound fiscal and monetary policies. Moreover, as long as the reserve currency countries follow prudent fiscal and monetary policies that also take into account cross-border effects, the countries can maintain their reserve currency status and share in the benefits of "exorbitant privilege" (see Box 12.1 in Chapter 12). Macroeconomic policy competition between the reserve currency countries should improve policy discipline, conditional on close policy coordination, preferably within the G7 and G20 frameworks.[21]

The lack of international policy coordination in providing adequate global liquidity has long been a problem. The gold standard set up under the original Bretton Woods system was abandoned mainly because of the overexpansion of fiscal deficits and monetary policy in the United States. More recently the problem has become more complex, involving liquidity held by the private sector as well as the public

---

[21] European System of Central Banks (2010).

sector. Changes in global liquidity, reflecting the actions of regulated institutions and markets and the expansion of the shadow banking sector, can strongly influence the risks posed by capital flows.[22] Although the two components of global liquidity (international liquidity and domestic liquidity in reserve currency countries) were roughly equal at the end of the 1990s, the liabilities of the shadow banking system multiplied with the rapid increase in global liquidity and gross cross-border flows before the 2008–9 crisis, as a direct result of financial deregulation.

Shadow banks, mostly unregulated, were an important source of instability during the 2008–9 crisis.[23] Global banks in the reserve currency countries, often in collaboration with their related shadow banking units, collect funds globally and lend globally on the basis of an overall global asset allocation strategy. When perceived risks are low, these banks increase their leverage, expand their balance sheets, and expand global liquidity well beyond what the central bank authorities of the affected countries intended. Global banks also magnify the effects and international reach of a reserve currency country's monetary policy. When the reserve currency country increases its money supply, for example by lowering its policy rate, carry trades lead to large capital outflows to nonreserve currency countries (the reverse process occurs when the reserve currency country reduces its money supply). The rise of global banks following financial liberalization in the 1980s and 1990s and the loose monetary policy in the United States in the 2000s contributed to a large increase in cross-border capital flows before the global crisis in 2008 and 2009.

Many market participants expect the US Federal Reserve to embark on further quantitative easing in 2013 and beyond to help the US economy recover from the slow pace of growth and high unemployment, especially because of rising fears of possible deflation as consumers pay down their unsustainably high debts. Similarly, the central banks of Japan, the United Kingdom, and the European Union have expanded their unconventional monetary interventions or have signaled their intent to maintain very low interest rates over the next two years, given the slow pace of economic growth (Figure 14.2). As a form of financial repression that relieves the government of its debt burden – when real economic growth is sluggish, negative real interest rates can

---

[22] IMF (2011f).   [23] Bruno and Shin (2011).

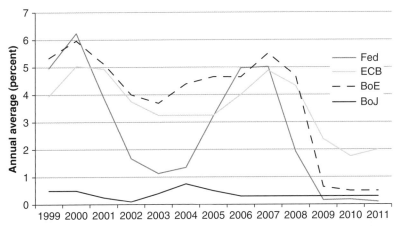

Figure 14.2 Policy rates of reserve currency central banks
Sources: Federal Reserve Board's "Economic research and data": www.
federalreserve.gov/econresdata/statisticsdata.htm; ECB's "Key ECB interest
rates" data: www.ecb.int/stats/monetary/rates/html/index.en.html; Bank of
England's "Interest and exchange rates" data (annual average of official bank
rate: IUAABEDR): www.bankofengland.co.uk/boeapps/iadb/index.asp?
Travel=NIxSTxTIx&levels=1&XNotes=Y&A3688XNode3687.x=4&A3688
XNode3687.y=6&XNotes2=Y&Nodes=X4052X4053X4097X3687X3764X
3765X3691&SectionRequired=I&HideNums=-1&ExtraInfo=false#BM;
Bank of Japan's "Basic discount rate and basic loan rate" data: www.boj.or.jp/
en/statistics/boj/other/discount/index.htm.

be the "solution" for stabilizing or lowering debt to GDP ratios – these
policies are likely to continue.[24]

Experience during 2008 to 2011 suggests that these highly accommodative monetary policies are likely to set off another round of massive capital flows from the advanced economies to emerging market
economies, resulting in new credit, asset, and commodity price bubbles
and causing exchange rates in capital-receiving countries to appreciate
(Figure 14.3).

In global financial markets, the international dimension of credit goes
well beyond monetary policy. For a few key currencies (the US dollar

---

[24] Reinhart, Kirkegaard, and Sbrancia (2011); Reinhart and Rogoff (2009);
Reinhart and Sbrancia (2011).

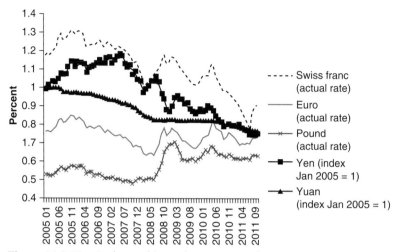

Figure 14.3 Nominal monthly exchange rates of currencies against the US dollar

Note: Swiss franc, euro, and pound data are actual exchange rates per dollar; yen and yuan rates are indices (January 2005 = 1) in order to fit the same scale and to show trends and volatility.

Source: Based on data from World Bank's "Global economic monitor" database: http://data.worldbank.org/data-catalog/global-economic-monitor.

and the euro), credit use extends well beyond the issuing country.[25] The stock of dollar-denominated credit to borrowers outside the United States amounted to $5.8 trillion in 2010, or 12 percent of global (non-US) GDP; the stock of euro-denominated credit outside the Eurozone stood at €2.1 trillion.[26] In larger countries the stock of credit denominated in foreign currency tends to be a small share of overall credit, but its volume can rapidly grow beyond policymakers' control. Cross-border credit has grown more rapidly than overall credit in many countries experiencing a credit boom.

The transition to a truly multiple reserve currency system could thus be marred by periods of substantial short-term instability and high volatility in exchange and interest rates worldwide. The currencies of current and potential future reserve currency countries are affected by

[25] Domanci, Fender, and McGuire (2011).
[26] Domanci, Fender, and McGuire (2011).

continuing economic weaknesses, including high levels of debt, and structural problems that stifle faster economic growth, particularly in Europe and the United States. China's participation in the emerging multiple reserve currency system will be gradual, because of its need first to reform its financial sector and remove other structural rigidities over the next five to ten years and because the process must await the independent decisions of private investors and the monetary authorities.[27]

The main advantage of the emerging multiple reserve currency system is its potential to enable countries to diversify their reserve holdings and to provide more global liquidity during a crisis. But these advantages may come at the cost of the additional instability arising from exchange rate volatility among currencies used as reserve assets.[28]

---

[27] See Eichengreen (2011b) and Eichengreen and Flandreau (2008).
[28] United Nations (2009).

15 | *The thinking behind the main reform proposals*

As international economic and financial integration deepened in the decades following the Bretton Woods conference, the international monetary system changed. Calls for more radical reform have intensified since the global financial crisis of 2008–9. In evaluating various reform proposals, it is important to keep in mind how the international monetary system differs from national systems. Some of its functions resemble those of a national monetary authority: a payment system, acting as lender of last resort, and provider of liquidity as part of overall management of the global money supply. But these roles are more limited at the international level, because of the constraints of national sovereignty and the absence of an international government. This implies that the international monetary system must always operate by consensus. The coordination of monetary policy and exchange rate regimes would thus be an additional function at the international level.

The international payments system

The payments system of the international monetary system is anchored by the Bank for International Settlements, which settles foreign exchange and gold transactions between member central banks.[1] The BIS also provides money market instruments: sight and fixed-term deposits and tradable instruments denominated in a variety of major currencies and Special Drawing Rights. The BIS handles these functions well, and there are no major reform proposals currently on the table.

---

[1] The BIS was established in 1930 to facilitate transactions for the war reparation payments imposed on Germany after World War I.

This purely financial "bank of banks" role has diminished over time, however, relative to the size of global financial markets. The BIS still has a balance sheet of about SDR 260 billion,[2] and for some countries it is an important repository for reserves and provides vital central bank services. Most foreign exchange transactions are now conducted through private sector cooperative mechanisms, however. For example, the Continuous Linked Settlement (CLS) Bank, founded in 2002 to reduce counterparty risk in the settlement of financial transactions in foreign currency, provides settlement services in seventeen currencies to thirty-nine large private sector financial institutions. It now settles some 58 percent of global foreign exchange trading,[3] and serviced $1.4 trillion in foreign currency transactions in 2010.

As the BIS's foreign exchange transaction business has declined, so the BIS has become a critical research and data center for financial policy coordination through the Basel accords, and it hosts the Financial Stability Board. These deliberations go well beyond payment systems and monetary policy to focus on financial regulatory policy and financial supervision reforms.

As economic integration deepens, countries might transition to a unified payment system – a process that would likely require a common currency. The European Union is moving toward the integration of payment systems with the Single Euro Payments Area project. Security measures are already progressing at the national level to facilitate such integration, but improved interoperability between national payment infrastructures is also needed.[4] "E-payment" systems are also advancing – but slowly.

Other payment settlement issues to be considered include settling payments for new instruments that might arise with reform of the international monetary system and, if a new international currency is created, facilitating payments between central banks on international transactions. For example, if the International Monetary Fund were to issue tradable securities denominated in SDRs or in some new global currency unit, a market-maker role might be needed until deep and

---

[2] BIS (2011a).

[3] The 58 percent is a share of a reduced base (rather than of BIS survey reports of total foreign currency trading activity), which eliminates transactions that do not present any settlement risk and thus have no need for a specialized settlement counterparty. See CLS Group (2011).

[4] ECB (2010).

liquid markets had been established for those securities. The IMF would be the likely candidate.[5] Another option would be to establish a more permanent role for transacting swap arrangements, through either the IMF or the BIS. Payment system integration could be a natural consequence of establishing a new international currency – whether as a substitute or a complement to existing national currencies.

Lender of last resort

The second principal function of the international monetary system is as a lender of last resort, which was an intense focus of the Bretton Woods conference. Without a global lender of last resort, countries need to self-insure against potential losses from terms of trade shocks. Imperfections in international capital markets imply imperfect access to credit, meaning that borrowing to smooth consumption during such shocks is not always possible. Sudden stops in access to foreign currency flows pose a risk.[6] Countries without an internationally accepted currency self-insure against these shocks by accumulating foreign exchange reserves.

The IMF is a lender of last resort to sovereign nations through their central banks. Purpose V of the articles of agreement states that the IMF makes general funds available to its members, "thus providing them with opportunity to correct maladjustments in their balance of payments without resorting to measures destructive of national or international prosperity." These "resources" are gold, major international currencies, and other national currencies that countries have subscribed to the IMF. In this sense, the IMF is a fund for pooling international reserves.[7] Because commercial banks and other financial institutions in member countries do not have direct access to IMF resources, the IMF's role as a lender of last resort is more circumscribed than that of central banks at the national level.

Several initiatives for lender of last resort functions are at various stages of implementation or under discussion. They include providing enhanced direct funding for the IMF to adapt to trade and international

---

[5] IMF (2011a: annex 2) describes how the settlement process might work for SDR-denominated assets.

[6] Calvo (1998); Calvo, Izquierdo, and Mejía (2004).

[7] Article I of the IMF's articles of agreement (adopted in 1944) refers to six purposes for the IMF's establishment.

capital flows that have far outpaced its balance sheet; creating contingent financing mechanisms – either bilaterally through swap arrangements between central banks or new contingent funding arrangements for the IMF (along with the accompanying contingent loan instruments); pooling reserves or emergency lending arrangements regionally rather than internationally; and creating an international monetary authority with its own currency that could be a lender of last resort.

The IMF's resources for providing foreign-currency financing to countries under stress have not kept pace with the size of the global economy, global trade, or global financial flows. One option for increasing IMF resources is to raise quotas. Quotas now total SDR 217.4 billion (about $335 billion), or about 0.5 percent of world GDP. The quota is paid 25 percent in SDRs or major currencies and 75 percent in the country's own currency. Another option, used sparingly, is sales of the IMF's vast store of gold – managed carefully so as not to disturb gold markets. The IMF has 90.5 million ounces of gold,[8] currently worth about $164 billion – the third largest gold holdings in the world.[9] A third direct approach would be to issue IMF bonds (regional development banks already issue bonds for leveraging their membership's paid-in and contingent capital). If these bonds were denominated in SDRs, that could be a first step toward making the SDR a global currency.[10] (This is discussed in more detail below.)

Another approach, tried tentatively during the recent global crisis, was contingent lending: IMF members made commitments to lend to the IMF in case of a need for additional resources to conduct IMF lending programs. The commitments, called the New Arrangements to Borrow, total SDR 367.5 billion (about $585 billion).[11] These arrangements seem particularly well suited for funding the relatively new contingent loan instruments, such as the Flexible Credit Line; funds are needed only if a country wants to use the credit line. Bilateral contingent funding arrangements were also established during the global financial crisis.[12] Large banks in Europe had dollar liabilities contracted with US

---

[8] See IMF (2012a). The value stated above is the end-August 2011 gold price.

[9] The United States and Germany have larger holdings (according to World Gold Council data; see www.gold.org).

[10] See, for example, Cooper (1984, 2000, 2006, 2010).

[11] In April 2012 commitments were made for more than $430 billion in additional resources to the IMF.

[12] IMF (2010b).

banks (and vice versa). Central banks agreed to swap national currencies if there was a surge in domestic banks' financing needs in dollars.[13] As part of a broader lender of last resort function, these sorts of arrangements could be formalized ahead of the next financial crisis bilaterally or multilaterally, with IMF assistance. Such precommitment might help prevent the panic-induced freezing of swap markets during future episodes of financial stress.

Following the Asian crisis, some countries expressed a need for regional rather than international pooling of reserves. The ASEAN Plus Three Chiang Mai initiative to set up swap lines was a step in that direction. To date, no country programs have been established or funds disbursed under the initiative.[14] There have also been proposals to establish an Asian Monetary Fund as a regional equivalent of the IMF. There are no financial advantages to a regional rather than international fund, but many disadvantages – among them less funding and less risk diversification.[15] The initiative reflects concerns about IMF governance among the initiative's supporters, though some of these concerns could be addressed through IMF governance reforms. Other regional arrangements, the European Financial Stability Facility and the European Stability Mechanism, have been established recently as a complement to IMF programs to channel emergency funding to several European Union countries suffering extreme balance of payments difficulties.

The most comprehensive reform would establish a central-bank-style lender of last resort, giving individual banks access to emergency resources. To function as a central bank, such an institution would need its own currency or payment note that would be generally accepted as payment by creditors of troubled financial institutions. In principle, access could be restricted to banks with a substantial cross-border presence or substantial debt exposure to financial institutions in other countries. Reasonable technical criteria could be established for determining such exposure. Banks below the exposure threshold would rely on national central banks for lender of last resort functions, and presumably for regulatory and supervisory functions as well.

---

[13] BIS (2008).   [14] Henning (2009); Sussangkarn (2010).
[15] Stiglitz and Greenwald (2010) argue that the close economic links and "greater sense of solidarity" of a regional arrangement would assure countries that access would be available when needed.

While it would be theoretically possible to establish such an idealized international lender of last resort, it might also be able to function using several existing currencies – say, by granting the IMF authority to lend directly to commercial banks. But, in that case, the lender of last resort would also have to regulate and supervise those banks. Therefore, there are a number of additional advantages and potential complications with the creation of a global currency; these are discussed later.

For use in a lender of last resort function, a new global currency would need to be at least as credible as existing reserve currencies, freely usable by national central banks, and accepted by commercial banks for liquidity support and the settling of claims between banks. The SDR as currently constituted cannot serve this function, as it is only a unit of account. SDR-denominated bonds – issued by international financial institutions or countries – might eventually serve that role, but this would require market development. Developing a liquid market for the new instruments would involve lower bid–ask spreads; the IMF estimates an initial cost of 80 to 100 basis points for this liquidity premium.[16] Coordination between several sovereign institutions and multilateral institutions could substantially reduce the costs.

In addition to these international (and regional) proposals, there are go-it-alone proposals for emerging economies. They can accumulate reserves, take initial steps toward internationalizing their currencies, and then draw on international reserves to pay foreign obligations when access to foreign currency capital markets is tight. Once a country makes its currency acceptable to foreigners as payment for transactions, it can borrow from foreigners in their own currency, bypassing the need to access foreign currency when external shocks strike. This is not easy to do, and indeed few countries have been able to internationalize their currencies fully.

Why do countries hold foreign currency reserves at all? In principle, under a pure floating exchange rate regime and with perfect international capital markets, reserves are not needed, central banks would not execute purchases or sales of foreign currency on the foreign exchange market, and central banks would be able to borrow whenever they needed foreign currency. Under the gold standard, a negative balance of payments resulting from an external or domestic shock would result in a loss of gold. If the imbalance persisted, the loss of gold would lead to

---

[16] IMF (2011a: annex 2).

an eventual parity adjustment or outright abandonment of the gold standard. Today, with much larger international capital flows, reserves can provide self-insurance against sudden stops in access to foreign currency flows. In an IMF survey of central bankers, 80 percent cited "buffer for liquidity needs" as a motivation for increasing reserves, and 60 percent cited "smoothing of exchange rate volatility."[17]

Following the financial crises of the 1980s and 1990s, reserve adequacy guidelines were established to forestall fears of a sudden stop in access to foreign currency. For example, the Guidotti–Greenspan rule suggests that countries keep international reserves equal to their stock of short-term (less than one year) external liabilities. Others use modeling techniques to evaluate the optimal level of foreign currency reserves – particularly in the context of the recent massive rise in reserve holdings in emerging economies.[18] There is a cost to holding high levels of international reserves, however: higher inflation if the reserves are not sterilized, and quasi-fiscal costs if they are sterilized using domestic securities with a higher interest rate than the return on reserve assets.[19] More recent analyses focus on risks arising from the "double drain." Weaknesses in the domestic financial system can cause national residents to flee the system (the first "drain"), and, if those depositors try to convert their local currency into foreign currency, a second, external "drain" develops. One model of optimal reserve holdings provides empirical evidence that emerging markets with larger banking systems tend to hold more international reserves.[20] Concerns about the domestic banking system can also prompt reserve accumulation that might otherwise be considered "excessive."

Much of this discussion at the country level relates to what has been called the macroeconomic policy "trilemma," or the impossibility of simultaneously achieving more than two of the three policy objectives: an independent monetary policy, exchange rate stability, and capital account openness. China maintains exchange rate stability with sterilized reserve accumulation to limit inflation, but it retains strong capital controls. The United States has open capital accounts and independent monetary policy but a relatively unstable exchange rate with other key

---

[17] IMF (2011b).   [18] Jeanne and Rancière (2008); Alfaro and Kanczuk (2009).

[19] See Saraiva and Canuto (2009) on the case of Brazil's prepayment of debt to the IMF in early 2006. The IMF estimates that average reserve costs for the median country were about 0.5 percent of GDP from 2001 to 2009 (IMF 2011b).

[20] Obstfeld, Shambaugh, and Taylor (2010).

currencies. Most countries attempt to allow some adjustment to the exchange rate and some capital mobility rather than strictly seeking to achieve both objectives. There is empirical evidence, however, that the trilemma broadly applied over the last century.[21]

Along with the trend toward more open capital accounts has come greater international financial integration – and new risks for the global economy and new challenges for international safety net arrangements. The quality and effectiveness of financial sector regulation and supervision directly affect risk and the need for an international lender of last resort, as well as the degree of reliance on safety net services. There are numerous proposals for strengthening financial sector regulation and supervision – all of which are beyond the scope of this book.

Provider of global liquidity – during "normal" times

Total liquidity in the global economy is determined by the independent actions of national monetary authorities around the world. Monetary authorities in reserve currency countries – particularly the US Federal Reserve – carry more weight than do others and have a more direct impact on international transactions. Pure international liquidity – comprising transactions by residents across countries – is determined by the monetary policy of reserve currency countries. Because of the potential conflict in reserve currency countries between national and international interests, expansionary national monetary and fiscal policies, pursued to achieve domestic policy objectives, may create instability in global financial and currency markets by exceeding global reserves demand based on global economic growth alone.[22]

There are two basic ways to moderate the effects of this decentralized system for determining international liquidity: more voluntary cooperation or greater centralization of decisionmaking. Some voluntary cooperation has begun under the auspices of the G7, the G20, the International Monetary and Financial Committee of the IMF, and other such forums. These cooperative arrangements focus largely on the lender of last resort function, however, such as coordinating national bailouts of large banks with global links during the 2008–9

---

[21] Obstfeld, Shambaugh, and Taylor (2010).

[22] For a discussion of reserve currency countries "debasing" their currency through asset creation, see Pozsar (2011).

financial crisis and setting up central bank swap lines. National autonomy still prevails in the more mundane, daily monetary policy decisions. Expanding voluntary cooperation will require that countries anticipate mutually beneficial outcomes – a global win-win.

Increases over the years in the general allocation of SDRs (by SDR 9.3 billion in 1970–2, SDR 12.1 billion in 1979–81, and SDR 161.2 billion in 2009) might appear to have created additional liquidity, but they simply represent a claim on other IMF members' international reserves.[23] Thus they are a reserve-pooling mechanism to reallocate the global supply of reserves to countries that need it most – in line with the lender of last resort function. Substantial changes would be required to make the SDR a workable form of international liquidity.

The other alternative is for national governments to give up some policy autonomy to an international monetary authority, which would make the day-to-day monetary policy decisions. To conduct monetary policy, the international monetary authority would need a composite currency or a purely international currency. A decision would be needed on what to do about national currencies: abandon them,[24] retain them but peg them to an international composite or international currency, or retain them along with some more flexible arrangement in which national and international currencies coexist.[25] A more flexible arrangement might not solve the coordination problem while adding yet another actor: the international monetary authority.

Under one proposal that calls for abandoning national currencies, a new international Bank of Issue would conduct open market operations with securities of member countries and lend directly to banks as the lender of last resort.[26] The new international currency could be a new instrument, an evolution of the dollar, or an evolution of a composite such as the SDR. There are advantages to an international currency, but the hurdle of abandoning national currencies, and with them national monetary policy, may not be surmountable.

---

[23] Obstfeld (2011b).   [24] Cooper (1984, 2000, 2006).
[25] Mundell (2005) prefers a currency board arrangement – a tightly fixed exchange rate – as a transition to a global currency union.
[26] Cooper (2000, 2006).

16 | *Costs and benefits of major reform proposals*

This chapter reviews some of the major proposals for reform of the international monetary system and provides a rough assessment of their costs and benefits. The criteria for assessment should include efficiency, stability (incentives to correct external imbalances), equity, and feasibility, but quantifying each criterion would be extremely difficult – an entire research agenda in its own right. The chapter considers three reform proposals: a bigger and better IMF, a global central bank with international currency, and international policy coordination.

A bigger and better International Monetary Fund

There have been many proposals to reform the IMF with the objective of improving the performance of the international monetary system. The discussion here focuses on funding, instruments, surveillance, and governance.

Funding

The lending capacity of the IMF as a lender of last resort for sovereign countries has declined as a share of global GDP. Establishing automatic quota increases, perhaps combined with a one-off initial increase, could automatically adjust the size of the IMF to the size of the rapidly growing international economy. One proposal calls for automatic quota increases that, on average, equal average annual real global GDP growth but with a countercyclical wrinkle: countries would contribute more during high growth years and less during subpar growth years.[1]

---

[1] Eichengreen (2009).

The IMF could also leverage its capital base by issuing bonds. If they were denominated in SDRs and sold both to central banks and private investors, these bonds could also gradually establish private sector demand for the SDR as a near-currency. Because this arrangement would change the financial model of the IMF, it would require enhanced balance sheet management and staffing for Treasury operations to support the bond issues.

Contingent borrowing along the lines of the New Arrangements to Borrow could also be expanded. This option would be particularly useful if there were an expansion or greater use of contingent lending through the Flexible Credit Line or the Precautionary Credit Line. Capital would not have to be provided up-front – only the commitment to provide it when needed.

It would be more controversial to add teeth to the IMF's surveillance function by fining countries for inappropriate macroeconomic policies that disrupt international financial stability. During the Bretton Woods conference, Keynes suggested escalating interest rates on larger imbalances in an international clearing bank, and several people have revived the idea of taxing excess reserve accumulation or extreme current account surpluses.[2] The revenue from these taxes could be used to fund and strengthen surveillance, as discussed below.

Instruments

Expanding SDR allocations could complement international reserves by serving as an insurance mechanism.[3] Used this way, the SDR could make liquidity flow where and when it is needed. Substitution accounts, discussed previously, could also serve this function.

Indexing is another way to create new global reserve assets, whether from a liability-managing or asset-managing approach. During the debt crises of the 1990s there were proposals for limiting the impact of the "original sin" of borrowing in dollars by indexing public debt to a country's ability to pay. One way would be to link debt service directly to GDP growth, as was done with some of Argentina's restructured debt during the early 2000s. A more comprehensive approach would create an index of emerging market currencies to be used as a unit of account for denominating debt – first for multilateral development bank loans

---

[2] Eichengreen (2009).   [3] See Williamson (2009) for an appraisal.

and eventually for sovereign bond issues.[4] From an asset management perspective, central banks could invest in assets linked to the value of global GDP. Such an asset has built-in risk diversification, as it is not linked to any individual country's income and creditworthiness.[5] The IMF could take the lead in creating the instrument and, as a market maker, in implementing it.

Surveillance

Several proposals call for the IMF to get tougher on individual countries that are unsettling international financial stability. One way is through direct "naming and shaming" under article IV consultations and press releases. Another way – agreed to in G20 deliberations, endorsed by the IMF board, and already being implemented – is the production of "spillover reports" for systemically important economies. A more forceful approach would be to fine countries for persistent external imbalances, as mentioned above. Spillover reports are one way to enhance IMF surveillance of reserve currency countries that face structural imbalances and pursue excessively expansionary monetary policies. It could be difficult moving from surveillance to policy action, however, because of the IMF's limited leverage with the reserve currency countries.

Governance

There are both technical and political reasons for changing the IMF's governance structure. Technical issues reflect the lessons from inflation targeting by central banks. The IMF could set up a decisionmaking body of experts to serve like the board of governors of a central bank.[6] There are also largely political motivations for changing the governance structure to increase the fairness of representation on the IMF's board. Countries would accept new reserve-pooling mechanisms as a substitute for national stockpiles of reserves only if they accepted and trusted the decisionmaking process that governs the pooling arrangements. For special SDR allocations to work, countries would have to go through the IMF to use them.

---

[4] Eichengreen and Hausmann (2005). [5] Eichengreen (2011b).
[6] Eichengreen (2009).

Assessment

The cost of increasing the IMF's access to resources would be modest. In the end, the new, higher quotas would still be counted as part of each country's international reserves. And the IMF would need only limited additional staffing to enhance its surveillance role. But getting member countries to accept stronger surveillance would depend on governance reforms.[7] To the extent that representation is proportional to financing, funding reforms provide an opportunity to make needed adjustments at the margin.

The cost of experimenting with using the SDR as an international reserve asset would also be modest,[8] but the size of the benefits is less clear. The SDR is a composite currency, and central banks can manage their reserves to mimic the currency composition of the SDR. In addition, using the SDR as an international reserve asset does not avoid volatility problems arising from structural imbalances and expansionary macroeconomic policies in reserve currency countries. The SDR is not an asset external to the monetary system, as gold is, with an independent value, so expanding the supply of SDRs expands claims on the underlying currency. As a composite fiat money, the SDR's role as a store of value depends on the credible solvency of the sovereigns that issue the underlying currencies.

The IMF is the key institution in the current international monetary system – a system that saw a steady increase in global trade and capital flows before the 2008–9 financial crisis. Even with a bigger and better IMF, the international monetary system would still be based on reserve currencies, with the same risk of fragility that led to the crisis. Governance reforms might generate greater confidence in the IMF and greater willingness to pool international reserves that could enable a more rapid and effective response to specific country crises. Governance reforms might also prevent national central banks from accumulating excess reserves. In addition, with more resources, the IMF might be able to coordinate central bank swap lines, though it is difficult to say whether this would have been more efficient or effective in responding to the immediate impact of the 2008–9 crisis. The political feasibility of creating a bigger and better IMF depends on how far the reforms go.

---

[7] Eichengreen (2009).   [8] IMF (2011a).

Simple governance reforms might increase confidence in the IMF, but they would not address the underlying weaknesses of the system.

A global central bank with international currency

There are essentially three options for a new international currency. One is fiat money, whose value is based on the full faith and credit of the international issuer. A second is a composite of existing currencies – essentially, the evolution of the SDR into a banknote that is accepted for the payment of goods, services, and assets by governments and the private sector. A third is a commodity-linked currency, such as Keynes's bancor, whose value is tied to the physical quantities of a commodity or basket of commodities.

An international issuing entity could be created from scratch or it could evolve from an existing international organization, such as the IMF. A key issue would be the credibility of the governance structure – especially if the international currency issued is fiat money.

Another element to consider is whether the new international currency would replace or complement national reserve currencies. In principle, the new international currency could evolve gradually, with countries first fixing their national currencies to a band around the international currency, then fixing it to a hard peg, and finally adopting the new currency. But exchange rate regimes and exchange rate coordination are always contentious issues.

If a fiat international currency could be created, it would have several advantages. It would create a safe asset that avoids the conflict between national and global interests inherent in using national currencies as reserve currencies. It could lower transaction costs for international trade and finance and promote long-term stability in the financial system. There would still be a need for an international lender of last resort (discussed below). The problem is creating a global governance structure to administer the currency that engenders confidence in its "full faith and credit" backing of the currency. The issue is important, and deserves further consideration and analysis. The main question is political feasibility. An international treaty would be required, likely entailing a long process of ratification. If a multiple reserve currency is a lose-lose proposition, as argued here, it will be easier to win agreement for an international currency.

A composite currency that circulates along with national currencies might provide a stabilizing alternative to reserves denominated in national currencies. And a number of international organizations, including the IMF, could issue bonds denominated in the composite currency that central banks could hold as a reserve asset. But that benefit would likely be small, since national central banks could diversify their reserve holdings in a way that mimicked the underlying currency composition of the composite currency. The benefit would then be the creation of an additional supply of safe assets. Because the composite currency still represents claims on the underlying currencies, though, its value would still depend on the perceived solvency of the issuing countries.[9] In addition, the seigniorage would be shared only by the countries whose currencies are in the basket, and, perhaps more importantly, the inherent conflicts of interest in using national currencies as a reserve currency would persist.

Several proposals call for increasing the use of the SDR – already a quasi-currency and a composite – in transactions and thus moving it closer to currency status. One proposal suggests converting SDRs into national currencies through the central banks of reserve currency countries.[10] In some ways, this would be similar to formalizing the bilateral central bank swap arrangements that emerged during 2008 and 2009 and centralizing them at the IMF.[11]

Because a composite currency's value is, in essence, based on the value of the component national currencies, an alternative approach would be to tie the value of the currency to a commodity, such as gold. This would have the same problems as before, however, arising from the finite supply of a scarce commodity resource. If nonmetallic commodities – such as foodstuffs – were included, the new asset's claims on the supply of those commodities could drive up their prices at a time when there is already substantial volatility in global food prices.

Another important design consideration is whether to have the exchange rate between national currencies and the international currency pegged, dirty floating, or fully floating. Pegging the rate would be similar to the original Bretton Woods system, while a full float or dirty float would resemble the current system. The tradeoffs between fixed and floating rates are complex – and the subject of long-standing debate. Factors influencing a country's choice for its

[9] Obstfeld (2011a).   [10] Truman (2010).   [11] Obstfeld (2011a).

exchange rate regime include its size, openness, trade patterns, and degree of development.

Finally, if countries did drop their national currencies and adopt the international currency domestically, fiscal policy coordination would be an issue. Business cycles in industrial countries are largely synchronized, and these economies do not generally suffer from asymmetric shocks.[12] To the extent that there are shocks, they could be managed, in principle, through independent fiscal policy. The Eurozone's recent experience suggests that a supranational fiscal authority may be needed as well, however – yet another daunting political challenge at the global scale.

Global policy coordination

There are several current mechanisms for global policy coordination. They include the IMF's articles of agreement and board discussions of article IV consultations with member governments. The G20 was a critical forum for coordinating monetary policy responses and emergency support to financial systems during the 2008–9 financial crisis. Its Mutual Assessment Process provides a forum for discussing short-term macroeconomic imbalances and longer-term structural policies to support "strong, sustainable, and balanced growth." As part of that process, countries agreed that the IMF would provide multilateral surveillance reports as well as country-specific reports and that it would develop a new Precautionary and Liquidity Line.

The ongoing fixed/flexible exchange rate debate notwithstanding, a consensus is emerging that countries may need different policy regimes at different stages of development or according to the structure of their economy.[13] And, whatever the choice, the trilemma remains: policymakers will still have to choose which two of the three objectives of monetary policy to pursue fully – an independent monetary policy, exchange rate stability, or capital account openness.

Intermediate regimes could also be considered. Under a proposal for a system of reference rates, central banks could be allowed to intervene in foreign exchange markets as long as the currency is within a band

[12] Cooper (2006).
[13] For example, Frankel (2008) has suggested that commodity exporters should peg to the export price.

around its reference rate.[14] The IMF could periodically revise the reference rate.

Finally, countries could be free to "internationalize" their currencies as part of a broadly decentralized system with policy coordination mechanisms.[15] This option has the potential to create new reserve assets and meet some of the demand for these assets. In addition, currency "competition" in itself could enhance discipline in national macroeconomic policy. This mechanism will work only if each reserve currency country is structurally "healthy." In the final analysis, however, this option is really just a continuation of the current non-system. Left unanswered is the question of whether competition between reserve currencies could incentivize sustainable macroeconomic policies – especially among systemically important countries and countries that issue reserve currencies. Recent history indicates that this could be a risky path.

[14] Williamson (2007).   [15] Maziad *et al.* (2011).

17 | A proposal for a new global reserve currency: paper gold ("p-gold")

The survey of the evolution of the international monetary system and options for reform in previous chapters of this part provides a reminder of the complexity of designing global governance for a global economy. And that is without considering the equally important and challenging issues raised by the broader global financial architecture, including cooperation on the regulation and supervision of financial institutions. The recent transmission of the effects of the weaknesses in US housing finance across international borders is a painful reminder of how difficult – and vital – this issue is. The fiscal dimension of reforming the international monetary system is yet another potential sticking point.[1] Any increase in the size and role of the IMF, expansion in the role of SDRs, or attempt to create new international currencies will require fiscal backing by national governments.

This book has amply demonstrated the fragility of the international monetary system, which has experienced periodic crises over the past two centuries. The rapid swings in market perceptions, the fiscal challenges in high-income countries, and the development challenges of emerging market economies could all lead to regional and global instabilities even greater than those of the past decade. Complicating the situation is the difficult political process involved in addressing such looming issues as pension and health reforms in rich countries and income inequality and other social stresses in emerging market economies.

The odds favor continuing periodic crises accompanied by highly volatile financial flows. The consequences would be grave for developing countries, as the global financial crisis demonstrated.

---

[1] Obstfeld (2011a).

More ambitious reforms of the international monetary system and of the broader financial architecture are needed if we are to avoid repeating the mistakes and outcomes of the past. And we need to start planning now, because setting up and implementing a global currency system requires considerable lead time – and, as recent events have shown, we may have very little time to do it before another crisis strikes.

The two key services that should be provided by the international monetary system are interrelated and complementary: a credible and well-functioning adjustment mechanism for correcting excessive deficits and surpluses in the balance of payments; and a mechanism for providing international liquidity that meets the needs of the international economy. Both these services are global public goods.

Correcting external imbalances

For the adjustment mechanism for correcting excessive deficits and surpluses in the balance of payments, a key issue is the diagnosis of the main cause of persistent external imbalances. These imbalances were created by the macroeconomic policies of the reserve currency countries and were facilitated by the international monetary system. Under the current system, reserve currency countries have privileged, nearly unrestrained access to low-cost financing for expansionary policies. A reformed international monetary system that eliminates this privilege would be a big step in the right direction. And, because countries will still have enough policy flexibility to need additional international liquidity occasionally, the new system will need to provide such liquidity as well.

Continuing with the current international monetary system would be a lose-lose situation for reserve currency countries and other countries alike. Following the recent global financial crisis, it is hard to argue that the current system is working. Even the United States might agree that the discipline imposed by an international currency could improve the intertemporal consistency of its monetary and fiscal policies. There is growing concern that the emerging multiple reserve currency system based on national currencies has led to high volatility in exchange rates and other financial prices. Further (perhaps more brutal) global macroeconomic and financial instability is a likely scenario.

A truly international currency could avoid many of these shortcomings. Appropriately designed, an international currency can avoid the conflicts inherent in using national currencies as an international reserve currency, and it can have some of the desirable properties of precious metals used for that purpose while avoiding the limitations that inadequate supply growth imposes on global liquidity.

I propose the adoption of an international currency that has the flexibility of paper money, in that it could support liquidity growth as the global economy expands, but that – like a commodity such as gold – would be "outside" the system of national currencies. This would offer stable exchange rates without the deflationary tendency of the gold standard. In addition, it would eliminate the inherent conflict of interest between reserve currency countries' domestic policy concerns and the global public good of economic stability. This new currency would have the advantages of fiat paper money plus the stability of gold, and so could be called paper gold (p-gold).

Although the political process of agreeing on a governance structure for a new international currency would likely be complex, the economic structure of such a system is fairly straightforward.

- P-gold would be an international reserve currency, issued by an international central bank, according to the provisions of an international treaty. Countries would agree that p-gold could be used to settle all international transactions for goods and services, commodities, and securities. P-gold would serve as a store of value, a medium of exchange, and a unit of account for international transactions.
- The supply of p-gold would follow Friedman's k percent rule[2] (or a modified Taylor rule[3]) based on a projected measure of global economic and asset transaction growth. The precise value of k would be determined by an independent expert council created by the foundational international treaty.
- Also to be determined by an international treaty, the seigniorage created by issuing p-gold could be used to pay for the operations of the international issuer and for producing international public goods, perhaps through international development institutions.
- Countries could retain their national currencies but would have to fix their exchange rate to p-gold. Parity adjustments would require the permission of the international monetary authority and could be granted only in cases of severe balance of payments imbalances

---

[2] Friedman (1960).   [3] Taylor (1993).

(when p-gold reserves had reached critical levels – either too high or too low relative to an agreed norm).

- To capitalize the international central bank, current reserve currency countries would turn over a combination of existing foreign currency reserves, gold, SDRs, and a predetermined amount of their national currency to the new international monetary authority. In exchange, these countries would hold equivalent p-gold reserves in a deposit reserve account at the international monetary authority. Other countries would place their existing foreign reserves – currency and securities – at the international central bank in exchange for a p-gold-denominated account. Countries would still have access to these funds – now denominated in p-gold – to finance their balance of payments.

Setting up the new international monetary system and creating p-gold would require a credible treaty – especially if p-gold is to serve as a store of value. The k percent rule (discussed below) will work only if economic agents believe that the rule will not be tinkered with in politically motivated ways. Finally, any governance issues concerning the decision to allow the use of p-gold-denominated emergency liquidity support could be managed with a set of rules about the size of the imbalances concerned.

Ensuring adequate global liquidity

Providing the second service of an international currency would require a fixed rule governing monetary policy that would ensure adequate global liquidity without causing inflation. The initial p-gold issuance could be based on an estimate of the current liquidity provided by international currencies and the value of trade and financial transactions. The agreement to use p-gold for all currencies would create instant demand for the new currency.

Thereafter, a simple rule of thumb could be devised along the lines of Friedman's k percent rule. The value of k could be tied to growth in world GDP and world trade. An expert commission, using selection criteria laid out in the foundational international treaty, could periodically review the value of k and suggest any needed adjustments.

P-gold would enter the international monetary system through purchases and expenditures related to the operations of the international central bank and the production of global public goods. This would be a way of broadly sharing the seigniorage from the new currency across the international community. The foundational international treaty could specify the types of global public goods that would be eligible for p-gold seigniorage. Examples might be purchases of carbon credits, the creation of internationally valuable environmental reserves, and basic research related to mitigating and adapting to the effects of climate change.

Total world currency in circulation is a small fraction of world GDP of $65 trillion, and only a small fraction of that is now used for international rather than national transactions. For example, there is about $1 trillion in US currency in circulation, representing about 6 percent of the US economy; only about one half is held inside the United States. Extrapolating these figures internationally suggests that a stock of about $2 trillion (times an international multiplier) would be needed to support international transactions. If the k percent figure is 3, the annual seigniorage flow would be about $60 billion.

As part of the international treaty, countries would agree to fix the parity of their national currency to the new global currency.[4] The trilemma would still hold, and, with a fixed exchange rate, countries would have less control over their monetary policy. A country's degree of capital account liberalization would have to be chosen carefully, based on the degree of monetary policy independence that makes sense for the country's structure, trade patterns, and level of development. Current reserve currency countries follow a broadly flexible exchange rate and hold relatively low levels of international reserves (other than their own currencies). To support a fixed exchange rate system, these economies would now require international reserves to finance temporary balance of payments deficits. An adequate initial level of reserves could be estimated for each current reserve currency country, based on standard measures such as the ratio of

---

[4] Some countries might adopt p-gold as their national currency (as some small economies have dollarized their economies today). Because this would eliminate the option of adjusting parity with the support of the international monetary authority during a balance of payments crisis provoked by an external shock, possible "euro" problems could emerge. The new p-gold-based international monetary system should experience less frequent and less severe shocks than the current national-currency-based reserve system, however.

reserves to short-term external debt and months of imports, or some combination of measures.

In this new international monetary system, national central banks and regulators could retain the bank regulation, supervision, and lender of last resort functions domestically. In addition, as part of the foundational international treaty, all countries would undergo annual surveillance and consultations in the spirit of IMF article IV surveillance, in order to avoid a drift toward unsustainable fiscal and monetary policies and to maintain macroeconomic stability in each country. The international monetary authority could also set up a facility for emergency liquidity support, according to a pre-agreed rule.

If a multiple reserve currency system is as volatile as predicted, countries might be able to succeed in negotiating an international treaty to create p-gold and a new international monetary system in the medium term – for two main reasons. First, for reserve currency countries, the seigniorage in the current system is small, but the benefits from avoiding harmful speculative flows could be large. Second, for nonreserve currency countries, the harmful effects of using national currencies as international reserves will worsen. As financial globalization deepens, unstable blocs could form around key reserve currencies as the nonreserve currency countries fix their exchange rate against a particular reserve currency. Meanwhile, exchange rates among reserve currencies would fluctuate widely against each other in response to shifts in macroeconomic policies, external shocks, and currency wars to gain global market share at the expense of other countries. The resulting volatility of capital flows and financial prices (exchange rates, interest rate, and equity prices) could slow growth in both advanced and emerging market economies.

The proposed p-gold, by reducing volatility and transaction costs, would be more conducive to long-term growth. The move to an international reserve currency would be a win-win situation for reserve currency and nonreserve currency countries alike. The global community should consider it now.

18 | *Why it still matters*

Only if we understand the roots of the global financial crisis of 2008 and 2009 and its probable evolution can we prevent a recurrence. The crisis originated in the international monetary system – in the global imbalances arising from the wealth effect of the excess liquidity created by US financial deregulation and loose monetary policy. How could the imbalances be so large and so long-lasting? Because the US dollar was the major reserve currency, and the United States creates reserves through its current account deficit and capital outflows. The way to prevent future crises is to establish a more stable international monetary system. This book proposes such a system based on a new global reserve currency: paper gold.

The economic crisis took almost everyone by surprise. Despite large and widening global imbalances in current accounts, confidence prevailed – confidence in the US financial and political system and its financial regulations; in its capital market, the largest in the world; and in its rock-steady monetary policy institutions. Few economists expressed serious concerns about the US housing bubble and a disorderly unwinding of rising global imbalances.

There were a few doomsayers, however, and their concerns were dramatically validated when the financial crisis erupted in September 2008. The coordinated policy response by the G20 countries – cash infusions, debt guarantees, and other forms of assistance on the order of $10 trillion – helped avoid a global depression. But the causes of the crisis remain the subject of fierce debate.

Once the crisis had hit, hindsight singled out as its cause the enormous rise in global imbalances preceding the crisis. But economists disagreed about how important the imbalances were – and whether they were the primary cause or an accelerator. Many observers blamed the East Asian countries' export-oriented strategies, their protective accumulation of foreign reserves following their 1997–8 financial crisis, and in particular China's undervalued exchange rate. The global imbalances and reserve accumulations, so the thinking went, led to cheap credit and a housing bubble in the United States.

But there is another explanation – one that points to excess liquidity in the United States and its causes. US financial deregulation – which allowed higher leverage – when combined with low interest rates vastly increased liquidity and inflated the housing bubble. Household consumption soared, feeding off the wealth effect of the housing bubble and innovative financial instruments. This consumption surge, and the fiscal deficits needed to finance the wars in Iraq and Afghanistan, generated large US trade deficits and global imbalances. Only the dollar's reserve currency status enabled the United States to maintain these severe imbalances for so long.

The excess liquidity in the United States also contributed to large gross capital outflows to other countries, fueling investment and equity market booms. Countries converted the dollars they earned through trade surpluses and capital inflows into their local currency, held as reserves by the central banks. Those reserves then flowed back to the United States as investments in US Treasury bills and financial markets, giving the impression that the excessive accumulation of reserves in those nonreserve currency countries was behind the low interest rates. When the US housing bubble burst and the financial system collapsed, a global crisis erupted.

Meanwhile, financial deregulation and liberalization had also swept through Europe. Major European banks established branches in eastern and southern Europe, using high leverage to support housing bubbles and consumption spending. The spread of the euro exacerbated intra-European imbalances. Fiscal positions that had been manageable before the crisis, when government revenues were rising, became unsustainable in the recession, setting the stage for the Eurozone sovereign debt crisis that began with Greece in 2010.

Financial deregulation and liberalization were driven principally by policymakers under the influence of the financial industry, and the flourishing innovations in the financial sector were instrumental in transmitting the collapse of key financial sector institutions to the global economy and causing disruptions in output, from which many countries have yet to recover.

As early as 2003 academics and policymakers in high-income countries began blaming China for the mounting global imbalances, even though China did not begin to accumulate large trade surpluses until

2005. In fact, China's large current account surplus reflects mainly its high domestic saving rate. Had the real causes of the crisis been understood and dealt with earlier, it could have been averted or at least mitigated.

How can countries revive growth and prevent another crisis? Structural reform is the conventional answer. Without structural reforms to enhance competitiveness, the debt-ridden countries in southern Europe will require repeated and increasingly large rescue packages. And, without structural reform in Japan and the United States, they will continue their loose monetary policies to keep interest rates low to support the financial system, help indebted households, and reduce the cost of public debt. The likely outcome is that all these economies will be trapped in a protracted "new normal" of slow growth, high risks, and low returns on financial investment. Low interest rates will also encourage short-term speculative capital flows to international commodity markets (resulting in volatile prices) and to emerging economies (resulting in asset bubbles, currency appreciations, and difficulties in macroeconomic management).

The problem is that structural reform is contractionary in the short run, and thus not politically feasible in the many countries in which unemployment is already at historical highs. Public or private debt restructuring and fiscal consolidation cannot be the immediate priority. Instead, high-income countries need to stimulate demand in order to create space for structural reforms.

This means that countercyclical fiscal policies should focus on projects that create jobs now and enhance productivity in the future, especially through investments in infrastructure, green sectors, and education. But productivity-enhancing investment opportunities are limited in advanced economies and may not be large enough to pull the countries out of crisis. In developing countries, however, opportunities for productivity-enhancing infrastructure investments abound, and they will generate demand for the exports of high-income countries. Funds for such investments can come from both reserve-issuing and reserve-rich countries. In today's global economy, infrastructure projects are good investments for private sector funds, including pension funds, and for sovereign wealth funds. Multilateral development banks and governments could help make infrastructure projects attractive to private investors through innovative arrangements that leverage private funds.

A global push for infrastructure investments in developing countries will work only if developing countries can grow dynamically in the coming decades. But do they have the space to do so in today's uncertain global economy? And, if so, how do they seize the opportunity?

The pervasive failures of government interventions guided by structuralism in the period since World War II have discredited policies aimed at "picking winners" – policies that created unsustainable and socially costly distortions and led to rent-seeking, stagnation, and frequent crises. The prevailing view is that the private sector is better at identifying new industries. But much of the literature fails to distinguish policies supporting new industries that do not align with an economy's comparative advantage from policies supporting new industries that do. The first set of policies generally fails; the second often succeeds.

The "new structural economics" focuses on developing countries' endowments and on what these countries can do well on the basis of their (latent) comparative advantage (as determined by their endowments), to start them on the road to dynamic structural change. For low-income countries, opportunities for economic transformation abound in a globalized world. If countries follow their comparative advantage and tap the potential of the latecomer's advantage in adopting or adapting new technologies, they can transform their economies and grow dynamically for decades, advancing to middle- or even high-income economies in just a generation or two.

In coming years the Chinese economy, with some 85 million labor-intensive manufacturing jobs, will climb the industrial ladder from low-skilled, low-wage sectors into more capital- and technology-intensive industries. This will free up an enormous reservoir of employment possibilities that low-income countries can tap to start their own dynamic industrialization.

Indeed, low-income countries can grow at 8 percent or more a year for several decades if their governments follow the recommendations of the new structural economics, adopting policies that nurture private business on the basis of each country's comparative advantages and that tap into the potential left by the leading developing economies, such as China. This dynamic transformation will require huge infrastructure investments to release growth bottlenecks. These policies can turn the global crisis into an opportunity for win-win outcomes for developing countries and developed countries alike, creating jobs today and boosting productivity tomorrow.

The financial crisis highlighted major deficiencies in the international monetary system. Although the system weathered the initial shock, it remains fragile and threatens a full recovery.

After World War II, with the memory of the Great Depression still fresh, policymakers in the leading economies created new institutions to oversee international transactions. Referred to as the Bretton Woods system, these institutions were designed to promote growth and stability in international trade and finance. For nearly two decades the system relied on exchange rates fixed indirectly to a gold standard. What was effectively a gold exchange standard collapsed in the early 1970s, however, and global economic governance has since fallen into benign neglect.

Countries now follow their own monetary and exchange rate policies, and the US dollar has established itself as the predominant international reserve currency. This system stimulates highly volatile capital flows and exchange rates. It also creates large and persistent payments imbalances and exchange rate misalignments. And it lacks adequate global adjustment mechanisms. What is needed instead is an international monetary system that allows countries to run temporary surpluses and deficits on the current account and accumulate net claims – a task accomplished by the current system – while also creating incentives for countries to return to a balanced position. The inability to achieve this balance is the biggest deficiency of the current system.

The world is moving toward an international monetary system, mounting evidence suggests, with multiple reserve currencies that will compete for use in international transactions and as international reserves. Would such an international monetary system be more stable than the current system – or less? Some economists believe that competition among major reserve currencies can be a disciplining mechanism. If a reserve currency country follows a monetary policy that accommodates domestic interests only and that is irresponsible from a global perspective, reserve holders would switch to other reserve currencies, and the offending currency would lose the privilege of being a reserve currency.

This argument might be valid if all major reserve currency countries had strong and healthy economies. But most potential reserve currency countries have some intractable structural weakness that, once exposed, could trigger a swift exodus of short-term funds to other reserve currencies, causing a sharp appreciation of the other reserve currencies.

Appreciation weakens the real economy and exacerbates its structural flaws. The short-term funds might then move out of the next reserve currency with the most apparent structural weakness. As a result, a multiple reserve currency system will likely be even less stable than the current one, to the detriment of reserve currency countries and non-reserve currency countries alike.

This book has offered a way out of this impasse that could benefit both groups of countries. It has proposed creating a new global reserve currency, called paper gold (p-gold), to replace the current "nonsystem" of reserve currencies. If countries agree to a single supranational reserve currency issued by an international monetary authority, the global economy could return to stability, resolving the conflicts between national interests and global interests inherent in using national currencies as reserves. Central banks would hold p-gold as reserves and issue domestic currency according to a fixed exchange rate. The increase in p-gold each year – the global seigniorage – could be used by the international monetary authority to finance its operating costs and by international development institutions to finance global public goods.

The p-gold system would avoid the fatal limitations of a gold standard (an inability to expand to meet the needs of a growing global economy) and of the use of national currencies as reserves (the inherent conflict between national and global interests). It would have a disciplinary effect on national monetary authorities while still allowing them to devalue their national currency when circumstance required.

The time is right for reforming the international monetary system. We should seize it now, before another crisis deals the system a lethal blow.

References

Abramowitz, Moses. 1983. "Notes on international differences in productivity growth rates." In Dennis C. Mueller (ed.), *The Political Economy of Growth*, 79–89. New Haven, CT: Yale University Press.

Agenor, Pierre-Richard, and Blanca Moreno-Dodson. 2006. "Public infrastructure and growth: new channels and policy implications," Policy Research Working Paper no. 4064. World Bank, Washington, DC.

Aghion, Philippe. 2006. "A primer on innovation and growth," Policy Brief no. 2006/06. Bruegel, Brussels.

Aghion, Philippe, Nick Bloom, Richard Blundell, Rachael Griffith, and Peter Howitt. 2005. "Competition and innovation: an inverted-U relationship." *Quarterly Journal of Economics* 120 (2): 701–28.

Aizenman, Joshua. 2008. "Large hoarding of international reserves and the emerging global economic architecture." *Manchester School* 76 (5): 487–503.

Aizenman, Joshua, and Jaewoo Lee. 2008. "Financial versus monetary mercantilism: long-run view of large international reserves hoarding." *World Economy* 31 (5): 593–611.

Akamatsu, Kaname. [1932] 1962. "A historical pattern of economic growth in developing countries." *Journal of Developing Economies* 1 (1): 3–25.

Alby, Philippe, Jean-Jacques Dethier, and Stéphane Straub. 2011. "Let there be light! Firms operating under electricity constraints in developing countries." Unpublished manuscript.

Alfaro, Laura, and Fabio Kanczuk. 2009. "Optimal reserve management and sovereign debt." *Journal of International Economics* 77 (1): 23–36.

Almunia, Miguel, Agustín S. Bénétrix, Barry Eichengreen, Kevin H. O'Rourke, and Gisela Rua. 2010. "From Great Depression to Great Credit Crisis: similarities, differences and lessons." *Economic Policy* 25 (2): 219–65.

American Petroleum Institute. 2011. "The facts about the US royalty collection system," fact sheet. American Petroleum Institute, Washington, DC.

American Society of Civil Engineers. 2009. *2009 Report Card for America's Infrastructure*. Reston, VA: American Society of Civil Engineers,

available   at   www.infrastructurereportcard.org/sites/default/files/
    RC2009_full_report.pdf.
Angeloni, Ignazio, Agnès Bénassy-Quéré, Benjamin Carton, Zsolt Darvas,
    Christophe Destais, Jean Pisani-Ferry, André Sapir, and Shahin Vallée.
    2011. "Global currencies for tomorrow: a European perspective,"
    Blueprint no. 13. Bruegel, Brussels.
Auerbach, Alan, and Yuriy Gorodnichenko. 2010. "Measuring the output
    responses to fiscal policy," Working Paper no. 16311. National Bureau
    of Economic Research, Cambridge, MA.
Avesani, Renzo G., Antonio García Pascual, and Elina Ribakova. 2007. "The
    use of mortgage covered bonds," Working Paper no. 07/20. IMF,
    Washington, DC.
Bagchi, Amiya Kumar. 1990. "Industrialization." In John Eatwell,
    Murray Milgate, and Peter Newman (eds.), The New Palgrave:
    Economic Development, 160–73. New York: W. W. Norton.
Barro, Robert J. 2009. "Government spending is no free lunch." Wall Street
    Journal, January 22, available at http://online.wsj.com/article/
    SB123258618204604599.html.
    2010. "The stimulus evidence one year on." Wall Street Journal,
    February   23,   available   at   http://online.wsj.com/article/
    SB10001424052748704751304575079260144504040.html.
Baxter, Marianne, and Robert King. 1993. "Fiscal policy in general
    equilibrium." American Economic Review 83 (3): 315–34.
Beck, Thorsten, and Asli Demirgüç-Kunt. 2009. "Financial institutions and
    markets across countries and over time: data and analysis," Policy
    Research Working Paper no. 4943. World Bank, Washington, DC.
Ben-Bassat, Avraham, and Daniel Gottlieb. 1992. "Optimal international
    reserves and sovereign risk." Journal of International Economics 33 (3/
    4): 345–62.
Bergsten, C. Fred. 2007. "The dollar and the renminbi." Statement before the
    hearing on "US economic relations with China: strategies and options on
    exchange rates and market access," Subcommittee on Security and
    International Trade and Finance, Committee on Banking, Housing,
    and Urban Affairs, US Senate, Washington, DC, May 23.
Bernanke, Ben. 2005a. "Global imbalances: recent developments and pros-
    pects." Speech at the Bundesbank lecture, Berlin, September 11.
    2005b. "The global savings glut and the US current account deficit."
    Speech at the Homer Jones lecture, St. Louis, MO, April 14.
Bernanke, Ben, Carol Bertaut, Laurie Pounder DeMarco, and Steven Kamin.
    2011. "International capital flows and the returns to safe assets in the
    United States, 2003–2007," International Finance Discussion Paper no.
    1014. Federal Reserve Board, Washington, DC.

Bernanke, Ben, and Kevin Carey. 1996. "Nominal wage stickiness and aggregate supply in the Great Depression." *Quarterly Journal of Economics* 111 (3): 853–83.

Berthelemy, Jean-Claude, and Ludvig Söderling. 2001. "The role of capital accumulation, adjustment and structural change for economic take-off: empirical evidence from African growth episodes." *World Development* 29 (2): 323–43.

Bhutta, Neil. 2008. "Giving credit where credit is due? The Community Reinvestment Act and mortgage lending in lower-income neighborhoods," Finance and Economics Discussion Working Paper no. 2008–61. Federal Reserve Board, Washington, DC.

BIS. 2008. "Central bank operations in response to the financial turmoil," Committee on the Global Financial System Paper no. 31. BIS, Basel.

2009. "The role of valuation and leverage in procyclicality," Committee on the Global Financial System Paper no. 34. BIS, Basel.

2010. *Triennial Central Bank Survey: Report on Global Foreign Exchange Market Activity in 2010*. Basel: BIS, available at www.bis.org/publ/rpfxf10t.pdf.

2011a. "Statement of account," June. BIS, Basel.

2011b. *BIS Quarterly Review, September 2011: International Banking and Financial Market Developments*. Basel: BIS.

2012. "Statistical release: OTC derivatives statistics at end-December 2011." BIS, Basel.

Bordo, Michael D. 1993. "The Bretton Woods international monetary system: a historical overview." In Michael D. Bordo and Barry Eichengreen (eds.), *A Retrospective on the Bretton Woods System: Lessons for International Monetary Reform*, 3–108. University of Chicago Press.

Bordo, Michael D., Ehsan U. Choudhri, and Anna J. Schwartz. 2002. "Was expansionary monetary policy feasible during the Great Contraction? An examination of the gold standard constraint." *Explorations in Economic History* 39 (1): 1–28.

Bordo, Michael D., and Ronald MacDonald. 2003. "The inter-war gold exchange standard: credibility and monetary independence." *Journal of International Money and Finance* 22 (1): 1–32.

Borio, Claudio, and Piti Disyatat. 2011. "Global imbalances and the financial crisis: link or no link?" Working Paper no. 346. BIS, Basel.

Bostic, Raphael, Stuart Gabriel, and Gary Painter. 2006. "Housing wealth, financial wealth, and consumption: new evidence from micro data." Draft. Lusk Center for Real Estate, Marshall School of Business and School of Policy, Planning and Development, University of Southern California, Los Angeles.

Boughton, James. 2002. "Why White, not Keynes? Inventing the postwar international monetary system," Working Paper no. 02/52. IMF, Washington, DC.

Briceño-Garmendia, Cecilia, Karlis Smits, and Vivien Foster. 2008. "Financing public infrastructure in sub-Saharan Africa: patterns and emerging issues," Africa Infrastructure Country Diagnostic Background Paper no. 15. World Bank, Washington, DC.

Bruno, Valentina, and Hyun Song Shin. 2011. "Capital flows, cross-border banking and global liquidity." Princeton University, NJ, available at www.princeton.edu/~hsshin/www/capital_flows_global_liquidity.pdf.

Buch, Claudia M., and Ralph P. Heinrich. 2002. "Financial integration in Europe and banking sector performance." Kiel Institute of World Economics.

Bullard, James. 2010. "Three lessons for monetary policy from the panic of 2008." *Federal Reserve Bank of St. Louis Review* 92 (3): 155–63.

Caballero, Ricardo J. 2006, "On the macroeconomics of asset shortages." In Andreas Beyer and Lucrezia Reichlin (eds.), *The Role of Money: Money and Monetary Policy in the Twenty-First Century*, 272–83. Frankfurt: ECB.

Caballero, Ricardo J., Emmanuel Farhi, and Pierre-Olivier Gourinchas. 2008. "Financial crash, commodity prices, and global imbalances." *Brookings Papers on Economic Activity* 2: 1–68.

Calderón, César, Enrique Moral-Benito, and Luis Servén. 2011. "Is infrastructure capital productive? A dynamic heterogeneous approach," Policy Research Working Paper no. 5682. World Bank, Washington, DC.

Calderón, César, and Luis Servén. 2010a. "Infrastructure and economic development in sub-Saharan Africa." *Journal of African Economies* 19 (S1): i13–i87.

2010b. "Infrastructure in Latin America." In José Antonio Ocampo and Jaime Ros (eds.), *The Oxford Handbook of Latin American Economics*, 659–89. Oxford University Press.

Calvo, Guillermo A. 1998. "Capital flows and capital market crises: the simple economics of sudden stops." *Journal of Applied Economics* 1 (1): 35–54.

Calvo, Guillermo A., Alejandro Izquierdo, and Luis Mejía. 2004. "On the empirics of sudden stops: the relevance of balance-sheet effects," Working Paper no. 10520. National Bureau of Economic Research, Cambridge, MA.

Carbó-Valverde, Santiago, David Marques-Ibanez, and Francisco Rodríguez Fernández. 2011. "Securitization, bank lending and credit quality: the case of Spain," Working Paper no. 1329. ECB, Frankfurt.

Case, Karl E., John M. Quigley, and Robert J. Shiller. 2005. "Comparing wealth effects: the stock market versus the housing market." *Advances in Macroeconomics 5* (1): 1–32.

Cecchetti, Stephen G., Hans Genberg, John Lipsky, and Sushil Wadhwani. 2000. "Asset prices and central bank policy," Geneva Report on the World Economy no. 2. International Centre for Monetary and Banking Studies, Geneva, and Centre for Economic Policy Research, London.

Chenery, Hollis B. 1979. *Structural Change and Development Policy*. New York: Oxford University Press.

Chenery, Hollis B., and Michael Bruno. 1962. "Development alternatives in an open economy: the case of Israel." *Economic Journal* 72: 79–103.

Chenery, Hollis B., and Alan M. Strout. 1966. "Foreign assistance and economic development." *American Economic Review* 56 (4): 679–733.

China Mobile. 2011. *Annual Report 2010*. Hong Kong: China Mobile.

Chinn, Menzie D., and Hiro Ito. 2008. "A new measure of financial openness." *Journal of Comparative Policy Analysis* 10 (3): 309–22.

Christiano, Lawrence, Martin Eichenbaum, and Sergio Rebelo. 2011. "When is the government spending multiplier large?" *Journal of Political Economy* 119 (1): 78–121.

Clarida, Richard. 2010. "The mean of the new normal is an observation rarely realized: focus also on the tails." Pacific Investment Management Company, Newport Beach, CA, available at www.pimco.com/ EN/Insights/Pages/TheMeanoftheNewNormalIsanObservationRarely RealizedFocusAlsoontheTails.aspx.

CLS Group. 2011. *CLS Market Share: February 2011*. London: CLS Group, available at www.cls-group.com/SiteCollectionDocuments/CLS% 20market%20share%20Feb%202011.pdf.

Collier, Paul. 2007. *The Bottom Billion: Why the Poorest Countries Are Failing and What Can Be Done about It*. Oxford University Press.

Consulate General of India, New York. 2010. "Double-digit growth within India's reach: prime minister Manmohan Singh." Consulate General of India, New York, March 23, available at www.indiacgny.org/php/ showHighLightDet.php?h_id=130&key=0.

Cooper, Richard. 1984. "A monetary system for the future." *Foreign Affairs* 63 (1): 166–84.

    2000. "Toward a common currency?" *International Finance* 3 (2): 287–308.

    2006. "Proposal for a common currency among rich democracies." *International Economics and Economic Policy* 3 (3): 387–94.

    2010. "Does the SDR have a future?" *Journal of Globalization and Development* 1 (2): article 11.

Council for Economic Planning and Development. 2011. *Taiwan Statistical Data Book: 2011.* Taipei: Council for Economic Planning and Development.

Dabla-Norris, Era, Jim Brumby, Annette Kyobe, Zac Mills, and Chris Papageorgiou. 2011. "Investing in public investment: an index of public investment efficiency," Working Paper no. 11/37. IMF, Washington, DC.

Dadush, Uri. 2010. *Paradigm Lost: The Euro in Crisis.* Washington, DC: Carnegie Endowment for International Peace.

Dadush, Uri, and Vera Eidelman. 2011. "The international monetary system: if it ain't broke, don't fix it." Centre for Economic Policy and Research, London, www.voxeu.org/index.php?q=node/6156.

Dailami, Mansoor, and Robert Hauswald. 2003. "The emerging project bond market: covenant provisions and credit spreads," Policy Research Working Paper no. 3095. World Bank, Washington, DC.

Dang, Hai-Anh, Steve Knack, and Halsey Rogers. 2009. "International aid and financial crisis in donor countries," Policy Research Working Paper no. 5162. World Bank, Washington, DC.

Datta, Bhabatosh. 1952. *Economics of Industrialization.* Calcutta: World Press.

Darwin, Charles. [1859] 1964. *On the Origin of Species: A Facsimile of the First Edition.* Cambridge, MA: Harvard University Press.

DeLong, J. Bradford, and Lawrence H. Summers. 2012. "Fiscal policy in a depressed economy." Paper presented to the Brookings Institution, Washington, DC, March 20.

Diebolt, Claude, and Antoine Parent. 2008. "Bimetallism: the 'rules of the game.'" *Explorations in Economic History* 45 (3): 288–302.

Dobbs, Richard, David Skilling, Wayne Hu, Susan Lund, James Manyika, and Charles Roxburgh. 2009. "An exorbitant privilege? Implications of reserve currencies for competitiveness," discussion paper. McKinsey Global Institute, Chicago.

Domanci, Dietrich, Ingo Fender, and Patrick McGuire. 2011. "Assessing global liquidity." In *BIS Quarterly Review, December 2011: International Banking and Financial Market Developments*, 57–71. Basel: BIS, available at www.bis.org/publ/qtrpdf/r_qt1112g.pdf.

Dorrucci, Ettore, and Julie McKay. 2011. "The international monetary system after the financial crisis," Occasional Paper no. 123. ECB, Frankfurt.

Duhigg, Charles. 2008. "Pressured to take more risk, Fannie reached tipping point." *New York Times*, October 4.

Easterly, William. 2001. "The lost decades: explaining developing countries' stagnation in spite of policy reform 1980–1998." *Journal of Economic Growth* 6 (2): 135–57.

2005. "What did structural adjustment adjust? The association of policies and growth with repeated IMF and World Bank adjustment loans." *Journal of Development Economics* 76 (1): 1–22.

ECB. 2009. "Housing finance in the euro area," Occasional Paper no. 101. ECB, Frankfurt.

2010. *Single Euro Payments Area Seventh Progress Report: Beyond Theory into Practice*. Frankfurt: ECB.

Economist Intelligence Unit. 2011. "China in focus: moving on up." Economist Intelligence Unit, London, available at www.eiu.com/index. asp?layout=info&info_name=China_moving_on_up.

Eichengreen, Barry. 1987. "Hegemonic stability theories of the international monetary system," Working Paper no. 2193. National Bureau of Economic Research, Cambridge, MA.

1992a. *Golden Fetters: The Gold Standard and the Great Depression, 1919–1939*. Oxford University Press.

1992b. "Three perspectives on the Bretton Woods system," Working Paper no. 4141. National Bureau of Economic Research, Cambridge, MA.

2009. "Out of the box: thoughts about the international financial architecture," Working Paper no. 09/116. IMF, Washington, DC.

2010a. *Globalizing Capital: A History of the International Monetary System* (2nd edn.). Princeton University Press.

2010b. "The renminbi as an international currency." University of California, Berkeley, available at http://emlab.berkeley.edu/~eichengr/ renminbi_international_1-2011.pdf.

2011a. *Exorbitant Privilege: The Rise and Fall of the Dollar and the Future of the International Monetary System*. New York: Oxford University Press.

2011b. "What can replace the dollar?" Project Syndicate, August 11, www. project-syndicate.org/commentary/what-can-replace-the-dollar-.

2012. "Implications of the euro's crisis for the international monetary system." *Journal of Policy Modeling* 34 (4): 541–8.

Eichengreen, Barry, and Marc Flandreau. 2008. "The rise and fall of the dollar, or when did the dollar replace sterling as the leading international currency?" Working Paper no. 14154. National Bureau of Economic Research, Cambridge, MA.

Eichengreen, Barry, and Ricardo Hausmann. 2005. "Original sin: the road to redemption." In Barry Eichengreen and Ricardo Hausmann (eds.), *Other People's Money: Debt Denomination and Financial Instability in Emerging Market Economies*, 266–88. University of Chicago Press.

Eichengreen, Barry, and Douglas A. Irwin. 2009. "The slide to protectionism in the Great Depression: who succumbed and why?" Working Paper no. 15142. National Bureau of Economic Research, Cambridge, MA.

Eichengreen, Barry, and Kevin H. O'Rourke. 2010. "A tale of two depressions: what do the new data tell us?" Centre for Economic Policy and Research, London, available at www.voxeu.org/index.php?q=node/3421#jun09.

Eichengreen, Barry, and Jeffrey Sachs. 1985. "Exchange rates and economic recovery in the 1930s." *Journal of Economic History* 45 (4): 925–46.

Eichengreen, Barry, and Peter Temin. 2010. "Fetters of gold and paper." *Oxford Review of Economic Policy* 26 (3): 370–84.

Eifert, Benn, Alan Gelb, and Vijaya Ramachandran. 2005. "Business environment and comparative advantage in Africa: evidence from the investment climate data," Working Paper no. 56. Center for Global Development, Washington, DC.

Eisenhower, Dwight. 1919. "Memorandum from Lt. Col. Dwight D. Eisenhower to the chief, Motor Transport Corps, with attached report on the trans-continental trip." Rock Island, IL, Rock Island Arsenal, available at www.fhwa.dot.gov/infrastructure/convoy.cfm.

   1963. *Mandate for Change, 1953–1956: The White House Years: A Personal Account*. New York: Doubleday Press.

Engel, Eduardo, Ronald Fischer, and Alexander Galetovic. 2010. "The economics of infrastructure finance: public–private partnerships versus public provision." *EIB Papers* 15 (1): 40–69.

Esfahani, Hadi Salehi, and Maria Teresa Ramirez. 2003. "Institutions, infrastructure, and economic growth." *Journal of Development Economics* 70 (2): 443–7.

European Commission. 2011. "Stakeholder consultation paper on the Europe 2020 Project bond initiative," working paper. European Commission, Brussels.

European System of Central Banks. 2010. "Strengthening the international monetary system: reserves," report of the International Relations Committee Task Force on IMF Issues. Frankfurt, European System of Central Banks.

Fay, Marianne, Michael Toman, Daniel Benitez, and Stefan Csordas. 2011. "Infrastructure and sustainable development." In Shahrokh Fardoust, Yongbeom Kim, and Claudia Sepúlveda (eds.), *Postcrisis Growth and Development: A Development Agenda for the G-20*, 329–82. Washington, DC: World Bank.

Federal Reserve Board. 2009. "Flow of funds accounts of the United States: flows and outstandings third quarter 2009," Federal Reserve statistical release. Federal Reserve Board, Washington, DC.

Fei, John C. H., and Gustav Ranis. 1964. *Development of the Labor Surplus Economy*. Homewood, IL: Irwin.

Ferguson, Niall, and Moritz Schularick. 2009. "The end of Chimerica," Working Paper no. 10–037. Harvard Business School, Cambridge, MA.

Fernald, John. 1999. "Roads to prosperity? Assessing the link between public capital and productivity." *American Economic Review* 89 (3): 619–38.

Ferreira, Pedro, and Carlos Araujo. 2008. "Growth and fiscal effects of infrastructure investment in Brazil." In Guillermo Perry, Luis Servén, and Rodrigo Suescún (eds.), *Fiscal Policy, Stabilization, and Growth: Prudence or Abstinence?*, 297–318. Washington, DC: World Bank.

Ferri, Giovanni, and Li-Gang Liu. 2009. "Honor thy creditors before thy shareholders: are the profits of Chinese state-owned enterprises real?" Working Paper no. 16/2009. Hong Kong Institute for Monetary Research.

Financial Crisis Inquiry Commission. 2011. *The Financial Crisis Inquiry Report: Final Report of the National Commission on the Causes of the Financial and Economic Crisis in the United States*. Washington, DC: US Government Printing Office.

Financial Times. 2001. "Lex – the Greenspan put." *Financial Times*, January 4.

Fishback, Price, and Valentina Kachanovskaya. 2010. "In search of the multiplier for federal spending in the states during the New Deal," Working Paper no. 16561. National Bureau of Economic Research, Cambridge, MA.

Fisher, Irving. 1894. "The mechanics of bimetallism." *Economic Journal* 4 (15): 527–37.

Flandreau, Marc. 2002. "'Water seeks a level': modeling bimetallic exchange rates and the bimetallic band." *Journal of Money, Credit and Banking* 34 (2): 491–519.

[1995] 2004. *The Glitter of Gold: France, Bimetallism, and the Emergence of the International Gold Standard, 1848–1873* (trans. Owen Leeming). Oxford University Press.

Foster, Vivien, and Cecilia Briceño-Garmendia (eds.). 2010. *Africa's Infrastructure: A Time for Transformation*. Washington, DC: World Bank.

Foster, Vivien, and Jevgenijs Steinbuks. 2009. "Paying the price for unreliable power supplies: in-house generation of electricity by firms in Africa," Policy Research Working Paper no. 4913. World Bank, Washington, DC.

Frankel, Jeffrey A. 2008. "Peg the export price," Policy Insight no. 25. Centre for Economic Policy Research, London.

Friedman, Milton. 1960. *A Program for Monetary Stability*. New York: Fordham University Press.

1990. "Bimetallism revisited." *Journal of Economic Perspectives* 4 (4): 35–104.

Friedman, Milton, and Anna Jacobson Schwartz. 1971. *A Monetary History of the United States, 1867–1960*. Princeton University Press.

Funke, Michael, and Jörg Rahn. 2005. "Just how undervalued is the Chinese renminbi?" *World Economy* 28 (4): 465–89.

Gerschenkron, Alexander. 1955. "Notes on the rate of industrial growth in Italy, 1881–1913." *Journal of Economic History* 15 (4): 360–75.

　 1962. *Economic Backwardness in Historical Perspective: A Book of Essays*. Cambridge, MA: Belknap Press.

Gersovitz, Mark, and Christina H. Paxson. 1990. *The Economies of Africa and the Prices of Their Exports*. Princeton University Press.

Goldberg, Linda. 2010. "Is the international role of the dollar changing?" Current Issues in Economics and Finance no. 16–1. Federal Reserve Bank of New York.

Goldstein, Morris, and Nicholas R. Lardy (eds.). 2008. *Debating China's Exchange Rate Policy*. Washington, DC: Peter G. Peterson Institute for International Economics.

Goodman, Peter S. 2008. "Taking hard new look at a Greenspan legacy." *New York Times*, October 8.

Gordon, Robert J. (ed.). 1990. *The American Business Cycle: Continuity and Change*. University of Chicago Press.

Gorton, Gary B., and Andrew Metrick. 2010. "Regulating the shadow banking system." *Brookings Papers on Economic Activity* 41 (2): 261–312.

Gourinchas, Pierre Olivier, and Hélène Rey. 2005. "From world banker to world venture capitalist: US external adjustment and the exorbitant privilege," Working Paper no. 11563. National Bureau of Economic Research, Cambridge, MA.

Greenspan, Alan. 2004. "Risk and uncertainty in monetary policy." *American Economic Review* 94 (2): 33–40.

Greenspan, Alan, and James E. Kennedy. 2008. "Sources and uses of equity extracted from homes." *Oxford Review of Economic Policy* 24 (1): 120–44.

Guajardo, Jaime, Daniel Leigh, and Andrea Pescatori. 2011. "Expansionary austerity: new international evidence," Working Paper no. 11/158. IMF, Washington, DC.

Guasch, J. Luis. 2004. *Granting and Renegotiating Infrastructure Concessions: Doing It Right*. Washington, DC: World Bank.

Gwartney, James D., Joshua Hall, and Robert Lawson. 2010. *Economic Freedom of the World: 2010 Annual Report*. Vancouver: Fraser Institute.

Habib, Maurizio M. 2010. "Excess returns on net foreign assets: the exorbitant privilege from a global perspective," Working Paper no. 1158. ECB, Frankfurt.

Hall, Robert, and Charles Jones. 1999. "Why do some countries produce so much more output than others?" *Quarterly Journal of Economics* 114 (1): 83–116.

Haraguchi, Nobuya, and Gorazd Rezonja. 2009. "Patterns of manufacturing development revisited," Working Paper no. 22/2009. UNIDO, Vienna.

2010. "In search of general patterns of manufacturing development," Working Paper no. 02/2010. UNIDO, Vienna.

Hausmann, Ricardo, Dani Rodrik, and Andrés Velasco. 2005. "Growth diagnostics." In Joseph Stiglitz and Narcís Serra (eds.), *The Washington Consensus Reconsidered: Towards a New Global Governance*, 324–55. Oxford University Press.

Hausmann, Ricardo, and Federico Sturzenegger. 2006. "Global imbalances or bad accounting? The missing dark matter in the wealth of nations," Working Paper no. 124. Harvard Center for International Development, Cambridge, MA.

Heckscher, Eli F., and Bertil Ohlin. 1991. *Heckscher–Ohlin Trade Theory*. Cambridge, MA: MIT Press.

Heintz, James, Robert Pollin, and Heidi Garrett-Peltier. 2009. "How infrastructure investment supports the US economy: employment, productivity and growth." Political Economy Research Institute, Amherst, MA.

Henning, C. Randall. 2009. "The future of the Chiang Mai initiative: an Asian Monetary Fund?" Policy Brief no. 09–5. Peter G. Peterson Institute for International Economics, Washington, DC.

Hördahl, Peter, and Oreste Tristani. 2007. "Inflation risk premia in the term structure of interest rates," Working Paper no. 228. BIS, Basel.

Hoselitz, Bert F. 1960. "Theories of stages of economic growth." In Bert F. Hoselitz, Joseph J. Spengler, John M. Letiche, Edward McKinley, John Buttrick, and Henry J. Bruton (eds.), *Theories of Economic Growth*, 193–238. New York: Free Press.

Hsieh, Chang-Tai, and Christina Romer. 2006. "Was the Federal Reserve constrained by the gold standard during the Great Depression? Evidence from the 1932 open market purchase." *Journal of Economic History* 66 (1): 140–76.

Huang, Yiping, May Yan, Jin Chang, Lingxiu Yang, and Shujin Chen. 2011. "China beyond the miracle part 2: the coming financial revolution." Barclays Capital, London.

Hulten, Charles, and Anders Isaksson. 2007. "Why development levels differ: the sources of differential economic growth in a panel of high and low income countries," Working Paper no. 13469. National Bureau of Economic Research, Cambridge, MA.

Iarossi, Giuseppe. 2009. "Benchmarking Africa's costs and competitiveness." In Jennifer Blanke, Marilou Uy, Giuseppe Iarossi, and Peter Ondiege (eds.), *The Africa Competitiveness Report 2009*, 83–108. Geneva: World Economic Forum.

Igan, Deniz, and Prachi Misra. 2011. "Three's company: Wall Street, Capitol Hill, and K Street," working paper. IMF, Washington, DC.

Imbs, Jean, and Romain Wacziarg. 2003. "Stages of diversification." *American Economic Review* 93 (1): 63–86.

IMF. 2007. *World Economic Outlook April 2007: Spillovers and Cycles in the Global Economy*. Washington, DC: IMF.

    2008. *World Economic Outlook October 2008: Financial Stress, Downturns, and Recoveries*. Washington, DC: IMF.

    2009. "The state of public finances cross-country fiscal monitor: November 2009," Staff Position Note no. SPN/09/25. IMF, Washington, DC.

    2010a. "Ireland: 2010 article IV consultation: staff report and public information notice on the executive board discussion," Country Report no. 10/209. IMF, Washington, DC.

    2010b. "Proposed decision to modify the new arrangements to borrow." IMF, Washington, DC.

    2010c. *World Economic Outlook October 2010: Recovery, Risk, and Rebalancing*. Washington, DC: IMF.

    2011a. "Enhancing international monetary stability: a role for the SDR?" policy paper. IMF, Washington, DC.

    2011b. "Assessing reserve adequacy," policy paper. IMF, Washington, DC.

    2011c. "Strengthening the international monetary system: taking stock and looking ahead," policy paper. IMF, Washington, DC.

    2011d. *World Economic Outlook April 2011: Tensions from the Two-Speed Recovery: Unemployment, Commodities, and Capital Flows*. Washington, DC: IMF.

    2011e. *World Economic Outlook September 2011: Slowing Growth, Rising Risks*. Washington, DC: IMF.

    2011f. "The multilateral aspects of policies affecting capital flows," policy paper. IMF, Washington, DC.

    2012a. "Gold in the IMF," factsheet. IMF, Washington, DC, available at www.imf.org/external/np/exr/facts/pdf/gold.pdf.

    2012b. "World economic outlook update January 2012: global recovery stalls, downside risks intensify." IMF, Washington, DC.

    2012c. *World Economic Outlook April 2012: Growth Resuming, Dangers Remain*. Washington, DC: IMF.

    2012d. *Global Financial Stability Report April 2012: The Quest for Lasting Stability*. Washington, DC: IMF.

International Road Federation. 2010. "Rural transport," IRF Bulletin, special edition 1. International Road Federation, Geneva.

Izaguirre, Ada Karina. 2010. "Assessment of the impact of the crisis on new PPI projects," Private Participation in Infrastructure Data Update Note no. 36. World Bank, Washington, DC.

Jarocinski, Marek, and Frank R. Smets. 2008. "Housing prices and the stance of monetary policy." *Federal Reserve Bank of St. Louis Review* 90 (4): 339–65.

Jeanne, Olivier. 2011. "Capital account policies and the real exchange rate," working paper. Johns Hopkins University, Baltimore.

Jeanne, Olivier, and Romain Rancière. 2008. "The optimal level of international reserves for emerging market countries: new formula and some applications," Discussion Paper no. 6723. Centre for Economic Policy Research, London.

Ju, Jiandong, Justin Yifu Lin, and Qing Liu. 2011. "Real exchange rates and current account imbalances in an economy with excess supply of labor," working paper. World Bank, Washington, DC, University of Oklahoma, Norman, OK, and Tsinghua University, Beijing, available at https://editorialexpress.com/cgi-bin/conference/download.cgi?db_name=FEMES11&paper_id=748.

Kalemli-Ozcan, Sebnem, Elias Papaioannou, and Jose Luis Peydro. 2010. "What lies beneath the euro's effect on financial integration? Currency risk, legal harmonization, or trade." *Journal of International Economics* 81 (1): 75–88.

Kenen, Peter. 1983. "The role of the dollar as an international currency," Occasional Paper no. 13. Group of Thirty, Washington, DC.

Klein, Brian P., and Kenneth Neil Cukier. 2009. "Tamed tigers, distressed dragon: how export-led growth derailed Asia's economies." *Foreign Affairs* 88 (4): 8–16.

Klein, Michael. 2005. "Managing guarantee programs in support of infrastructure investment," Policy Research Working Paper no. 1812. World Bank, Washington, DC.

Klitzing, Espen, Diaan-Yi Lin, Susan Lund, and Laurent Nordin. 2010. "Demystifying sovereign wealth funds." In Udaibir S. Das, Adnan Mazarei, and Han van der Hoorn (eds.), *Economics of Sovereign Wealth Funds: Issues for Policy Makers*, 3–14. Washington, DC: IMF.

Kojima, Kiyoshi. 2000. "The 'flying geese' model of Asian economic development: origin, theoretical extensions, and regional policy implications." *Journal of Asian Economics* 11 (4): 375–401.

Koo, Richard. 2009. *The Holy Grail of Macroeconomics: Lessons from Japan's Great Recession*. Singapore: John Wiley.

Kreps, Theodore J. 1934. "The price of silver and Chinese purchasing power." *Quarterly Journal of Economics* 48 (2): 245–87.

Krugman, Paul. 1996. *Pop Internationalism*. Cambridge, MA: MIT Press.

  1999. "Balance sheets, the transfer problem, and financial crises." In Robert Flood, Peter Isard, Assaf Razin, and Andrew Rose (eds.), *International Finance and Financial Crises: Essays in Honor of Robert P. Flood, Jr.*, 31–44. Amsterdam: Kluwer.

  2009a. "Revenge of the glut." *New York Times*, March 2.

  2009b. *The Return of Depression Economics and the Crisis of 2008*. New York: W. W. Norton.

  2010a. "Chinese New Year." *New York Times*, January 1.

  2010b. "Taking on China." *New York Times*, March 15.

Krugman, Paul, and Maurice Obstfeld. 2002. *International Economics: Theory and Policy* (6th edn.). Boston: Addison Wesley.

Krugman, Paul, and Robin Wells. 2010. "The slump goes on: why?" *New York Review of Books* 57 (14): 57–60.

Kuijs, Louis. 2006. "How will China's saving–investment balance evolve?" Policy Research Working Paper no. 3958. World Bank, Washington, DC.

Kuijs, Louis, William Mako, and Chunlin Zhang. 2005. "SOE dividends: how much and to whom?" Policy Note no. 56651. World Bank, Washington, DC.

Kuznets, Simon. 1966. *Modern Economic Growth: Rate, Structure and Spread*. New Haven, CT: Yale University Press.

  1971. *Economic Growth of Nations: Total Output and Production Structure*. Cambridge, MA: Harvard University Press.

Laibson, David, and Johanna Mollerstrom. 2010. "Capital flows, consumption booms and asset bubbles: a behavioral alternative to the savings glut hypothesis." *Economic Journal* 120: 354–74.

Lane, Philip R. 2011. "The Irish crisis," Discussion Paper no. 8287. Centre for Economic Policy Research, London.

Lane, Philip R., and Gian Maria Milesi-Ferretti. 2007. "The external wealth of nations mark II: revised and extended estimates of foreign assets and liabilities, 1970–2004." *Journal of International Economics* 73 (2): 223–50.

  2008. "Where did all the borrowing go? A forensic analysis of the US external position," Working Paper no. 08/28. IMF, Washington, DC.

Lapper, Richard. 2010. "Brazil accelerates investment in Africa." *Financial Times*, February 9.

Lardy, Nicholas R. 2005. "Exchange rate and monetary policy in China." *Cato Journal* 25 (1): 41–7.

  2007. "China: rebalancing economic growth." In C. Fred Bergsten, Bates Gill, Nicholas R. Lardy, and Derek J. Mitchell (eds.), *The China Balance Sheet in 2007 and Beyond*, 1–24. Washington, DC: Center for Strategic and International Studies.

Leavens, Dickson H. 1936. "The silver clause in China." *American Economic Review* 26 (4): 650–9.

Lederman, Daniel, and William F. Maloney. Forthcoming. *Does What You Export Matter? In Search of Empirical Guidance for Industrial Policies.* Washington, DC: World Bank.

Lee, Matthew R. 2008. "Subprime stoked by deregulation and bipartisan greed, not Community Reinvestment Act." Inner City Press, September 28.

Lewis, Michael. 2010. *The Big Short: Inside the Doomsday Machine.* New York: W. W. Norton.

Lewis, William Arthur. 1954. "Economic development with unlimited supplies of labour." *Manchester School of Economic and Social Studies* 22 (2): 139–91.

Libecap, Gary D., and Marie C. Thursby (eds.). 2008. *Technological Innovation: Generating Economic Results.* Amsterdam: Elsevier.

Ligthart, Jenny, and Rosa Martin Suarez. 2011. "The productivity of public capital: a meta-analysis." In Wouter Jonkhoff and Walter Manshanden (eds.), *Infrastructure Productivity Evaluation*, 5–32. New York: Springer.

Lin, Justin Yifu. 2003. "Development strategy, viability and economic convergence." *Economic Development and Cultural Change* 53 (2): 277–308.

   2009. *Economic Development and Transition: Thought, Strategy, and Viability.* Cambridge University Press.

   2011a. "From flying geese to leading dragons: new opportunities and strategies for structural transformation in developing countries," Policy Research Working Paper no. 5702. World Bank, Washington, DC.

   2011b. "New structural economics: a framework for rethinking economic development." *World Bank Research Observer* 26 (2): 193–221.

   2012a. *Demystifying the Chinese Economy.* Cambridge University Press.

   2012b. *The Quest for Prosperity: How Developing Economies Can Take Off.* Princeton University Press.

   2012c. *New Structural Economics: A Framework for Rethinking Development and Policy.* Washington, DC: World Bank.

Lin, Justin Yifu, Hinh Dinh, and Fernando Im. 2010. "US–China external imbalance and the global financial crisis." *China Economic Journal* 3 (1): 1–24.

Lin, Justin Yifu, Xifang Sun, and Ye Jiang. 2009. "Toward a theory of optimal financial structure," Policy Research Working Paper no. 5038. World Bank, Washington, DC.

Lin, Justin Yifu, and Volker Treichel. 2012. "The unexpected global financial crisis: researching its root cause," Policy Research Working Paper no. 5937. World Bank, Washington, DC.

López-Córdova, José Ernesto, and Christopher M. Meissner. 2003. "Exchange-rate regimes and international trade: evidence from the classical gold standard era." *American Economic Review* 93 (1): 344–53.

Maddison, Angus. 1995. *Monitoring the World Economy, 1820–1992*. Paris: OECD.

2010. "Historical statistics of the world economy: 1–2008 AD." www. ggdc.net/.../Historical_Statistics/horizontal-file_02-2010.xls.

Mallaby, Sebastian. 2010. *More Money than God: Hedge Funds and the Making of a New Elite*. New York: Penguin Books.

Matthews, Robert Charles Oliver, Charles H. Feinstein, and John Odling-Smee. 1982. *British Economic Growth 1856–1973: The Post-War Period in Historical Perspective*. Oxford University Press.

Maziad, Samar, Pascal Farahmand, Shengzu Wang, Stephanie Segal, and Faisal Ahmed. 2011. "Internationalization of emerging market currencies: a balance between risks and rewards," Staff Discussion Note no. 11/17. IMF, Washington, DC.

McKibbin, Warwick, Andrew Stoeckel, and Ying Ying Lu. 2011. "Global fiscal adjustment and trade rebalancing," Policy Research Working Paper no. 6044. World Bank, Washington, DC.

McKinnon, Ronald I. 2010. "Why exchange rate changes will not correct global trade imbalances," policy brief. Stanford Institute for Economic Policy Research, Stanford, CA.

McMillan, Alex Frew. 2011. "China's role as 'world's factory' coming to an end." CNBC, February 6, available at www.cnbc.com/id/41035650/ China_s_Role_as_World_s_Factory_Coming_to_an_End.

McMillan, Margaret, and Dani Rodrik. 2011. "Globalization, structural change, and productivity growth," Working Paper no. 17143. National Bureau of Economic Research, Cambridge, MA.

MDB Working Group on Infrastructure. 2011. "Infrastructure action plan: submission to the G20 by the MDB Working Group on Infrastructure." World Bank, Washington, DC, available at www.boell.org/downloads/ MDBs_Infrastructure_Action_Plan.pdf.

Mian, Atif, and Amir Sufi. 2009. "The consequences of mortgage credit expansion: evidence from the US mortgage default crisis." *Quarterly Journal of Economics* 124 (4): 1449–96.

Mian, Atif, Amir Sufi, and Francesco Trebbi. 2010. "The political economy of the US mortgage default crisis." *American Economic Review* 100 (5): 1967–98.

Miller, Marcus, Paul Weller, and Lei Zhang. 2002. "Moral hazard and the US stock market: analyzing the 'Greenspan put.'" *Economic Journal* 112 (3): C171–86.

Ministry of Finance. 1995. "Provisional regulations on the payment by Sino-foreign cooperative joint ventures of royalties for the exploitation of onshore oil resources." Beijing: Ministry of Finance.

Monga, Celestin. 2006. "Commodities, Mercedes-Benz, and adjustment: an episode in west African history." In Emmanuel Kwaku Akyeampong (ed.), *Themes in West Africa's History*, 227–64. Oxford: James Currey.

Mundell, Robert A. 1995. "The international monetary system: the missing factor." *Journal of Policy Modeling* 17 (5): 479–92.

2005. "The case for a world currency." *Journal of Policy Modeling* 27 (4): 465–75.

2011. "International monetary reform 2011." Presentation at G20 seminar, Nanjing, March 31.

NASSCOM. 2011. "The IT-BPO sector in India: strategic review 2011." NASSCOM, New Delhi.

National Bureau of Economic Research. 2010. "US business cycle expansions and contractions." National Bureau of Economic Research, Cambridge, MA, available at www.nber.org/cycles/cyclesmain.html.

National Bureau of Statistics of China. 1998. *China Statistical Yearbook 1998*. Beijing: China Statistics Press.

1999. *China Statistical Yearbook 1999*. Beijing: China Statistics Press.

2000. *China Statistical Yearbook 2000*. Beijing: China Statistics Press.

2001. *China Statistical Yearbook 2001*. Beijing: China Statistics Press.

2002. *China Statistical Yearbook 2002*. Beijing: China Statistics Press.

2003. *China Statistical Yearbook 2003*. Beijing: China Statistics Press.

2004. *China Statistical Yearbook 2004*. Beijing: China Statistics Press.

2005. *China Statistical Yearbook 2005*. Beijing: China Statistics Press.

2006. *China Statistical Yearbook 2006*. Beijing: China Statistics Press.

2007. *China Statistical Yearbook 2007*. Beijing: China Statistics Press.

2008. *China Statistical Yearbook 2008*. Beijing: China Statistics Press.

2009. *China Statistical Yearbook 2009*. Beijing: China Statistics Press.

2010. *China Statistical Yearbook 2010*. Beijing: China Statistics Press.

2012. *China Statistical Abstract 2011*. Beijing: China Statistics Press.

Ndulu, Benno, Stephen O'Connell, Robert Bates, Paul Collier, and Chukwuma C. Soludo (eds.) 2007. *The Political Economy of Economic Growth in Africa, 1960–2000*, vol. I. New York: Cambridge University Press.

Obstfeld, Maurice. 2011a. "International liquidity: the fiscal dimension," Working Paper no. 17379. National Bureau of Economic Research, Cambridge, MA.

2011b. "The SDR as an international reserve asset: what future?" University of California, Berkeley, available at http://elsa.berkeley.edu/~;obstfeld/SDR_Obstfeld.pdf.

Obstfeld, Maurice, and Kenneth S. Rogoff. 2010. "Global imbalances and the financial crisis: products of common causes." In Reuven Glick and Mark M. Spiegel (eds.), *Asia and the Global Financial Crisis: Asia Economic Policy Conference*, 131–72. Federal Reserve Bank of San Francisco.

Obstfeld, Maurice, Jay C. Shambaugh, and Alan M. Taylor. 2010. "Financial stability, the trilemma, and international reserves." *American Economic Journal: Macroeconomics* 2 (2): 57–94.

Obstfeld, Maurice, and Alan M. Taylor. 2004. *Global Capital Markets: Integration, Crisis, and Growth*. Cambridge University Press.

OECD. 2006. *Infrastructure to 2030: Telecom, Land Transport, Water and Electricity*. Paris: OECD.

2011a. Economic Outlook no. 90. OECD, Paris.

2011b. *Making the Most of Public Investment in a Tight Fiscal Environment: Multi-Level Governance Lessons from the Crisis*. Paris: OECD.

ORC International. 2001. "SIPC/investment clubs investor survival quiz." ORC International, Princeton, NJ, available at www.sipc.org/Portals/1/PDF/Survey_results.pdf.

Ozawa, Terutomo. 2011. "The (Japan-born) 'flying-geese' theory of economic development revisited – and reformulated from a structuralist perspective." *Global Policy* 2 (3): 272–85.

Pack, Howard, and Kamal Saggi. 2006. "Is there a case for industrial policy? A critical survey." *World Bank Research Observer* 21 (2): 267–97.

Padoan, Pier Carlo. 2011. "The policy imperative: rebuild confidence." In Economic Outlook no. 90, 7. OECD, Paris.

Parker, Jonathan. 2011. "On measuring the effects of fiscal policy in recessions." *Journal of Economic Literature* 49 (3): 703–18.

Parkin, Brian, and Tony Czuczka. 2010. "Merkel seeks 'decisive' German cuts as US urges spending." Bloomberg, June 6, available at www.bloomberg.com/news/2010-06-06/merkel-seeks-decisive-german-budget-cuts-putting-her-at-odds-with-u-s-.html.

Pauschert, Dirk. 2009. "Study of equipment prices in the power sector," Energy Sector Management Assistance Program Technical Paper no. 122/09. World Bank, Washington, DC.

Portes, Richard. 2009. "Global imbalances." In Mathias Dewatripont, Xavier Freixas, and Richard Portes (eds.), *Macroeconomic Stability and Financial Regulation: Key Issues for the G20*, 19–26. London: Centre for Economic Policy Research.

Pozsar, Zoltan. 2011. "Institutional cash pools and the Triffin dilemma of the US banking system," Working Paper no. 11/190. IMF, Washington, DC.

Prasad, Eswar S. 2011. "Rebalancing growth in Asia." *International Finance* 14 (1): 27–66.

Pritchett, Lant. 1997. "Divergence, big time." *Journal of Economic Perspectives* 11 (3): 3–17.

Rajan, Raghuram G. 2005. "The Greenspan era: lessons for the future." Speech at a symposium sponsored by the Federal Reserve Bank of Kansas City, Jackson Hole, WY, August 27.

2010. *Fault Lines: How Hidden Fractures Still Threaten the World Economy*. Princeton University Press.

Ramey, Valeria. 2011. "Can government purchases stimulate the economy?" *Journal of Economic Literature* 49 (3): 673–85.

Ravallion, Martin, and Shaohua Chen. 2007. "Absolute poverty measures for the developing world, 1981–2004." *Proceedings of the National Academy of Sciences* 104 (43): 16757–62.

Reinhart, Carmen M., Jacob F. Kirkegaard, and M. Belen Sbrancia. 2011. "Financial repression redux." *Finance and Development* 48 (1): 22–6.

Reinhart, Carmen M., and Kenneth S. Rogoff. 2009. *This Time Is Different: Eight Centuries of Financial Folly*. Princeton University Press.

Reinhart, Carmen M., and M. Belen Sbrancia. 2011. "The liquidation of government debt," Working Paper no. 16893. National Bureau of Economic Research, Cambridge, MA.

Roberts, Mark, Uwe Deichmann, Bernard Fingleton, and Tuo Shi. 2010. "On the road to prosperity? The economic geography of China's national expressway network," Policy Research Working Paper no. 5479. World Bank, Washington, DC.

Rogoff, Kenneth. 1983. "New evidence on the free banking era." *American Economic Review* 73 (5): 1080–91.

Roller, Lars Hendrik, and Leonard Waverman. 2001. "Telecommunications infrastructure and economic development: a simultaneous approach." *American Economic Review* 91 (4): 909–23.

Rolnick, Arthur J., and Warren E. Weber. 1983. "New evidence on the free banking era." *American Economic Review* 73 (5): 1080–91.

1988. "Explaining the demand for free bank notes." *Journal of Monetary Economics* 21 (1): 47–71.

Romp, Ward, and Jakob de Haan. 2005. "Public capital and economic growth: a critical survey," *EIB Papers* 10 (1): 40–71.

Rostow, Walt W. 1960. *The Stage of Economic Growth: A Non-Communist Manifesto*. Cambridge University Press.

Roubini, Nouriel. 2008. "The rising risk of a systemic financial meltdown: the twelve steps to disaster." Roubini.com, www.roubini.com/analysis/ 44763.php.

Roubini, Nouriel, and Stephen Mihm. 2010. *Crisis Economics: A Crash Course in the Future of Finance*. New York: Penguin Books.

Rowthorn, Robert, and Ramana Ramaswamy. 1997. "Deindustrialization: causes and implications," Working Paper no. 97/42. IMF, Washington, DC.

Russell, Henry. 2009. "The World Bank guarantee: leveraging private financing for emerging markets." Presentation at "Public–private partnership" conference, Damascus, October 30.

Sachs, Jeffrey D. 2009. "Achieving global cooperation on economic recovery and long-term sustainable development." *Asian Development Review* 26 (1): 3–15.

Sahoo, Pravakar, Ranjan Dash, and Geethanjali Nataraj. 2010. "Infrastructure development and economic growth in China," Discussion Paper no. 261. Institute of Developing Economies, Chiba City, Japan.

Saraiva, Bruno, and Otaviano Canuto. 2009. "Vulnerability, exchange rate and international reserves: whither Brazil?" EconoMonitor, www.economonitor.com/blog/2009/09/vulnerability-exchange-rate-and-international-reserves-whither-brazil.

Schroeppel, Christian, and Nakajima Mariko. 2002. "The changing interpretation of the flying geese model of economic development." *Japanstudien* (German Institute for Japanese Studies) 14: 203–36.

Schultz, Theodore W. 1964. *Transforming Traditional Agriculture*. New Haven, CT: Yale University Press.

Schwartz, Jordan, Luis Andres, and Georgeta Dragoiu. 2009. "Crisis in LAC: infrastructure investment, employment and the expectations of stimulus," Policy Research Working Paper no. 5009. World Bank, Washington, DC.

Servén, Luis. 2011. "The global dimensions of saving in China." Presentation at conference "China and the world economy," Rio de Janeiro, March 18.

Sherman, Matthew. 2009. *A Short History of Financial Deregulation in the United States*. Washington, DC: Center for Economic and Policy Research.

Shiller, Robert J. 2005. *Irrational Exuberance* (2nd edn). Princeton University Press.

Smith, Penelope, and Peter M. Summers. 2009. "Regime switches in GDP growth and volatility: some international evidence and implications for modeling business cycles." *B. E. Journal of Macroeconomics* 9 (1): 1–36.

Solow, Robert. 2005. "Rethinking fiscal policy." *Oxford Review of Economic Policy* 21 (4): 509–14.

Speller, William, Gregory Thwaiter, and Michelle Wright. 2011. "The future of international capital flows," Financial Stability Paper no. 12. Bank of England, London.

Spence, Michael. 2011. *The Next Convergence: The Future of Economic Growth in a Multispeed World*. New York: Farrar, Straus & Giroux.

State Council. 2010. "China–Africa economic cooperation," White Paper. State Council, Beijing, available at http://china-wire.org/?p=9109.

Steverman, Ben, and David Bogoslaw. 2008. "The financial crisis blame game." *BusinessWeek*, October 18, available at www.businessweek.com/investor/content/oct2008/pi20081017_950382.htm?chan=top+news_top+news+index+-+temp_top+story.

Stiglitz, Joseph, and Bruce Greenwald. 2010. "Towards a new global reserve system." *Journal of Globalization and Development* 1 (2): article 10.

Stock, James H., and Mark W. Watson. 2002. "Has the business cycle changed and why?" Working Paper no. 9127. National Bureau of Economic Research, Cambridge, MA.

Straub, Stéphane. 2008. "Infrastructure and growth in developing countries: recent advances and research challenges," Policy Research Working Paper no. 4460. World Bank, Washington, DC.

Subramanian, Arvind. 2011. "Renminbi rules: the conditional imminence of the reserve currency transition," Working Paper no. 11–14. Peter G. Peterson Institute for International Economics, Washington, DC.

Summers, Lawrence H. 2008. "Commentary." In Morris Goldstein and Nicholas R. Lardy (eds.), *Debating China's Exchange Rate Policy*, 349–53. Washington, DC: Peter G. Peterson Institute for International Economics.

Sussangkarn, Chalongphob. 2010. "The Chiang Mai initiative multilateralization: origin, development and outlook," Working Paper no. 230. Asian Development Bank Institute, Tokyo.

Swiss National Bank. 2012. "Monthly statistical bulletin," September. Swiss National Bank, Zurich, available at www.snb.ch/en/iabout/stat/statpub/statmon/stats/statmon.

Syrquin, Moshe. 1986. "Sector proportions and economic development: the evidence since 1950." Paper presented at the 8th World Congress of the International Economic Association, New Delhi, December 3.

1988. "Patterns of structural change." In Hollis B. Chenery and T. N. Srinivasan (eds.), *Handbook of Development Economics*, vol. I, 203–74. Amsterdam: Elsevier Science.

Syrquin, Moshe, and Hollis B. Chenery. 1986. *Patterns of Development: 1950 to 1983*. Washington, DC: World Bank.

Tahilyani, Naveen, Toshan Tamhane, and Jessica Tan. 2011. "Asia's $1 trillion infrastructure opportunity." *McKinsey Quarterly*, March.

Taylor, John. 1993. "Discretion versus policy rules in practice." *Carnegie-Rochester Conference Series on Public Policy* 39 (1): 195–214.

Triffin, Robert. 1960. *Gold and the Dollar Crisis*. New Haven, CT: Yale University Press.

Truman, Edwin M., 2010. "The G20 and international financial institution governance," Working Paper no. 10–13. Peter G. Peterson Institute for International Economics, Washington, DC.

Tschetter, John. 2010. "Exports support American jobs: updated measure will quantify progress as global economy recovers," International Trade Research Report no. 1. International Trade Administration, US Department of Commerce, Washington, DC, available at http://trade.gov/publications/pdfs/exports-support-american-jobs.pdf.

UNCTAD. 2006. *World Investment Report 2006: FDI from Developing and Transition Economies: Implications for Development.* Geneva: UNCTAD.

UNIDO. 2009. *Industrial Development Report 2009: Breaking In and Moving Up: New Industrial Challenges for the Bottom Billion and the Middle-Income Countries.* New York: UNIDO.

United Nations. 2009. *Report of the Commission of Experts of the President of the United Nations General Assembly on Reforms of the International Monetary and Financial System.* New York: United Nations, available at www.un.org/ga/econcrisissummit/docs/FinalReport_CoE.pdf.

US Congress. 2003. American Dream Downpayment Act of 2003. S. 811, 108th Congress, 1st session.

2005a. Federal Housing Finance Reform Act of 2005. H.R. 1461, 109th Congress, 1st session.

2005b. Prohibit Predatory Lending Act of 2005. H.R. 1182, 109th Congress, 1st session.

2005c. Responsible Lending Act of 2005. H.R. 1295, 109th Congress, 1st session.

US Department of Housing and Urban Development. 2004. "HUD finalizes rule on new housing goals for Fannie Mae and Freddie Mac," News Release no. 04–133. US Department of Housing and Urban Development, Washington, DC, available at http://archives.hud.gov/news/2004/pr04-133.cfm.

US Department of Transportation Federal Highway Administration. 2008. *2008 Status of the Nation's Highways, Bridges, and Transit: Conditions and Performance.* Washington, DC: US Department of Transportation, available at www.fhwa.dot.gov/policy/2008cpr/index.htm.

US Environmental Protection Agency. 2002. "The clean water and drinking water infrastructure gap analysis," factsheet. US Environmental Protection Agency, Washington, DC, available at http://epa.gov/ogwdw000/gapfact.pdf.

US National Archives and Records Administration. 2004. "HUD's housing goals for the Federal National Mortgage Association (Fannie Mae) and the Federal Home Loan Mortgage Corporation (Freddie Mac) for the years 2005–2008 and amendments to HUD's regulation of Fannie Mae and Freddie Mac: final rule." *Federal Register* 69 (211): 63579–887.

US Office of Management and Budget. 2010. *Historical Tables: Budget of the US Government, Fiscal Year 2011.* Washington, DC: US Government Printing Office.

Velde, François R. 2002. "Following the Yellow Brick Road: how the United States adopted the gold standard." *Economic Perspectives* 26 (2): 42–58.

Walsh, James, Chanho Park, and Jiangyan Yu. 2011. "Financing infrastructure in India: macroeconomic lessons and emerging markets case studies," Working Paper no. 11/181. IMF, Washington, DC.

Wang, Tao. 2004. "Exchange rate dynamics." In Eswar Prasad (ed.), "China's growth and integration into the world economy: prospects and challenges," Occasional Paper no. 232, 21–8. IMF, Washington, DC.

Wang, Yan. 2009. "Development partnerships for growth and poverty reduction." Synthesis of the first event organized by the China–DAC Study Group, Beijing, October 29.

Warnock, Francis E., and Veronica Cacdac Warnock. 2006. "International capital flows and US interest rates," Working Paper no. 12560. National Bureau of Economic Research, Cambridge, MA.

Weidmann, Jens. 2012. "Rebalancing Europe." Speech to Royal Institute of International Affairs, London, March 28.

Williams, Jonathan (ed.). 1997. *Money: A History.* New York: St. Martin's Press.

Williamson, John. 1983. *The Exchange Rate System.* Washington, DC: Institute for International Economics.

1987. "International capital flows." In John Eatwell, Murray Milgate, and Peter Newman (eds.), *The New Palgrave: A Dictionary of Economics,* vol. II, 894–8. London: Palgrave Macmillan.

2002. "Did the Washington consensus fail?" Peter G. Peterson Institute for International Economics, Washington, DC, available at www.petersoninstitute.org/publications/papers/paper.cfm?ResearchID=488.

2007. "Reference rates and the international system," Policy Analysis in International Economics no. 82. Peter G. Peterson Institute for International Economics, Washington, DC.

2009. "Why SDRs could rival the dollar," Policy Brief no. 09–20. Peter G. Peterson Institute for International Economics, Washington, DC.

Wolf, Martin. 2011. "In the grip of a Great Convergence." *Financial Times,* January 4, available at www.ft.com/intl/cms/s/0/072c87e6-1841-11e0-88c9-00144feab49a.html#axzz1xV3WYb37.

2012. "The German response." *Financial Times,* June 7, available at http://blogs.ft.com/martin-wolf-exchange/2012/06/07/the-german-response.

Woodford, Michael. 2011. "Simple analytics of the government expenditures multiplier," Discussion Paper no. 7704. Centre for Economic Policy Research, London.

World Bank. 1996. "Kingdom of Morocco impact evaluation report: socio-economic influence of rural roads." World Bank, Washington, DC.

2004. *Doing Business in 2004: Understanding Regulation.* Washington, DC: World Bank.

2005a. *Economic Growth in the 1990s: Learning from a Decade of Reform.* Washington, DC: World Bank.

2005b. "Lesotho: growth and employment option study," country economic memorandum. World Bank, Washington, DC.

2007. "The nexus between infrastructure and environment; from the Evaluation Cooperation Group of the international financial institutions," Evaluation Brief no. 5. World Bank, Washington, DC, available at http://siteresources.worldbank.org/INTOED/Resources/infrastructure_environment.pdf.

2009a. *World Development Indicators 2009.* Washington, DC: World Bank.

2009b. *World Development Report 2009: Reshaping Economic Geography.* Washington, DC: World Bank.

2010. *Global Economic Prospects 2010: Fiscal Headwinds and Recovery.* Washington, DC: World Bank.

2011a. *Global Development Horizons 2011: Multipolarity: The New Global Economy.* Washington, DC: World Bank.

2011b. "Supporting infrastructure development in low-income countries," interim report submitted to the G20 by the MDB Working Group on Infrastructure. World Bank, Washington, DC.

2011c. "Transformation through infrastructure," issues and concept note. World Bank, Washington, DC.

2011d. *World Monitoring Report 2011: Improving the Odds of Achieving the MDGs: Heterogeneity, Gaps, and Challenges.* Washington, DC: World Bank.

2012. *Global Economic Prospects January 2012: Uncertainties and Vulnerabilities.* Washington, DC: World Bank.

World Bank and IMF. 2009. *Global Monitoring Report 2009: A Development Emergency.* Washington, DC: World Bank.

World Economic Forum. 2011b. *The Global Competitiveness Report 2011–12.* Geneva: World Economic Forum.

Xafa, Miranda. 2007. "Global imbalances: do they matter?" *Cato Journal* 7 (1): 59–68.

Yepez-García, Rigoberto Ariel, Todd M. Johnson, and Luis Alberto Andrés. 2010. *Meeting the Electricity Supply/Demand Balance in Latin America and the Caribbean.* Washington, DC: World Bank.

Zoellick, Robert. 2010a. "The end of the Third World: modernizing multi-lateralism for a multipolar world." Speech at the Woodrow Wilson Center for International Scholars, Washington, DC, April 14, available at http://go.worldbank.org/MI7PLIP8U0.

2010b. Transcript of a press conference with the Foreign Correspondents Association. Singapore, November 10, available at http://web.world-bank.org/WBSITE/EXTERNAL/NEWS/0,, contentMDK:22760007 ~menuPK:34476~pagePK:34370~piPK:34424~theSitePK:4607,00.html.

Index